·· THE ··
· SIMON & ·
SCHUSTER
POCKET GUIDE TO
WHITE
WINES

J I M   A I N S W O R T H

A Fireside Book
Published by Simon & Schuster Inc.
New York London Toronto
Sydney Tokyo Singapore

FIRESIDE
Simon & Schuster Building
Rockefeller Center
1230 Avenue of the Americas
New York, New York 10020

The Simon & Schuster Pocket Guide to White Wines
Edited and designed by Mitchell Beazley International Limited, Artists House, 14-15 Manette Street, London W1V 5LB.

Published simultaneously in the United Kingdom by Mitchell Beazley under the title *The Mitchell Beazley White Wine Guide*.

10 9 8 7 6 5 4 3 2 1

Library of Congress Catalog Card Number: 90-3598
ISBN 0-671-69622-X

Editor	Rupert Joy
Art Editor	Paul Drayson
Additional Material	Rosalind Cooper
Research	Paul Dymond, Andrew Jefford
Proofreader	Alison Franks
Indexer	Anne Barratt
Production	Barbara Hind
Managing Editor	Chris Foulkes
Senior Art Editor	Tim Foster

Typeset in Caslon by Servis Filmsetting Ltd, Manchester, England
Produced by Mandarin Offset
Printed in Singapore

CONTENTS

HOW TO USE THIS BOOK

This book is divided into two sections. The first section is a short introduction explaining the climatic and winemaking factors that influence the taste of wine, the key style factors to be aware of in choosing wine, and the culinary and temperature guidelines to follow when enjoying wine. The second section consists of an A-Z directory of white wine styles, from Adelaide Hills to Zinfandel (White).

In the directory a wine "style" is taken to mean anything from a distinctive individual wine (such as Château-Grillet) to a major grape variety, "appellation" or wine-producing region (such as Chardonnay, Vinho Verde or Burgundy). There are also introductions to the wines of the main white wine producing countries – France, Germany, Italy, Spain, Portugal, the United States, Australia and New Zealand – and to the sparkling wines of the world.

A white wine is taken to mean any wine that is made principally from white grapes (including Australian Liqueur Muscat, which, though dark in colour, is made from white grapes) and wines labelled white (such as "White Zinfandel", which is in fact made from red grapes).

Each entry in the directory follows a similar pattern, describing the taste of the wine together with any significant variations in style or production method, offering advice on vintages and food partnerships where appropriate, and comparing the wine with other styles in the book. Reliable wines/producers are listed, with basic quality and price bands, as follows:

QUALITY		PRICE	
★	everyday	■	cheap
★★	superior	■■	medium-priced
★★★	top-class	■■■	expensive

The quality bands assess each wine or producer on a world-wide, rather than a regional, scale of worth. The price bands reflect approximately the retail cost of a wine, rather than its cost in a restaurant, where it will usually rise in price to a higher band.

At the end of each entry is a sub-section entitled **Where next?** This suggests taste paths to follow, directing the reader towards other entries in the directory, where information on similar styles of wine can be found. The recommended wines may be slightly lighter or heavier, a little oakier or less oaky, cheaper or more expensive, but each recommendation is designed to encourage confident experimentation with similar, though not identical, tastes.

INTRODUCTION

We have never had such abundant choice. There are more wines available today than there have ever been. Brilliant! Aren't we lucky?

So we walk into a shop and ask for a bottle of Chardonnay. We follow the sweep of the assistant's arm as it waves airily towards a shelf crowded with 50 Chardonnays. We groan inwardly while trying not to appear ungracious for the unparalleled selection.

Where do we start? How do we pick the right one? We only have five minutes – that's six seconds to examine each bottle – so we take a blind stab, disguising it with our best I-do-this-sort-of-thing-every-day look and worrying afterwards whether we might have been better off with one of the 49 we left behind. What a jerk we shall look, too, if it doesn't go with the grilled salmon or chicken chasseur that we have come out to find a bottle specifically to match.

We could have narrowed it down by price. With the money we had to spend we could have bought a bottle from California, or a Mâcon Blanc, or one from Australia, or two from Bulgaria. But that still doesn't help us decide on the best wine for the occasion. There is a world of difference between a light, crisp, fresh, appley-lemony Chardonnay from Alto Adige and a great hulking brute from the Hunter Valley tasting like a whole breakfast of pineapple juice and well-done toast, dripping butter and honey.

This book helps to narrow the choice by working from the point of view of taste or style. If you want a big fat Chardonnay, or a zingily crisp Sauvignon Blanc or whatever, it will help you find them. That is not meant to make the whole business of choosing and drinking wine too predictable, because if the taste is a foregone conclusion there seems hardly any point in opening the bottle.

Because of the risk involved, we can very easily become too conservative once we find a wine we like. We buy lots of the new discovery and drink it every day, certain in the knowledge that we have found a winner and are spending our money wisely. And then one day we discover that the wine has become boring. We want a change, but cannot face a 50-Chardonnay mega-choice. What do we do then?

The idea behind this book is to help with both problems: to pinpoint the style of a wine, and thereby reduce the risk of bringing one home that will disappoint or be inappropriate to the circumstances. At the same time it aims to broaden choice and embrace variety. Too often we rely on well-known names – Muscadet perhaps, or Sancerre – without realizing that similar styles of wine, from elsewhere in France or from other countries, might be less expensive, or more interesting, or might just help to vary the diet. It is more fun to have a range of wines to choose from than to bore ourselves silly drinking the same old stuff, however good, the whole time.

THE COMPONENTS OF
A WINE STYLE

A wine tastes, smells and looks the way it does because of the unique combination of circumstances surrounding its production: the soil on which the grapes are grown, the grape variety, the climate, and the countless winemaking decisions the producer takes.

GRAPE VARIETY Perhaps the biggest single influence on flavour is the grape variety, or varieties, used to make the wine. From a drinker's point of view, therefore, selecting the appropriate grape is, in broad terms, the key to finding a suitable wine. Sauvignon Blanc, for example, generally produces strongly aromatic wines reminiscent of blackcurrant leaves and gooseberries, with crisp, refreshing acidity. Freshness is paramount, and the wines are usually best drunk within a year or two of the harvest.

The Sauvignon Blanc entry describes the style of wine that the grape makes, where to find particularly good examples, how it varies around the world, and how it differs when combined with other grape varieties. The same goes for the other principal grapes: Chardonnay, Chenin Blanc, Gewürztraminer, Müller-Thurgau, Muscat, Pinot Blanc, Pinot Gris, Riesling, Sémillon, Silvaner and Trebbiano.

The variety of tastes in wine is one of its great glories. Once we have got the hang of the basic grapes and their tastes, then it makes sense to break out and explore alternatives. The adventurous drinker will want to taste light, crisp and fresh Chardonnays; elegant, steely ones; buttery, toasty, cinnamon-and-honey ones; pineapple and fruit-salady ones, and so on. France, Alto Adige, California, Australia and New Zealand are particularly fertile territory in which to hunt.

CLIMATE AND SOIL Even the basic grapes, however, can vary considerably in the style of wine they produce: from country to country, between regions, from one village or vineyard to another, even within the same vineyard when vinified by two different people.

Hot growing conditions are particularly difficult for white grapes, especially when combined, as in some traditional wine-producing regions, with the use of open fermenters and a lack of temperature control. Acidity is low, so the wines taste flabby and uninteresting; sugar is high, so there is an excess of alcohol; delicate flavour components are burned off.

Where such wines have been drunk for generations they are considered normal, but for the rest of the world a white wine should normally be refreshing, which requires either good acidity or something else to perk it up, such as a slight prickle of bubbles. Alcohol, whether moderate or high, should be in balance with the other components: a feather-light Mosel Riesling, for example, needs much less than a big, weighty California Chardonnay.

Generally, these key stylistic requirements point us away from warmer climates such as North Africa, the Middle East, Greece, southern Spain and Italy, and towards northern Europe, the higher latitudes of North America, New Zealand and the coastal regions of Australia, or anywhere with vineyards at high altitude. These so-called "cool climates" are increasingly sought after for vine-growing: a long cool growing season brings about a better balance between those components of alcohol, acidity and flavour.

In fact the term "cool climate" rather oversimplifies the case. Some warm regions may be rescued by a climatic quirk: the fogs from California's San Francisco Bay that creep up the valleys and protect Napa's grapes from sunburn for example. Then there are ways to offset the ravages of heat: by picking the grapes early while acidity is still high and sugar is moderate; or by harvesting the grapes at night.

On top of this, some grape varieties benefit more than others from cool conditions. Riesling seems to need them more than Sémillon for instance, while Chardonnay is pretty adaptable. There are also less apparent temperature variations that play a crucial role. The larger the difference between day-time high and night-time low, the better the grapes respond.

The biggest drawback about cultivating vines in the cooler regions is frost. Vines can survive down to around -13°F (-25°C), but severe winters dip below that, destroying the vines completely. It can then take years for them to be replanted and grow to the point where winemaking is again possible. Even without such extremes, a relatively light but late winter frost can destroy the buds and make a mess of a whole year's crop. It is a risky business. For this reason, some varieties (such as those now grown in southern England) have been specifically engineered to survive cold conditions.

The other end of the season can be equally risky. If it rains just as the crop is about to be picked the grapes will suck up the moisture, growing plump but diluting the flavour. If the grower waits, hoping for sun to dry them out and concentrate the juice a bit, he may just get more rain and rotten grapes that make rotten wine. Given, on the other hand, a long, dry, warm and sunny autumn, some grapes such as Riesling and Sémillon can produce wines with a wonderful honeyed richness. If they are affected by the *Botrytis* rot, like the grapes of Sauternes, Tokay and other regions, then the results can be even more splendid. Given all these differences in weather pattern from one year to the next, it is not surprising that vintage variation can mean the difference between a stunningly good and an extremely ordinary wine.

Wine style also varies according to the kind of soil in which the vines grow, although this is probably due less to its chemical make-up than to its physical properties such as drainage. The gravel of an old river bed helps Marlborough Sauvignon Blanc to achieve its superiority; the steep, slatey slopes of the Mosel mark its finest Riesling sites.

THE WINEMAKING PROCESS Making white wine is easy. Making good white wine is more difficult. The basic process, after the grapes have been picked, involves pressing out the juice to separate it from the pips and skins, fermenting the juice or "must", racking it off the dead yeast cells, maturing it if necessary, then filtering and cleaning it up before bottling.

This basic plan can be varied at every stage. The first level on which it can be varied concerns hygiene. It is standard practice now, in those wineries that can afford it, to install stainless steel equipment, which is much easier to keep clean than concrete vats or old wooden barrels; and they will have temperature-control, since white wines are best fermented at around 61-64°F (16-18°C). Once the fermentation gets under way, the heat produced can raise the temperature quite considerably, so some method of cooling – dribbling cold water down the outside, through a serpentine tube inside the tank, or by passing it through a heat exchanger – is essential.

Excluding air, or at least controlling the degree of contact carefully, is important at all stages of winemaking. Modern equipment achieves this comfortably, reducing the need to add the winemaker's all-purpose standby cleaning chemical, sulphur dioxide.

Although there are strict limits in the EEC about how much sulphur dioxide a wine may contain, it is used excessively in some cases: the smell of a struck match is sometimes detectable, with an unpleasant, cough-inducing, throat-burning sensation. In the United States, labels are required to state that a sulphured wine "contains sulfites", although this inevitably applies to most wines. On a different tack, some winemakers prefer to oxidize the must before it ferments, turning it a dirty brown colour, the idea being that those components which would have been capable of oxidizing the wine later will no longer be present. As it ferments the wine brightens to a normal colour.

On the whole, though, the winemaking world is agreed on the principles of good health management. Unfortunately not everybody is either willing or able to implement them. The New World countries are generally at the forefront. If the United States can put a man on the moon, then Californian wineries are not going to be without their space-age technology. And in Australia the show circuit, whereby wines are judged against their peers in a glare of publicity, has contributed to the largely "fault-free" wine industry. Sometimes, in countries such as Greece, Spain and Portugal, old practices continue to chase around a vicious circle: nobody outside the region is going to buy flabby, oxidized wines, so no money will be forthcoming for investment in new equipment.

The second level at which the winemaking process can be varied is more personal but no less crucial. It is up to the winemaker to decide, depending on the style of wine he or she is aiming to produce, precisely how to carry out each operation.

For instance, the grapes can be simply crushed or pressed and the juice run off. Generally it is only the lightest pressing that will produce a high-quality wine; more pressure will result in a harsher, more astringent wine. The winemaker can also intervene by leaving the crushed grapes and juice to macerate together for a few hours before separating them, in order to extract more of the aromatic and flavouring components; this is called "skin contact". Or again, fermentation might be carried out using either the natural yeasts, a home-grown culture, or a common international strain.

The great merit of cool-temperature stainless steel fermentation, allied to micropore filters and other state-of-the-art gadgets, is that the wines emerge appetizingly clean, bright, scrubbed and fresh. This suits many wines, and many people, perfectly. But sometimes, and Chardonnay is a prime example, more interest and complexity can result from either maturing – or better still fermenting – the wine in oak barrels. The wines are more expensive, and need to mature longer than others because they have picked up some tannin from the barrels, but Chardonnay and oak together make a classic combination that every wine drinker should experience sooner rather than later. Others, like Sauvignon Blanc and oak (a combination often called Fumé Blanc in the New World), don't seem to work half so well.

Another way in which winemakers are "putting some dirt back into the wine" and avoiding the monotony of squeaky-clean, clinically pure, laboratory-hatched wines, is to allow "yeast-lees contact". This little winemaker's phrase refers to the time that the wine spends before being racked off the spent yeast and nutrients that fall to the bottom of the tank or cask after fermentation. The more time it spends like that, the weightier, more buttery and complex the wine. The winemaker can also choose whether to allow or prevent malolactic fermentation, a bacteriological change affecting the acidity of the wine. If it goes ahead, the sharper malic acid (like that present in apples) will be converted into the softer lactic acid (as in milk).

MATURITY Most white wine is meant to be drunk young. Unlike red wine, which picks up the preservative tannin along with colour from the grape skins, most white wine is just fermented juice. It has acidity though, which is a good preserver, and wines made from grape varieties such as Riesling and Sémillon are capable of maturing over many years, sometimes decades.

Some wines rely almost entirely on their freshness for appeal: Muscadet for instance, or Vinho Verde, or those made from Sauvignon Blanc. Chardonnay is variable, and can be made light and fresh for early drinking, as in Alto Adige, or with altogether more serious intent, as in Burgundy. The tannin from the oak barrels in which some Chardonnays are fermented or matured will help to preserve them for a number of years, bringing interesting and complex favours.

Sweetness is a preserver too, so most sweet wines will keep for a long time. Some that are both sweet and fresh – Muscat-based wines like Asti Spumante for example – need to be drunk very young, while others, such as Sémillon-based Sauternes, positively need ageing if we are to get the best from them. Wines made from Riesling and Sémillon in particular can develop a fullness and flavour that barely seems possible when they start out. It would be a shame to drink these wines too young, just as it would to leave Asti too long.

CHOOSING WINE

White wines suit almost any occasion, and will partner almost any food. They range in colour from the palest water-white to the darkest chestnut-brown; from acerbically dry to lusciously sweet; from crisp and fresh to oaky and mature; from still or prickly to frothy and fully sparkling; from pure varietals to unfathomable blends. All we have to work out is which particular one we would like to drink now.

Sometimes the wine itself is the focus of attention. A venerable bottle needs no distraction. But we should be wary of being too reverential. The whole point of drinking is to enjoy ourselves, which usually means there are other people to share the wine with, food to eat with it and so on. The wine often takes second or third place. In this case both style and price may affect our choice: nothing too expensive, and nothing too concentrated or attention-seeking, just something lightly aromatic and fresh.

Wines do not always divide easily into clear-cut groupings: two producers can make quite different versions of a wine with the same *appellation* or other regional designation. Boundaries, quite properly, are fuzzy. But at least we can make a start.

The two main dimensions along which white wines vary are sweetness and weight. Some back labels employ a scale from 1 (driest) to 9 (sweetest). Examples from the United Kingdom's Wine Development Board's advisory leaflet are as follows:

1 Chablis, Champagne, Entre-Deux-Mers, Saumur
2 Dry sherry and Montilla, Riesling d'Alsace, Soave
3 Grüner Veltliner from Austria, Pinot Blanc d'Alsace
4 Chenin Blanc, Olasz Riesling, Vinho Verde
5 Austrian *Spätlesen*, Liebfraumilch
6 Demi-sec Champagne, Tokay Szamorodni
7 Asti Spumante, German *Auslesen*, Monbazillac
8 Sauternes and Barsac, Moscatels
9 *Trockenbeerenauslesen*, Málaga, Malmsey

Detailed as it is, such a scale does not concern itself with weight or body – Asti Spumante is much lighter than Monbazillac for example – nor does it attempt to deal with acidity. Two wines can be matched for sweetness, but if one has higher acidity then it will not actually taste as sweet. The sweeter the wine, the more important it is to have good acidity in order to keep it fresh and lively.

The following broad groups of suggested wines are based roughly on sweetness and weight, with an extra category to reflect the attractively aromatic and spicy character of some wines.

LIGHT DRY WINES Most wines made from the Trebbiano grape fit into this category, and there is an abundance of light, dry styles made in Europe, especially in Italy and France:
● Italy – most wines from Alto Adige, and other Italian wines such as Verdicchio, Bianco di Custoza, Gambellara, much Soave, Vermentino from Sardinia and Italian Pinot Bianco;

- France – Chardonnay from Haut-Poitou, some Mâcon and Chablis, Alsace Pinot Blanc, Entre-Deux-Mers, Bergerac Sec, Muscadet and Bourgogne Aligoté;
- Germany – many *trocken* and *halbtrocken* wines, especially up to *Kabinett* level;
- Vinho Verde in Portugal, Torres Viña Sol from Penedès in Spain, Austrian *heurige* wine, Swiss Fendant and some English wines.

MEDIUM-BODIED DRY WINES Many of the mid-price Chardonnays from Australia, New Zealand, California and Bulgaria fit the bill. The older producing regions also have much to offer:

- France – Alsace Pinot Gris and Riesling, some Mâcon and Chablis, some Graves, northern Rhône wines and much Champagne;
- Germany – *trocken* wines, particularly *Spätlesen* and *Auslesen*;
- California – some Johannisberg Riesling and some Fumé Blancs;
- Australia – Rhine Riesling and some Fumé Blancs;
- Frascati and dry Orvieto, some Rioja, Manzanilla and *fino* sherry.

FULL DRY WINES An awful lot of Chardonnay from Australia and California, and the best wines from Burgundy, are full and dry. Deep colour, evidence of oak-ageing and high alcohol all contribute to extra weight and fullness. Wines in this category include:

- Australia – mature Hunter Valley Semillon, many Chardonnays;
- California – many Chardonnays;
- France – the more serious Graves wines, much Burgundy, and some Alsace (especially *Vendange tardive*) wines;
- Spain – some Rioja, dry *amontillado* and *oloroso* sherry.

AROMATIC SPICY WINES Almost any Gewürztraminer is aromatic and spicy (*gewürz* means spice), as is most Muscat, especially when young and grapily fresh, and much Sauvignon Blanc. Some oakier Chardonnays, some Riesling, some Pinot Grigio and some German crossings such as Scheurebe also display these characteristics. Try these from the following regions:

- France – including Alsace Gewürztraminer, Sancerre, Pouilly-Fumé, Sauvignon de Haut-Poitou;
- Italy – including Alto Adige Gewürztraminer, and some Pinot Grigio from Alto Adige and Friuli-Venezia Giulia;
- New Zealand – Gewürztraminers and most Sauvignons;
- Germany – some Riesling from Rheinhessen;
- California – some Johannisberg Riesling;
- Australia – some Rhine Riesling;
- Greece – Retsina.

MEDIUM-DRY TO MEDIUM-SWEET WINES This is the place where many people begin. Fruity and flowery flavours abound, and the wines are easy and gentle without any hard edges from sharp acidity. Many branded wines address themselves to this taste range:

- Yugoslavia – Laski Riesling;
- Hungary – Olasz Riesling;
- Germany – Liebfraumilch and other Müller-Thurgau wines, QbA or "Bereich" wines and some *Kabinetten*;
- some English wines and Vinho Verde sold outside Portugal.

Rather fuller-bodied wines in this range include:

- California – Johannisberg Riesling;
- Australia – Rhine Riesling;
- France – Alsace *Vendange tardive* wines, some Chenin Blanc from the Loire such as Vouvray, and *demi-sec* Champagne.

SWEET WINES These include a wealth of fortified and *Botrytis*-affected wines from France, Germany and other parts of Europe, as well as a few from the New World:

● Germany and Austria – some *Spätlesen* and *Auslesen*, and all *Beerenauslesen* and *Trockenbeerenauslesen*;

● California and Australia – most late harvest and all *Botrytis*-affected wines, Liqueur Muscat;

● France – including Beaumes-de-Venise, Sauternes, Barsac, Monbazillac, Loupiac, Cadillac and Ste-Croix-du-Mont from southern France, and Vouvray *moelleux*, Coteaux du Layon, Bonnezeaux and Quarts de Chaume from the Loire;

● Italy – Vin Santo and Orvieto *abboccato*;

● Hungary – Tokay above 3 *puttonyos*;

● Bual and Malmsey Madeira, Málaga and Muscat of Samos.

ENJOYING WINE

Many of us are afflicted some of the time, and some of us are afflicted most of the time, by the fear that somebody else may be having more fun than we are. It is a terrible experience, especially if we are paying the same amount of money as they are. It may well be this feeling of insecurity that has led to some of the "rules" associated with wine drinking. If we follow the rules we must be enjoying ourselves, right?

Wrong. As with so many things in life, the fun only starts once we throw the rules out of the window. If you see anything masquerading as a rule in wine drinking, especially where food is concerned, the best thing to do is break it immediately.

There are guidelines, yes, but they are something else entirely. Guidelines get us off the ground, help us avoid disappointment and unnecessary expense in the early stages. But then we must follow our nose and fly wherever the fancy takes us, without apologizing to anyone. If we want to drink Champagne with curry, roast beef, or egg and chips, there is nothing to stop us. At least that is a more sensible use of a bottle than smashing it against the side of a ship.

WINE AND FOOD Considering how much time many people spend consuming wine and food together, we seem to have remarkably little insight into why it is that some combinations work better than others. At its most basic, any combination is good: the body can absorb, metabolize and deal more effectively with alcohol if it is poured down along with platefuls of food.

Beyond that, although there are no straight answers, we can at least consider questions about matching particular foods and wines. Should they, for example, be as similar as possible – the sweetest food with the sweetest wine? Well, that works to some extent. Few people would complain about a lovely gooey pud with a rich, sweet Sauternes. But Sauternes is also a classic accompaniment to a starter of *foie gras* in south-west France; *foie gras* isn't sweet. A German *Auslese* goes very nicely with a game casserole. Sweet white with dark red meat? Surely some mistake. Well try it and see.

In these cases it seems to be weight or richness that makes the marriage work. Other successful partnerships include smoked foods, such as salmon, with oaky Chardonnay: a charred oak barrel has a similar, although more subdued, effect on the wine as the smokehouse has on the salmon, and comparable richness plays a part here too.

Chocolate is a problem, but can be alleviated by spicy, orangey, Muscatty flavours and fairly rich, dense textures. Some wines, such as Quady's Essensia from California, have been developed on the drawing board specifically to bring vinous relief to chocoholics.

So what about opposites? A rich, oily fish like a sardine goes wonderfully with Vinho Verde: red or white Vinho Verde, it doesn't matter, so long as it is the crisp, astringently dry kind you find in Portugal and not the sweetened export version.

Just as white wines are a knee-jerk choice with fish (while many red wines go equally well), so red wines are often an automatic choice with cheese. In fact some white wines make splendid partners for cheese. Madeira with Norwegian *gjetost* cheese is one; pungent Sauvignon Blanc with goat's cheese is another.

Precise matching is all very well, but it can become pedantic if we are not careful. What we need a large chunk of the time is just a wine that will go with everything on the table. We can have a swig while we're cooking and call it an aperitif; carry on through the avocado and prawns and the beef casserole; then continue out the other side with a hunk of Cheddar and a chocolate mousse. In these cases consider the less aromatic, less characterful wines, those which do not have a distinctively individual flavour but which seem almost "neutral" when tasted by themselves. Many Italian wines fit the bill, perhaps not surprisingly in view of the Italian passion for gastronomy.

TEMPERATURE Whether or not you have a cellar (and let's face it, most of us don't), do remember that if you're going to go through the endurance test of keeping wine you must have a stable environment in which it can relax and twiddle its toes. Exactly where doesn't matter all that much so long as the temperature is fairly constant – preferably in the 45-50°F (7-10°C) bracket – and the wine is not exposed to too much vibration or direct sunlight.

White wine should generally be served cool. How cool, in theory, depends on the wine. In practice it is usually determined by how much notice we've got. Friends arriving in 20 minutes? Haven't got time to chill the Chardonnay, what shall I do? The way to beat the system is to keep a few bottles permanently in the fridge door, although the wine may get so cold that the first swig numbs our mouths and we can't taste anything. However, it may be the lesser of two evils since a super-cold wine can be pulled out to warm slowly, receiving a final boost if necessary from the warmth of our hands around the glass.

If time is unlimited, it is a simple matter to get the temperature correct. Just uncork the Champagne, drop in a thermometer, and leave it in the fridge until the temperature reads 45°F (7°C). Nothing to it. Cellar temperature (45-50°F) is a good average for most white wines. Of course, the Champagne might lose a bit of fizz, but that is a small price to pay for getting the temperature spot on, don't you agree? No, well perhaps you are right.

There are recommended temperatures for different wines, which may be a useful guide in the first instance, but most people just feel the bottle: if it feels right they open it. Experience, trial and error, and "feel" are the ways to find the temperature that suits both the wine and yourself. It is worth varying it slightly now and again to see what difference it makes.

The principles are straightforward. First, sweet wines can stand more chilling than dry wines; sweetness can sometimes seem a little harsh, certainly more pronounced, at warmer temperatures, while a cooler temperature makes the wines appear brisker and fresher. So a Sauternes might well stand to be chilled more than a dry white Burgundy, for example: say the lower end of 40-45°F (4-7°C) for Sauternes, and the upper end of 45-50°F for a good Meursault.

Then, the chillier a wine, the less likely we are to appreciate the more delicate smells and tastes. The pungent aroma of a Marlborough

Sauvignon Blanc or a sweet Muscat de Beaumes-de-Venise will make themselves apparent at cooler temperatures than we might serve, say, a Soave. That does not mean that the aromatic wines *need* to be cooler, just that they will tolerate it if necessary.

As a rule of thumb, the classier the wine the less it should be chilled. So a *premier cru* Sauternes might be served a few degrees warmer than a less exalted Monbazillac. Likewise if we are to get the best from a *grand cru* Burgundy, we should allow it a degree or two more warmth than a plain Mâcon-Villages. The other side of the coin is that we can minimize the effect of a poor wine by chilling it as close to freezing as possible.

Although it may sound like heresy to some wine buffs, you can always lob a couple of ice-cubes in, providing the wine isn't too special. It might dilute it a bit if you drink slowly enough, but you can always have more to compensate.

SERVING WINE A good corkscrew can save a great deal of agony when it comes to broaching that hallowed bottle of *grand cru* Burgundy. The most efficient corkscrews are those with a spiral winding around a hollow centre, like a spring that has been stretched a bit – particularly the Screwpull. Do take your time with old bottles, as old corks can crumble.

White wines are easier to serve than reds, if only because there is no sediment or decanting to worry about. Nobody agonizes over whether or not to let white wines "breathe"; they just pour and drink. (Except, perhaps, for Asti Spumante, which purists in Piedmont sometimes pour from a great height – not to swish away the bubbles, but to release even more of its glorious Moscato aroma.) The only point to beware when opening white wines is that, once exposed to the air, a very old wine can begin to oxidize relatively quickly, so it should be treated with circumspection.

Wine boxes vary considerably in quality, not so much due to the packaging as to the wine that is put inside them. Those from European countries can be all right, but they can also be just another way of flogging off excess stocks of lousy or indifferent wine. Australian wine boxes (or "casks") are much more reliable. All boxed wine should be consumed within three or four weeks; it is made and packaged for drinking, not keeping.

Glasses are very much a matter of personal taste, but the main prerequisite of a good wine glass is that it should display every aspect of the wine to the maximum. Clear glass shows off the colour of the wine; a largeish, tapering bowl helps the aromas to concentrate in the glass and improves our chances of smelling them; and a longish stem enables us to hold the glass without touching the bowl and thereby affecting the temperature of the wine.

Now, have we earned a drink, or have we earned a drink?

A–Z DIRECTORY OF
WHITE WINE STYLES

ADELAIDE HILLS

Up above the sprawling Adelaide Plain in South Australia, vineyards are dotted among the hills up to around 1,200 feet (365 m). They are on slopes. Slopes! In Australia, which is 99% flat! As if that is not rare enough, this is one of the country's coolest wine regions. Cool by Australian standards, that is.

White wines dominate. The best Rieslings are greeny-gold, flowery but full-flavoured, big and weighty by German standards but with good balancing lemon 'n' lime acidity, concentrated fruit, and a long, spicy finish. With age (and it can take as little as three years) they develop a honeyed richness but are still bright, lively and well-defined thanks to the acidity. A few *Botrytis*-affected Rieslings are made when conditions allow. They can achieve the rich, sweet, luscious essence-of-raisin quality that is more akin to a Sauternes than, say, a German *Auslese*, for which they would need rather more acidity.

Chardonnay is barrel-fermented. The deep, golden, fat, buttery wines of the early years are giving way to a leaner style with more spicy quince-like flavours. But they are still weighty, rounded and very stylish. Other Chardonnays edge towards the lemony-fresh end of the spectrum; firm, sometimes steely, sometimes lightly smoky.

The outstanding producer of the region is Petaluma [★★★/■■■], whose Brian Croser is a seminal figure in Australian winemaking. He buys his Riesling from Clare, but is using progressively more home-grown Chardonnay. Other leading local producers [★★/■■] include:

Henschke, Eden Valley	*Wynns, High Eden*
Mountadam	*Yalumba, Heggies Vineyard*
Orlando, Steingarten	

A step down in quality, but still good, are the wines produced by Ashbourne and Grand Cru [★/■■].

Petaluma makes a good *méthode champenoise* wine [★★/■■■], and the Champagne house Bollinger has a 50% stake in production. The first (1985) vintage, made from 90% Chardonnay, lacked the depth of flavour and structure that Pinot Noir brings. But Brian Croser is still experimenting with every aspect of production. The aim is for a youthful, fresh, appley style with perceptible fruit flavour.

WHERE NEXT? Contrast Adelaide Rieslings with those from **Clare**, Chardonnays with those from **Coonawarra**. An extravagant leap would be to **Champagne** for a bottle of Bollinger, to see if its influence has rubbed off on Croser.

ALBANA DI ROMAGNA

Albana di Romagna, made near Bologna in the heart of the Emilia-Romagna region of Italy, is a pleasant enough wine, but it had the misfortune to be elevated to DOCG status in 1987. The DOCG is supposed to guarantee consistent quality, but the wine is patently inconsistent. Drinkers are often disappointed because it fails to meet the high expectations it sets for itself and this, of course, calls into question the integrity of the whole DOCG system.

The Albana grape produces a wine with moderate acidity and a marked bitter note at the finish. At its best it has a golden colour and light fruity flavour which goes well with a variety of seafood dishes and with spicy fish soups.

Within the same area there is also a Trebbiano di Romagna, which is blander and sharper-tasting. Blended together the two grape types make an admirable sparkler. Producers of *secco* (dry), *amabile* (sweeter) and *spumante* (sparkling) wines locally [★/■■] include Fratelli Vallunga, F Ferrucci and Consorzio Romagnolo Vini Tipici (COROVIN), one of the world's largest winemaking complexes.

WHERE NEXT? Verdicchio is from nearby: it can have more character. Try **Gavi** as a still alternative, or turn to **Piave** for alternative Italian-accented sparklers.

ALGERIA

The white wines of Algeria have the benefit of modern technology and at their best resemble the clean, fruity wines made by co-operatives in southern France. Indeed, the style is very French here. The Mascara region [★/■] produces agreeable white wines with good fruit; those of the Coteaux de Tlemcen [★/■] are stronger but with a soft finish. Three-quarters of all wines emanate from Albert Camus' home town of Oran and are generic wines made by the state-controlled Office National de Commercialization des Produits Viticoles [★/■]. Much of the wine is exported to the USSR.

WHERE NEXT? Try **Vins de Pays** and Côtes du Rhône (see **Rhône**) from southern France as examples of what quite a few former Algerian winemakers did when they went home.

ALIGOTÉ

Aligoté is a grape from Burgundy, a poor neighbour of the aristocratic Chardonnay, that hangs out mainly in the run-down neighbourhoods of the Bourgogne Aligoté AC. And like living next door to any celebrity, it has to put up with all the paparazzi on the doorstep without a column inch to show for it.

THE ALIGOTÉ TASTE Aligoté's thin-skinned, highly acidic grapes turn out lemony, tart, tangy, unripe-tasting, pinched wines with at best medium body. Oh dear, that doesn't sound very promising does it? And in many years it isn't. One would expect it to make a good sparkling wine, and indeed some of it does go into Crémant de Bourgogne (see **Burgundy**); but then so does a lot of Chardonnay.

Why do the Burgundians bother, we might wonder, when there's all that lovely Chardonnay knocking about? Because they have to drink something themselves, that's why. Men in blue overalls who prune vines, harvest grapes and do odd jobs in the cellar do not stagger home every evening to a welcoming bottle of Bâtard-Montrachet (see **Côte d'Or**). They cannot afford the top wines any more than you or I, but they are not going to be done out of a drink. Aligoté is a crisply refreshing, relatively inexpensive wine for everyday drinking. And it doesn't aim to be anything more.

If, however, the jarring acidity becomes too much, day in, day out, then it can be rounded off with a drop of cassis, the local sweet blackcurrant liqueur, for a less nerve-jangling relaxative. Most people know the combination as *kir*. Even without the addition of cassis,

Aligoté can improve immeasurably if made from older vines in a good, ripe vintage, developing something of the light, creamy nuttiness of Chardonnay and greater weight.

BOURGOGNE ALIGOTÉ The Bourgogne Aligoté *appellation* covers Burgundy from the north near Chablis, to Mâconnais in the south. But the grape has been pushed out to the poorer sites by its grand neighbours and makes, in the small scattered pockets where it is grown, correspondingly poorer wines.

Bouzeron in the Côte Chalonnaise makes the best wines and has its own AC for Bourgogne Aligoté. Good producers [★★/■■] include Bouchard Père et Fils, de Villaine and Pierre Cogny.

Elsewhere, among the best producers of the Bourgogne Aligoté *appellation* [★★/■■] are:

Chanzy	Jobard
Côche-Dury	Monthelie-Domhairet
Confuron	Rion
Diconne	

OTHER ALIGOTÉ Some Aligoté is grown in other parts of the world – most notably in Bulgaria (which grows more than France) and in Romania, where it is occasionally bottled as a varietal.

ALIGOTÉ AND FOOD Apart from its role in a *kir*, Aligoté's acidity is welcome with local dishes such as *jambon persillée*, with *andouillettes*, or with richer foods like snails and some of the tangier cheeses.

WHERE NEXT? Aligoté's acidity would suggest young, dry **Chenin Blanc** and **Gros Plant** as soul mates, or, in better years, **Muscadet**. One of Burgundy's other white grapes, **Pinot Blanc**, is a more appropriate next step than **Chardonnay**. The absence of strong aromatic character proffers dry **Silvaner** as another candidate.

ALSACE

Ssshhh! Don't tell a soul. Alsace produces some of France's best white wines. They are skilfully made cool-climate wines, varied in style, drinkable without having to be cellared for yonks, and affordable. Whatever you do, don't go out and buy any. Well ... it's worth a try. Years of screaming the wonders of these wines from the rooftops seems to have done little to enhance their popularity, so perhaps a different tack might work.

It is best to forget that Alsatian wines have ever had anything to do with Germany. This is difficult, given the preponderance of wine styles based on grapes like Riesling and Gewürztraminer, producers with names like Trimbach, Zind-Humbrecht and Deiss, and villages named Kaysersberg, Pfaffenheim, Gueberschwihr and so on. But anybody looking for light, flowery, bland Liebfraumilch or delicate, ethereal, sweet Rieslings will not find them here. Alsace is in France, and the wines taste like it.

THE ALSACE TASTE Alsace's grape varieties are transformed into wines which are drier and fuller than their German counterparts, with alcohol levels in line with the rest of France. Direct fruit flavour is the main draw; oak is irrelevant. Alsace is a good place to start tasting varietals because the wines are uncontaminated by extraneous flavours. At one time they were unusual in being France's only varietally designated wines, and they beat California and Australia to the starting post as well; now half the world sells its wines this way.

Gewürztraminer may well be the best place to begin. The sock-it-to-me flavours are unmistakeable, the appeal is immediate, strong, colourful, intense. Gewürztraminer comes at you with rich, exotic, tropical fruit flavours of lychee and mango. It does not knock on the door and wait politely for the OK, it barges in and creates a strident, larger-than-life, hurly-burly you cannot ignore.

Alsace Gewürztraminer is dry, but never seems bone dry: the richness of fruit and fatness of texture see to that. If you want searing acidity, try Riesling; it is precisely the lack of obvious acidity that gives buxom Gewürztraminer its broad, ripe, leisurely style, and the feeling that it has never heard of girth control. *Vendange tardive* (late-picked) wines are almost a caricature of this style; they take it to its logical and distinctive extreme. The best Alsatian Gewürztraminers are light to medium-bodied, restrained rather than powerful, with a crispness that comes from picking early. Since they can be almost too full and rich in the "best" years such as 1983 and 1985, they provide excellent drinking in leaner years such as 1981 or 1984.

Muscat is one of the few grapes that tastes just as squishily, juicily fresh whether made into wine or stuffed into your mouth in its raw spherical state. Alsace Muscat is slightly different: it still has the freshness and the glorious Muscat fruit, but it is one step removed from fresh grape feeling because it is dry. It is not austere, and it is still light, but it is just a weeny bit more serious than most other Muscats. The acidity, because it is not blanketed by sweetness, is free to make itself felt; perhaps for this reason many people find Alsace Muscat perfect as an aperitif.

Pinot Blanc has perhaps been underrated in the past. It does not produce wines with ostentatious, gaudy, swaggering, look-at-me flavours, but rather everyday, nine-to-five tastes. You could easily overlook it, as many people have. But that is no reason to dismiss it. Whip off the bowler, throw away the furled umbrella, and underneath is a clean, sharp, fresh-faced, likeable, dependable, salt-of-the-earth, appley-flavoured, and definitely upwardly mobile sort of wine. It is bright, attractive, undemanding and unlike, say, Gewürztraminer, it will partner a wide range of dishes.

The dark horse of grape varieties here is Tokay, or Pinot Gris. Though unremarkable over short distances – it would break no records in a 100-yard sprint – given ten furlongs it romps home ahead of the field. It can even leave Riesling gasping a length or two behind. Like Sémillon it has the ability to age magnificently from a seemingly humble and unexceptional beginning of peaches and nectarines into undreamed-of opulence and power, yet it still remains dry. It is very much a rags-to-riches wine, acquiring along the way the cream to go with the peaches, and the honey to dribble over the cream. *Vendange tardive* and *sélection des grains nobles* wines, made only in the ripest years, are virtually indestructible.

As for the name, Tokay sounds unusually exotic for France, whereas Pinot Gris sounds like it might be a Burgundian cast-off. Alsatians prefer Tokay, but Brussels insists on Pinot Gris, so the accepted compromise is to call it Tokay-Pinot Gris. This, however, does not affect the taste.

Riesling is the most regal of the region's seven permitted varietals, though not the most approachable. Inexpensive Alsace Rieslings can usually be drunk young, having already at that age a style and weight, and a decisive cut, that sets them apart from other wines. But Riesling shows best when it has some bottle age. Riper, fuller, richer Rieslings develop from a steely beginning through honeyed adolescence to a kerosene- and petrol-like maturity. The grape's acidity can keep the

READING LABELS

The name of the producer and the grape variety will be prominent on the label of an Alsace bottle; it is worth deciphering some of the other information too:

● Most wine, whether varietal or blended, is entitled to the Alsace AC. Alsace Grand Cru AC covers specific vineyards for certain grape varieties or blends; only Gewürztraminer, Riesling, Muscat and Pinot Gris varietals will be considered. If the wine comes from just one vineyard, it will be named on the label.

● *Vendange tardive* means that the grapes were picked late, giving them a high sugar level and consequently a high level of potential alcohol; the wine may not necessarily be sweet, but it will be full and fairly alcoholic.

● *Sélection des grains nobles* means that individual grapes (some of them infected with noble rot) were picked to make a rich, sweet wine.

● Words such as *réserve*, *réserve exceptionelle*, *cuvée spéciale*, *sélection spéciale* have no legal force: they will generally indicate a producer's best wine.

wine alive for decades. *Vendange tardive* and *sélection des grains nobles* wines are the real stayers – especially those from super years like 1985, 1983 and 1976.

Sylvaner (see **Silvaner**) is rarely worth getting worked up about, although those from Trimbach and Faller are among the honourable exceptions. It is usually basic drinking wine, the sort you might put on the table along with the salt, pepper and ketchup; part of the furniture rather than a painting to display and admire.

Chasselas (sometimes called Fendant in Switzerland, Gutedel in Germany) is extremely ordinary and in Alsace is only used with other varieties, Edelzwicker being the name for these bucket-shop blends.

Alsace's sparkling wine, Crémant d'Alsace, is made mainly from Pinot Blanc although Riesling and Chardonnay can be used too. The *appellation* was introduced in 1976, and wines are still variable, but it should only be a matter of time before quality improves. In general, Crémant follows the Alsace style in being dry, medium-bodied, flavoursome but not overpowering, and fresh without being sharp.

CHOOSING ALSACE WINES Across the board, the best Alsace producers [★★→★★★/■■→■■■], some of whom grow the grapes themselves, and others of whom are *négociants* who buy their wines from growers, include:

Becker	Hugel
Léon Beyer	Klipfel
Blanck	Kreydenweiss
Cattin	Kuehn
Deiss	Kuentz-Bas
Dopff au Moulin	Muré
Dopff & Irion	Domaine Oestertag
Faller	Schleret
Rolly Gassmann	Schlumberger
Louis Gisselbrecht	Trimbach
Willy Gisselbrecht	Willm
Heim	Zind-Humbrecht

France's first wine co-operative opened for business in Alsace, at Ribeauvillé in 1895, and it is to be recommended, along with those [★★/■■] at Bennwihr, Eguisheim, Turckheim, Kientzheim-Kaysersberg, Béblenheim (Hoen), Pfaffenheim-Gueberschwihr, Sigolsheim.

In the forefront of Crémant d'Alsace producers [★★/■■→■■■] is Dopff au Moulin, which produced the first Alsace sparkler at the turn of the century. Blanck and Boeckel are also good, as are the co-operatives listed above.

ALSACE WINES AND FOOD Mildly spiced dishes from around the world – China, India, Mexico – have a ready-made partner in Alsace Gewürztraminer. Good old Gewürz is also brilliant with smoked foods, rich dishes such as goose, and fruit tarts. The powerful scent of Alsace Muscat makes it another good partner for oriental food with an exotic blend of spices. User-friendly Pinot Blanc is a good wine to have around: drink it with quiche, full-flavoured fish and white meat. Much Pinot Gris can be treated equally casually; try it with sweetish vegetable dishes such as leeks or onion tart. If you have a really fine Tokay-Pinot Gris you will probably want to drink it on its own or with *foie gras*. Alsace Riesling is a good partner for fish, poultry, *choucroute*, cured hams and robust patés; it also goes well with strong cheeses such as Munster.

WHERE NEXT? Cross the Rhine to **Baden** for some interesting variants on broadly similar soil and climate. Baden Ruländer (Pinot Gris) is increasingly good; the Rieslings can be almost as full and flavoursome as Alsace. Or move on east to **Austria** where the dry wine tradition parallels Alsace. Or on to the next entry. . .

ALTO ADIGE

Walk through Bozen in the Südtirol, where the Eisack river joins the Etsch. Admire the snow-capped mountains and the copper onion-domed churches. Listen to one of the many *lederhosen*-clad oompahpah bands. Where are you? Austria, obviously – except for one thing. Ask to see somebody's passport and it will say *passaporta*; look at a map and you will see that you're actually walking through Bolzano in Alto Adige, and that the rivers are called Isarco and Adige.

Alto Adige, part of Austria until 1921, was ceded to Italy in the aftermath of World War I. But the people, and the winemaking, have still not fully made the transition. Wines, for example, can be labelled DOC or QmP; Germanic Riesling and Gewürztraminer figure among the local grape varieties with Gallic Chardonnay and Sauvignon, while Italy's native vines are as plentiful as cheese on Mars.

Alto Adige makes some of Italy's cleanest, brightest, liveliest wines. Ten different white varietals take the Alto Adige DOC, and wines must be made from 95% of the variety named on the label (rather than the more usual proportion of 85%). Almost half of the wine produced here is made in co-operatives.

THE ALTO ADIGE TASTE The Alto Adige style is fresh, light, crisp, clean and dry; it is sometimes delicately perfumed, sometimes lightly oaked, but invariably as invigorating as the mountains themselves. High yields partly account for the lightness, but the South Tyroleans also share something of the German view that it is must-weight, rather than low yields, that determines quality. Alcohol levels vary, but can be as high as 13%. The freshness of the wines is so appealing that it is difficult not to drink them within two to three years of the vintage. Only a few are worth keeping longer.

CHOOSING ALTO ADIGE WINES Chardonnay is a good barometer of winemaking style, and Alto Adige's are among the lightest anywhere, well made and inexpensive. Most are vibrantly fresh; some lightly peppery from their hello-goodbye with an oak barrel. A few producers make more concentrated Chardonnays from lower yields in particular villages or vineyards. Lageder, one of the region's best producers, makes a Buchholz [★★/■■] from the village of that name, and a very classy oak-aged Löwengang [★★★/■■■], smelling of sweet cinnamon and nutmeg in youth, maturing to toast and butter.

Alto Adige Gewürztraminers are among the most ethereal in the world. Even the rich-tasting mature wines have a welcome lightness of touch. The village of Tramin in Alto Adige is the supposed source of Traminer, a less "spicy" variant of Gewürztraminer. Producers to look for [★★/■■] are Tiefenbrunner and Trattmanhof.

Riesling is one of the few wines that does need ageing to bring out its best. In youth it can be feather-light and undistinguished. But with time, and from a good producer – Tiefenbrunner's 1979 [★★★/■■] is an example – it deepens in colour and matures into a powerful, honeyed but dry wine of great class. Other producers [★★/■■] include Bellendorf, Eizenbaum and Hofstätter.

Müller-Thurgau does amazingly well in Alto Adige too; even simple own-label café versions are a delight. Tiefenbrunner makes the northern hemisphere's most distinguished Müller-Thurgau, called Feldmarschall after the tiny, 1,000 metre-high (3,280-ft) vineyard [★★/■■ → ■■■]. Though expensive by Müller-Thurgau standards, it is remarkable how piercingly austere, crisp, dry, steely and "serious" the wine is. Another good producer is Pojer e Sandri [★★/■■].

Even plain Silvaner can be perfumed and attractive here. Sauvignons are variable, most lacking the incisive fruit that the grape produces elsewhere, but Lageder makes one of the more nettley examples called Lehenhof [★★/■■■] under the Terlaner DOC. Pinot Grigio and Pinot Bianco (see **Pinot Gris** and **Pinot Blanc**) both make generally sound wines but without the racy, edgy excitement of other varietals. Muscat (called Moscato Giallo or Goldenmuskateller) makes pure and simple wines, varying from dry to sweet, which are freshly grapey and easy to enjoy. Good examples [★★/■■] are made by Bellendorf, Hofstätter and Hirschprunn.

Other good Alto Adige producers [★→★★/■■] include:

Brigl	*Reiterer*
Kettmeir	*Schloss Sallegg*
Laimburg	*Walch*
Niedermayr	

Also good are the co-operatives [★→★★/■■] at Girlan, Margreid-Entiklar, Muri-Gries, St-Michael-Eppan, Schreckbichl and Tramin.

ALTO ADIGE WINE AND FOOD Pasta, *gnocchi* (dumplings), *speck* (smoked bacon), game and wild mushrooms are among the region's varied culinary delights, all of which can find a match among the wide range of wines. The delicacy and freshness of Alto Adige's wines recommend them as aperitifs, or as partners for light dishes.

WHERE NEXT? Alto Adige suggests parallels with **New Zealand**, which is where the adventurous drinker should explore next. Lower yields (together with differences in soil and climate) give New Zealand's wines rather more definition and punchy vibrant life. For greater weight, try **Alsace**, which shares some varieties with Alto Adige, or a dry German **Silvaner**.

ANJOU

East of Muscadet, the vineyards of Anjou sprawl across the River Loire, encompassing Saumur and producing a lot of mainly uninspiring rosé wines, the lesser-known reds of the region, and several exciting white wines. The great grape of Anjou is the "difficult" Chenin Blanc, often known locally as Pineau de la Loire. The strident acidity of the grape can make short, sharp wines, yet it also acts to preserve the best wines into a brilliant maturity – sometimes after 20 or 30 years. The grape's big problem is ripening, which is not helped by the climate of the Loire Valley; nevertheless, the Anjou-Saumur area is where the Chenin Blanc gives some of its star performances, in styles ranging from dry to sweet and from still to sparkling, stopping at all points en route.

Growers are beginning to blend their Chenin with some Chardonnay or Sauvignon Blanc, giving a welcome lift of fruit to the blanket Anjou AC (dry and semi-sweet), whose wines have in the past often deserved their reputation for sourness. Good producers [★★/■■] include:

Domaine de Closel	*de Jessey*
Michel Gigon	*Soulez*

The best dry Chenin of all comes from Savennières. Here the grapes are picked very ripe, lower yields give more concentration, while the screaming acidity quietens down after a decade or so, developing into a creamy nuttiness. These wines show that dry Chenin can be as graceful and charming as the drinker can be patient. Good years are 1988, 85, 83, 82, 78, 76, 75 and 70. Two small vineyards steal the highest honours, warranting their own Savennières *appellations*: Coulée de Serrant [★★★/■■■] and La Roche aux Moines [★★★/■■■].

In the *appellations* of Coteaux du Layon, Bonnezeaux and Quarts de Chaume, Anjou also makes some of the greatest, most luscious and long-lived sweet wines in the world (see **Coteaux du Layon**).

The dry wines need food to take the edge off the acidity: fish fresh from the river are a standard accompaniment. The more graceful Savennières are good with *rillettes*, the local coarse-textured pork pâtés of the Loire.

WHERE NEXT? Contrast the sweet wines with **Rheingau** and **Rheinpfalz** *Auslesen*: similar growing conditions, different grape. Dry and medium Anjous suggest **Graves** as the next step.

ARGENTINA

Argentine wines have as great a potential as those of Chile, but it is as yet unrealized. The grapes are grown on the same latitude as Chile's, in the shadow of the Andes and the major European varieties dominate: Sémillon, Chardonnay, Chenin Blanc (confusingly called Pinot Blanc), Silvaner (often called Riesling) and even Trebbiano (or Ugni Blanc) for good measure.

The wines are rich in fruit like those of California, but with some crispness in the best wines. The basic table wines, grown in the Mendoza area, are made from Palomino like Spanish sherry and are flabby and dull. Producers [★→★★/■■] include:

Canale	*Peñaflor*
Crillon	*Proviar*
Giol	*Suter*
Norton	*Weinert*
Orfila	

Proviar, owned by the Champagne house Moët et Chandon, makes Champana from a blend of grapes; Suter is known for its Pinot Blanc.

WHERE NEXT? Cross the Andes to Chile where the accent is more French than Italian, or try **Australia**.

ASTI SPUMANTE

Italy's most famous sparkling wine is sweet, fizzy Moscato d'Asti or Asti Spumante from Piedmont. Because the wine is only partially fermented, it is low in alcohol – usually around 5-6%. The unfermented grape juice that remains accounts for the sweetness. And because it is fermented in a sealed tank (by the Charmat or *cuve close* method), the carbon dioxide produced during fermentation cannot escape; it dissolves in the wine, to be released when the cork is popped.

Freshness is paramount. Producers chill the must to 32°F (0°C) in order to prevent the yeasts from working, and may store it for some months before raising the temperature to around 41°F (5°C) to start the 30-day fermentation. It is done this way so as to reduce to a minimum the time between making the wine and drinking it. The younger and fresher the bottle, the greater the chance to appreciate its powerful but fugitive aromas. In Italy they sometimes decant it by pouring from a great height into a jug, to aerate the wine and release as much of the glorious smell as possible.

Good producers [★★/■■] include Fontanafredda, Riccadonna, Viticoltori dell'Acquese, Martini and Cinzano.

Its refreshing grapiness makes Asti ideal as an aperitif. In Italy, it serves as a pudding wine. You dip cake in it and try not to make a mess. This is impossible, but has a Lazarus-like moistening and revitalizing effect on a piece of dry old cake. Asti is also good with trifles and other fruit and cream concoctions.

WHERE NEXT? No other region makes such joyous sparklers, but Clairette de Die (Cuvée Tradition) comes as close as any (see **Rhône**). For even less alcohol, try Pétillant de Raisin from Listel (see **Vin de Pays**). Prosecco fizz from north-east Italy, with its pungent character, offers an interesting Italian alternative (see **Piave**). Or try the fun sparklers of the less-serious **California** makers.

AUSTRALIA

There are two quite different and apparently contradictory philosophies at work in the way Australians make wine. The first involves trucking and blending, which allows the winemaker maximum flexibility to make the style of wine he or she wants, to suit a particular market; the second, more in line with "European" winemaking, is the production of single-vineyard wines.

At its simplest extreme, the goal of trucking and blending might be a plastic "cask" or a bottled wine that has to be made to cheap budget. The winemaker is free to buy grapes or juice from wherever he likes, so if Murrumbidgee (New South Wales) can deliver 1,000 tonnes of Colombard at the right price, while Mildara (Victoria) and Riverland (South Australia) can chip in with some surplus Chenin Blanc at a knock-down rate, then the blend is as good as made. Despite the emphasis on price, the track record of these wines, in terms of being fault-free at least, is generally impressive.

At the other extreme, often in order to hang on to his sanity and self-respect, a winemaker will make a "best shot" blend. "I'll show them what I can really do," he says to himself, buying a small parcel of the best Chardonnay he can find in Coonawarra, a tiny quantity of cool-climate Yarra Valley grapes, and a barrow-load from the Adelaide Hills. There may be no more than 2,000 bottles, but if it wins a few gold medals or a trophy on the show circuit the kudos is undeniable.

There is nothing wrong, illegal or unsound about this sort of thing, no matter how odd it may appear to winemakers in Europe, who are hedged about with restrictions. Move a kilo of grapes in France without the right bit of paper and you are up before the Fraud Squad. In Europe it is the land, the vineyard site, the soil, that is all-important. The wines express this individuality, and vignerons had better not join together what Nature has kept asunder.

This view is now gaining currency in Australia too. Coonawarra, defined by its distinctive red soil, is an obvious example. Cool climates are in vogue, too, particularly for white grapes, because the raw material is immeasurably superior to that from hot, irrigated regions. Yarra Valley and Tasmania for example, although insignificant in terms of quantity, will come under the spotlight more during the next decade. The emphasis, the focus of attention, is shifting from the cellar out into the vineyard.

Single-vineyard wines are on the increase, and we shall see more of particular sites such as Yalumba's Heggies Vineyard in the Barossa or Brown Brothers' Whitlands in Victoria. Larger producers are now adding single vineyard wines to their range. Another development we shall increasingly witness is the matching of grape variety to vineyard site. The traditional fruit salad approach of planting half a dozen grape varieties in one spot will become refined as experience shows that Chardonnay performs better here, Sauvignon there and so on. All this is not replacing trucking or blending, but living comfortably alongside.

Inexpensive fault-free blends have been a success for some time: clean, well-made, fresh, sometimes with a hint of varietal character if one grape dominates, sometimes with a light seasoning of oak if that's what the customer wants. A few wines have been so clean and fault-free that they have lost all character. That is now seen as a fault, and the aim is currently "to put some dirt back into the wine," not by being any less hygienic but, for example, by allowing more contact between skins and juice, or yeast lees and wine, or by filtering less fastidiously and so on.

When it comes to single varietal wines, then flavour has been ladled on with a trowel and we have lapped it up: if some flavour is good, then surely more flavour must be better. Great big buttery Chardonnays have led the field, tasting like a whole breakfast of well-done toast, dripping butter, oozing honey, and a jug of pineapple juice on the side. Put it next to a bantamweight Burgundy of the same price, and the Australian heavy would walk away with the title after the first punch on the nose. No contest. Coonawarra and Hunter Valley are two sources of some of these bruisers.

But, as in California, it occurs to somebody that there is more to life than sheer brawn. Drinkers award marks for artistic interpretation as well as technical competence and pure power. So the tide is turning slowly. Heaven forbid that flavour should get pushed aside – we still want plenty of that – but there is more concern for balance, for structure, for elegance and complexity than there was. That is why the cooler sites matter, because they make such wines possible.

Chardonnay has carried the flag for quality and value, although there have been hiccups. A "vine-pull" scheme, to rid the country of surplus wine, failed to insist that only the viticultural junk should be grubbed up. A Chardonnay shortfall followed, with inevitable price increases. Then more Chardonnay was planted, and when this comes to fruition we should see prices drop. Well, have you ever seen wine prices drop? Still, if we get even better quality than we have so far, and that is entirely possible, then we might decide it is worth the higher price anyway.

There is more to Australian wine than Chardonnay, though. There are some rather individual flavours that we don't find anywhere else: Hunter Valley and Margaret River Semillon for instance, and Liqueur Muscat & Tokay. And there are odd pockets of less usual varieties, like Marsanne in Central Victoria or Verdelho in Western Australia.

Riesling, too, is a great Australian success, although there has been some confusion over the name. In Australia, Hunter Valley Semillon has perversely been called Riesling in the past. In order to distinguish the real, proper, German Riesling from impostors, the habit has developed of calling them Rhine Rieslings. They rarely, if ever, taste like Rieslings from the Rhine but have a true Australian flavour, often less delicately ethereal, with more weight and power. They really should be called Strine Rieslings.

Strine Rieslings can vary from dry to off-dry to medium-dry, to positively sweet when they are *Botrytis*-affected. The weight and concentration varies too, often according to how much we are prepared to pay. Less expensive wines may be simply light and fruity, but with a refreshing tang of citrus that makes them great thirst-quenchers. The sturdier, fuller wines share that lemony, limey acidity which keeps them in balance, and which is one of the Riesling grape's great hallmarks.

Two other things to note about Strine Rieslings are their success in cooler growing areas such as Clare and the Eden Valley, which gives them greater definition and finesse, and their ability to age remarkably well, which is another great quality of the grape world-wide. In Australia the ageing is typically faster than it might be in Germany, so they can reach a rich, honeyed, ripe peak in a matter of 4-5 years. Dry wines, and some Late Harvest wines, retain acidity extremely well, but sometimes the raisiny *Botrytis*-affected wines have less of the knife-edge sharpness of an equivalent *Auslese*, and may be closer to the lusciousness of, say, Sauternes.

Because of the way Australian winemaking is organized, there are different ways of choosing wine. We might want to taste something of the regional character, perhaps the direct and vivid flavours of Margaret River Chardonnay as against the more buttery Coonawarra style, or the fat, honey and pineapple taste of the Hunter, or the more restrained Yarra Valley wines. So we go to a specialist, large or small: Leeuwin Estate or Cape Mentelle in Margaret River; Wynns in Coonawarra; Tyrrell's Vat 47 from the Hunter; or Coldstream Hills from the Yarra Valley (see **Margaret River, Coonawarra, Hunter Valley** and **Yarra Valley**).

If they seem a bit pricey, or if we just want a good Chardonnay or Sauvignon Blanc without worrying too much about the finer points like where it comes from, then we should turn to one of the large, reliable companies for a good mid-price brand. The fruit may be blended from different regions or it may not, but the wine should be consistent from one year to the next.

Enjoyable bottles at reasonable prices come from producers such as Orlando and Lindemans (see **South Australia, Barossa Valley**). Both these are big companies, and it is worth remembering that in Australia large size emphatically does not mean poor quality. If anything, it means the reverse.

WHERE NEXT? See the specific entries on Australian wine styles: **Adelaide Hills, Barossa Valley, Clare, Coonawarra, Hunter Valley, Liqueur Muscat & Tokay, Margaret River, New South Wales, South Australia, Southern Vales, Tasmania, Victoria, Western Australia** and **Yarra Valley**.

AUSTRIA

By rights, Austria should make some of the best white wines in the world. It has the sort of cool climate that some New World producers would sell their grandmothers for, and slopes that would make a French grower spit with envy. But somehow the soil and the grapes don't add up to a package likely to topple Australia, New Zealand, California, Germany or France from their pre-eminence. Yet.

The case of Südtirol, though, shows how much potential there is. Over the Alps to the south, this former chunk of Austria became Italy's Alto Adige in 1921. Here grape varieties with an international following (such as Chardonnay, Pinot Bianco and Gewürztraminer) take on a crisp mountain freshness, while high yields keep them light and relatively inexpensive. They have made a far bigger splash in recent years than anything from Austria.

THE AUSTRIAN TASTE Yet Austria does make good wines, none more immediately appealing than its *heurige* wine – light, fresh and crisp – from the country's very own grape variety, Grüner Veltliner. The green-tinged, tinglingly spritzy, everyday quaffing wine is inseparable from the taverns in which it is served: you get the latest vintage only, drawn from a vat into a pitcher or *viertel* and plonked on the table along with a plate of sausage, pork, bacon and ham.

Grüner Veltliner invariably makes good, but not great, wine. Rather like Pinot Blanc (also known as Klevner), it is sound, dependable, dry, light to medium-bodied, and, thanks to generous yields, not too expensive. The more serious wine is bottled; the best – with a distinctly peppery taste – comes from Wachau, from beside the Danube and from Kamptal-Donauland.

Frühroter Veltliner makes rather lumbering, full-bodied wines that often want for acidity. Although it is Austria's second most widely planted variety, Müller-Thurgau is underrated; Gewürztraminer's bold personality, as ever, shines through differences in soil and climate to produce aromatic and flowery wines. Finicky though it is, and nervous as a thoroughbred racehorse, Riesling outclasses all other varieties, making wines with more finesse and greater character. There is a little Chardonnay too.

CHOOSING AUSTRIAN WINES Austria can be considered an eastward extension of Germany as far as winemaking is concerned, with *Tafelwein*, *Landwein*, and *Qualitätswein* from *Kabinett* to *Trockenbeerenauslese* (see **Germany**). It adopts a similar scale of natural grape-sugar level or "must-weight", but the minimum öchsle levels are higher. An extra category, *Ausbruch*, comes mid-way between *Beerenauslese* and *Trockenbeerenauslese* and has an affinity with the *Assú* wines of Hungarian Tokay.

The best Austrian producers [★★/■■→■■■] include:

Klosterkeller	Fritz Saloman
Lingenfelder	Siegendorf
Lenz Moser	

AUSTRIAN WINE AND FOOD Austria's tremendously rich dessert dishes are delicious with summer fruits. *Auslesen* are also particularly appealing with pork.

WHERE NEXT? Strike westwards to Germany's **Rheingau** and **Mosel-Saar-Ruwer** for a taste of the heights to which Austrian Riesling wines aspire; or, if Grüner Veltliner appeals, try a light wine from **Switzerland** or Italy's **Alto Adige**.

BADEN

Baden may not be in the first rank of Germany's wine regions; it doesn't make Rieslings of Rheingau stature for instance. But then neither does it rely on Liebfraumilch. In fact it embodies two of the best elements of the contemporary German approach. The wines are dry. And many of them are simply and unconfusingly labelled: Baden Dry sums up pretty well most of what we need to know.

The mix of grape varieties in this sunny southern region on the edge of the Black Forest is rather unusual for Germany. There are few crosses, and, apart from Müller-Thurgau (the most widely planted) and a little Gewürztraminer, no great emphasis on the aromatic and flowery varieties. It shares some with Alsace, which sits just across the Rhine, over the border in France. Silvaner is not one to set the pulse racing, but it makes a plain, no-nonsense style of wine to drink with food, as does Ruländer (Pinot Gris). The even plainer Gutedel (France's Chasselas, Switzerland's Fendant) performs well too.

The grapes achieve good ripeness, which makes them relatively full-flavoured, with less crisp acidity and a bit more body than some of the more anorexic wines from further north. Because of this, wines made from Gewürztraminer are often rather fat, but the ripeness of Riesling can be very attractive.

Regional names to look for include the *Bereiche* of Ortenau (*Grosslagen* Durbach and Ortenberg), Kaiserstuhl-Thuniberg and Markgräflerland. Production is dominated by co-operatives, which account for nine out of every ten bottles of Baden wine. The biggest, in fact Europe's biggest, the Zentralkellerei Badischer Winzergenossenschaften or ZBW [★→★★★/■■], makes over 400 different wines every year. Despite this, quality can be commendably high.

Other good producers [★★/■■] include the co-operatives at Sasbachwalden and Bickensohl, and:

Freiherr von Gleichstein	*Freiherr von und zu*
Hermann Dörflinger	*Franckenstein'sches*
Salwey	*Staatsweingut Meersburg*

WHERE NEXT? Strike out to **Alsace** in one direction, for wines made under much the same conditions, or off east to **Franken** in Germany's heartland, where the wines are drier and more austere, but recognizably neighbours.

BAROSSA VALLEY

Vines do grow in this heartland of South Australian viticulture – lots of them – but a Barossa style is difficult to pinpoint since it is more like a clearing house for grapes. They come in from far and wide (sometimes as juice, sometimes as wine) to the headquarters of some of the country's biggest companies, to be filtered, finished, blended and bottled on "tank farms", and then packed on their way.

There is nothing at all wrong with this, either legally or oenologically, indeed it is an integral part of the Australian way of winemaking. If a company owns vineyards in Coonawarra, Padthaway and McLaren Vale there is no point in building three expensive wineries, where one expensive winery and a truck will do the job just as well. Or, if you need something to fatten you basic Barossa Semillon, you might buy a few hundred kilos of Hunter Valley grapes to blend in. Go ahead, there is nothing to stop you. It just doesn't make for a recognizable Barossa style that's all.

It does usually make for good drinking though, and that is one of the key ways in which Australia differs from, say, Europe. They couldn't do that in France – or at least they could, but the resulting wine would only be classed as *vin de table* and thus beneath the dignity of most people who consider themselves "serious" winemakers. And who would pay good money to drink it?

CHOOSING BAROSSA WINES Companies in the Barossa typically have a range of wines, from single-vineyard wines and regional classics to inter-state blends, and the following are among the best.

Orlando owns vineyards in different regions and buys in huge quantities of grapes. It is an excellent example of how quality can be comfortably delivered in quantity. Jacob's Creek Semillon/Chardonnay blend and lightly perfumed Rhine Riesling are the starting point of the range [★/■■]. Orlando RF Chardonnay [★/■■] is next, light and fresh with a dash of oak for seasoning. The Saints range [★★→★★★/■■→■■■] is the pick: St Hilary Chardonnay is golden, buttery, and toasty; St Helga Rhine Riesling is ripe, concentrated but lemony fresh, and 4-5 years bottle age transforms this into a glorious honeyed, keroseney beaut. Orlando also makes a Semillon-based sparkler called Carrington [★/■■].

Seppelt is another large producer either owning or buying grapes all over the place. The Queen Adelaide range opens the batting with simple but good value Rhine Riesling and Chardonnay [★/■■]. Gold Label Chardonnay [★★/■■■] is more tropically fruity, Show Chardonnay [★★/■■■] rich and buttery. Drumbourg Riesling [★★/■■■] is a single-vineyard wine. Seppelt's Great Western sparklers [★★/■■■], made with varying amounts of Chardonnay and Pinot Noir in the blend, are also good.

Peter Lehmann [★★/■■] is one of the few wineries to use grapes exclusively from Barossa. His Dry Semillon is light and fresh, Fumé Blanc is less successful, but Rhine Riesling is a delicate "each way" wine, drinkable very young but keepable for 5 years, and there is a luscious *Botrytis*-affected version.

Wolf Blass wines [★→★★★/■■] appeal to a wide range of drinkers. They are well made, with a seductive combination of powerful fruit and rich oak flavours. Juice comes mostly from Clare and Eden Valleys. Rhine Riesling is made slightly sweet for wide and immediate appeal, and Chardonnay is utterly sound.

Yalumba's range of wines is rather bewildering, but the best come from specific vineyard sites: Pewsey Vale, Heggies and Hill-Smith Estate. Pewsey Vale Rhine Riesling [★★/■■] captures the clean, direct flavour of the grape, while Heggies [★★/■■] is more aromatic and vivid. Hill-Smith Estate Semillon [★★/■■] is wholesome, honest, consistent, while Yalumba Signature Chardonnay [★★/■■■] is a "best shot" blend from McLaren Vale and Coonawarra. The overall style is generally sound, solid and workmanlike rather than breezy and exciting, but Angas Brut [★★/■■] is a dashing sparkler.

Krondorf [★★→★★★/■■] is good for Chardonnay, especially the fat, golden, buttery Show Reserve and lighter, more restrained Limited Edition. Lees-contact, malolactic fermentation, must-oxidation and barrel-fermentation together produce a softness and mellowness that balances the greeny freshness of the fruit, while keeping flavour to the fore. Rhine Rieslings are dry and stylish.

Penfolds, the country's biggest wine firm, has traditionally been based at Magill in the Adelaide Plains, but more goes on at the Nuriootpa HQ in Barossa. It is best known for a string of world-class red wines, which totally outclass and overshadow the whites, but

Seaview fizz [★★/■■] – particularly the *méthode champenoise* – is extremely good and fairly priced. Penfolds Chardonnay [★★/■■■] is one of the more outrageously tropical mango and passion fruit styles, with a rich layer of butter slapped on top. Fumé Blanc and Traminer/Riesling [★★/■■] bring up the rear.

Tollana makes a lightly aromatic, summer-drinking Dry White blend [★/■■] of Semillon, Colombard and Rhine Riesling, and a slightly more characterful, zingy Semillon/Chardonnay [★/■■]. Its best vineyard site, in Eden Valley near Barossa, produces good dry Rhine Riesling [★★/■■]: light-to-medium bodied, straight, honest, crisp, lively and slightly peppery. Small quantities of *Botrytis*-affected Rhine Riesling [★★/■■■] are sometimes made.

Saltram varietals [★→★★/■■] include good Chardonnay and Rhine Riesling, superior Mamre Brook Chardonnay, and top-of-the-range Pinnacle Selection Gewürztraminer.

Other good Barossa producers [★★/■■] include:

Barossa Valley Estates	*Kaiser Stuhl*
Basedow's	*Leo Buring*

BAROSSA WINE AND FOOD Barossa Chardonnays – indeed most Australian Chardonnays – are flexible enough to match a wide variety of foods. They go especially well with rich sauces, with haddock, salmon, trout, lobster, crab and even with *sashimi*.

WHERE NEXT? **Adelaide Hills** producers say their wines are finer and less obvious than Barossa's: try them and see. California's **Napa Valley** whites are the northern hemisphere's equivalent.

BEAUMES-DE-VENISE

This is France's best *vin doux naturel* and best sweet Muscat wine, made in the southern Rhône village of Beaumes-de-Venise. Most of France's VDNs are produced along the Mediterranean coast, and most of the wines here are red, so it really is an oddity. But a splendid one.

Muscat à Petits Grains, the classy member of the Muscat family, is the grape variety, and the wine is stamped with its irresistibly fresh grapey hallmark. It can be rich too, and muskily ripe with the perfumed taste of sultanas rather than raisins, and delightfully perfumed, but what makes is come alive is the spike of orange zest and the acidity that keeps the whole thing in balance.

The fermentation is stopped with grape spirit when it is only partially complete. By itself the juice is sweet enough to produce 15% alcohol, but grape spirit jacks this up to 21.5%. It remains naturally sweet because of the unfermented grape sugar.

Best producers [★★/■■■] include the Beaumes-de-Venise co-operative, which makes the lion's share, and:

Domaine des Bernardins	*Guigal*
Domaine de Coyeux	*Jaboulet*
Domaine de Durban	*Domaine St-Sauveur*

Since its "discovery", Muscat de Beaumes-de-Venise has become the ubiquitous pudding wine – but who's complaining, as long as it's served well chilled? It's particularly apt with fruit-based puddings.

WHERE NEXT? Other sweet Muscat wines, besides the French **Vins Doux Naturels**, include Moscatel de Setúbal, Muscat of Samos and Moscato di Pantelleria (see **Muscat**). Malvasia delle Lipari from Sicily (see **Malvasia**) shares the Muscat fragrance. **Pineau des Charentes** is made slightly differently.

BERGERAC

Bergerac is a sad case of an "also ran" in the wine world. Despite the similarity of style it is not part of neighbouring Bordeaux, the last outpost of which is Ste-Foy-Bordeaux [★/■], a humble AC making respectable dry wines from the usual Bordeaux blend of Sauvignon Blanc and Sémillon.

Bergerac has been discriminated against in the past, having to send its wines down the Dordogne via Libourne, and paying extra taxes for the privilege of using somebody else's backyard in order to reach the world outside. Soils, climate and grape varieties are very similar to much of Bordeaux, so there is no reason why its wines should not be on a par with at least Entre-Deux-Mers.

But Entre-Deux-Mers has put on something of a spurt over the last decade, and Bergerac needs to do the same if it is not to drop out of the race; there is no shortage of competitors, either locally or around the world, making crisp, dry whites. Bergerac has a few good producers, and one excellent one, but that is not much for an AC of its size.

THE BERGERAC TASTE Bergerac Sec is made principally from Sauvignon Blanc, with some Sémillon and Muscadelle often thrown in. It is rather like Sancerre – fresh, green, nettley, with blackcurrant leaves shredded into it – but without the stinging bite of acidity. In the first year or two it is pungently aromatic; and when this tails off there is still enough weight from the Sémillon to keep it going for a further year or two.

CHOOSING BERGERAC The star property is Château La Jaubertie [★★/■■], which does exactly what everybody else should be doing: using hi-tech and New World savvy to squeeze the last ounce of flavour from the grapes. It makes a traditional blend and also a 100% Sauvignon Blanc. Other good châteaux [★★/■→■■] include:

Belingard	Court-les-Mûts
Le Caillou	Le Fagé
du Chayne	de Panisseau
Domaine Constant	Thénac

Nearby Montravel makes both dry and sweeter styles with Sémillon dominating the blend; Château du Bloy [★★/■■] is the best producer here.

Bergerac's steely quality comes into its own and is even enhanced by certain food. Its sharpness stands up well to *antipasto* and smoked trout or mackerel.

WHERE NEXT? After Bergerac Sec the next best thing on the Bordeaux fringe is **Côtes de Duras**. Or taste what **New Zealand's** up-and-coming wine industry does with the same grapes (Bergerac producers should try a similar exercise).

BLANQUETTE-DE-LIMOUX

This good sparkling wine, from the hills south of Carcassonne in France's Aude region, has been made for centuries and may have pre-dated Champagne as the earliest form of *méthode champenoise* fizz – or so local producers claim. One way or the other, Blanquette-de-Limoux has not since risen to the same heights. Nevertheless it is a reliable and good-value fizz.

Made from the Mauzac grape, along with Chardonnay, Chenin Blanc and Clairette, by the *méthode champenoise* (or should that be the *méthode limousine?*), Blanquette has a sharp appley freshness and bite that follows up the slight cidery aroma. The large co-operative [★★/■■→■■■] dominates production, accounting for some 80% of wines released. Other names to look for [★★/■■] include:

Aimery	*Cuvée Diaphane*
Cuvée Cedric	*Ets Salasar*

WHERE NEXT? Cross the Pyrenees to Catalonia for **Cava** sparklers, or look to **Loire** Crémants for a bit more taste and a slightly higher price. Those with easy access to New World fizz will find it often better value than Blanquette (see **Sparkling Wines**).

BORDEAUX

Bordeaux is best known for red wines, which is not at all surprising when you consider that the total output of white wine in the region is about half that of red. Fine claret is world-class, and not in particularly short supply; the famous sweet wines of Sauternes and Barsac always find a market among discerning drinkers. Dry whites, on the other hand, were until relatively recently so badly made and fruitless that you wonder how anybody had the nerve to sell them.

Come the 1980s, two factors helped to improve the fortunes not only of basic Bordeaux Blanc but also of Entre-Deux-Mers and Graves. Technology, in the form of stainless steel tanks and temperature-controlled fermentation, has dramatically improved freshness, fruit flavour and quality. It is the simplest way to smarten up any white wine; all it takes is money. And, as drinkers have shown that they will pay more for a quality wine, it has become worthwhile for producers to invest in the necessary equipment. The effect has been to release a stream of drinkable wines.

THE BORDEAUX TASTE The flavour of white Bordeaux can range through every shade and style from the driest of dry to the unctuously sweet. The driest are the whites made with a high proportion of Sauvignon Blanc and labelled either Bordeaux Blanc, Bordeaux Blanc Supérieur or Entre-Deux-Mers. The flavour is grassy and vegetal, a little like a green pepper, but not so powerful as a California Fumé Blanc or a flinty Pouilly-Fumé from the Loire. The presence of Sémillon in most of these dry wines adds a honeyed note which softens the effect.

The white wines of Graves are of a far finer quality, dry and rich, with a hint of oak age on the very best. The flavour is supposed to make you think of the sun-drenched gravel which is their source, but a simpler comparison might be a bread-like aroma. There is plenty of fruit but less floral or vegetal fragrance; the blends are subtle.

Sweeter wines like those made at Cérons, Ste-Croix-du-Mont, Loupiac and Cadillac are generally soft and attractive on the nose with a scent of honey and perhaps a hint of fresh mushroom indicating the presence of "noble rot". These wines offer a cheaper alternative to the celebrated sweet wines of Sauternes and Barsac.

DRY BORDEAUX: BEGIN WITH ENTRE-DEUX-MERS Entre-Deux-Mers is made in the rolling countryside between the Rivers Garonne and Dordogne, and often has the quality edge over Bordeaux Blanc, which can be produced anywhere within the Gironde *département*. Though its wines lack the seriousness of Graves, they are generally fresher, lighter and more approachable; they also tend to be more affordable than the wines of Graves, and thus make a good starting-point for discovering the dry white wines of Bordeaux (see **Entre-Deux-Mers**).

OTHER DRY BORDEAUX Across the river, and a step up from Entre-Deux-Mers is Graves, which triumphed over its once-dismal reputation during the 1980s and now produces the region's (and some of France's) crispest, fruitiest dry white wines (see **Graves**).

Basic Bordeaux Blanc must have an alcohol level of at least 10.5 degrees and meet certain planting requirements; Bordeaux Supérieur is a little stronger at 11.5 degrees and the grapes are harvested more sparingly, but flavour differences are not remarkable. Both of these wines are based on Sauvignon Blanc, Sémillon and a little Muscadelle; neither is any great shakes. Reliable co-operative producers for the two styles [★/■→■■] include:

Espiet	*Ste Radegonde*
Rauzan	*Sauveterre*

A few apparently humdrum Bordeaux Blanc wines made at the great châteaux of the Médoc and Sauternes can be more significant, but they still have to be called simply Bordeaux or Bordeaux Supérieur. In the Médoc, fine dry white wines include: Caillou Blanc, from the fourth-growth Château Talbot [★★★/■■→■■■], a clean "flinty" wine as its name might suggest; Pavillon Blanc, made at the illustrious Château Margaux from 100% Sauvignon Blanc to the highest of standards [★★★/■■■]; and the white wine of Château Loudenne, one of the best-value white Bordeaux around, crisp and clean [★★/■■]. Good dry wines are also made by the great Sauternes estates, best known for their sweet wines (see **Sauternes & Barsac**).

Bordeaux is not made up entirely of châteaux that bottle their own wine. An important and traditional role is played by the *négociants* who buy wine from different producers, then blend it to their customers' specifications. Such merchants are often shippers as well. Just as with any vineyard or château it is possible for a blending merchant to make a hash of it: by buying whatever he can from growers who are desperate to sell and turning out very cheap tasteless wine. If it has a Bordeaux label, somebody, somewhere, will buy it.

But it is equally possible to be good at the job, which is to provide straightforward, drinkable and affordable wines. This may involve blending wines from villages miles apart, even from different years, to compensate for Nature's uneven gifts; the resulting wine may not have much individual character, but it gives us something to swig from Monday to Friday.

Négociant names to look for [★★/■→■■■] include:

Barton & Guestier	*Louis Eschenauer*
Borie-Manoux	*Ginestet*
Calvet	*Mouton-Cadet*
Cordier	*Schroder & Schyler*
Cruse	*Maison Sichel*

The white wines of Blaye, across the river from the Médoc – which may be labelled as Côtes de Blaye, Premières Côtes de Blaye, Blayais or simply Blaye – offer a variation on the Bordeaux theme. Sauvignon Blanc and Sémillon are the main grape varieties, but there is some crinkle-fresh Colombard too, the grape that was dismissed until it started to make zippy wines such as those from the Côtes de Gascogne. It doesn't perform quite so well here, but it perks up the other varieties a bit. Co-ops [★/■■] dominate production here, notably:

Generac	*St-Savin-de-Blaye*
Pugnac	*Tauriac*
St Gervais	

SWEET BORDEAUX: BEGIN WITH SAUTERNES The sweet wines of Sauternes-Barsac at the southern end of Graves are, by common consent, the greatest dessert wines in the world. Intensely sweet, opulent, honeyed and capable of developing in bottle over many decades, this is *the* classic sweet white wine. They are seldom cheap, and the cheap examples are seldom good, but splash out on a half-bottle from a good-value château such as Bastor-Lamontagne and from a good vintage such as 1983, 1986 or 1989 and see what all the fuss is about (see **Sauternes & Barsac**).

OTHER SWEET BORDEAUX Wines from the other regional *appellations*, made from the same trio of grapes as Sauternes and still sweet, are lighter, less syrupy, since they are allowed higher yields and are not affected by *Botrytis* to the same extent. Much of the Cérons crop is now made into dry Graves, but what little sweet wine there is can be good value, as can other sweet wines from Graves labelled Graves Supérieur (see **Graves**).

On the opposite (northern) bank of the Garonne are the Premières Côtes de Bordeaux, sandwiched between the river and the Entre-Deux-Mers *appellation*. The Premières Côtes is itself an AC, but also encloses the tiny ACs of Ste-Croix-du-Mont, Loupiac and Cadillac. Wines labelled Premières Côtes are much lighter than Sauternes and tend to be simply sweet with no noble rot flavours and little distinctive style. The area now tends to emphasize red wines. White wines are used to make generic blends for the big *négociants* and shippers.

Good Premières Côtes producers [★→★★/■■], some of which make dry wines too, include:

Beau Site	*Peyrat*
Biac	*Poncet*
Birot	*Reynon*
Lamothe	*Suau*
Monprimblanc	*Tanesse*

Ste-Croix-du-Mont, the best sweet AC of the Premières Côtes, and the next-door AC of Loupiac also make some extremely attractive and relatively inexpensive wines that resemble Sauternes quite closely.

Good Ste-Croix and Loupiac producers [★★/■■→■■■] include:

Bel-Air	*Ricud*
Loubens	*Morange*
Loupiac-Gaudiet	*de Tastes*

The tiny AC of Cadillac, a short hop along the northern bank from Loupiac, does not have the high reputation that automobile fans might expect, but it does have one excellent property, Château Fayau [★★/■■].

BORDEAUX AND FOOD The dry wines are often served with seafood, notably the excellent local oysters and other small shelled creatures found on a *plateau de fruits de mer*; for the sweeter styles try a blue cheese such as Roquefort or some *pâté de foie gras*.

WHERE NEXT? Kick off with **Côtes de Duras**; farther east are the agreeable dry whites of **Bergerac** and the sweet wine **Monbazillac** which more than rivals many Premières Côtes de Bordeaux.

Try **Sancerre & Pouilly-Fumé** for a really crisp dry Sauvignon Blanc; or be venturesome and compare Bordeaux white wine with other examples made of **Sémillon** or **Sauvignon Blanc** from around the world.

BULGARIA

A fish-and-chip shop proprietor once explained his success thus: "The customers want lots of it, they want it now, and they don't want any bones." So that is what he gave them. Bulgaria is a bit like that with wine. We want plenty of it, with lots of flavour, and we want it cheap. And that's just what we've got.

While classic Western red grape varieties have been producing steadily more impressive alternatives to Bordeaux, the whites have lagged some way behind. The native East European and Russian vine, Rkatziteli, is widely planted but not widely admired. Instead, we all look to Chardonnay to give us cheap white Burgundy on a plate, and it is beginning to assert itself, although if it has a distinctive style it is keeping it up its sleeve for the time being. The wines hover around medium-bodied, and are very drinkable, but they don't yet display the buttery richness of which Chardonnay is capable. Oak is often Chardonnay's saviour, but so far it has been applied with little finesse.

Eastern Bulgaria, towards the Black Sea, is prime white wine country, and the Schumen region shines with Chardonnay: wines from Preslav, Novi Pazar and Khan Krum are among the best [★★/■→■■], although it might help if Khan Krum carried a government oak warning. What the better wines do carry is the name of one of the eight white Controliran regions, which are rather like France's *appellations contrôlées*. Most wines are produced and sold by the Bulgarian state monopoly.

Other international varieties grown in Bulgaria include Riesling, Gewürztraminer, Sauvignon Blanc, Aligoté and Trebbiano.

WHERE NEXT? Try **New Zealand** where Chardonnay and Sauvignon Blanc are grown with more finesse – but the prices are higher. Or try **Mâcon** and the **Côte Chalonnaise** for Chardonnay. Look elsewhere in south-east Europe – **Yugoslavia**, **Romania** – for other wines struggling to make the grade.

BURGUNDY

Burgundy produces some of the greatest white wine in the world – Chablis, Puligny-Montrachet, Meursault – from what many people consider to be the greatest white grape, Chardonnay.

Quantities are small, or at least too small to satisfy a thirsty world, and prices can be high, so Burgundy has been copied, emulated and reproduced around the world. At one time it was the names that were borrowed, leading to claims that as much "Chablis" was consumed in a single day as was produced in the village of Chablis in a whole year. Now Chardonnay has established itself world-wide, and most respectable winemakers aim to make a wine to reflect their own circumstances rather than just another Burgundy look-alike. But Burgundy is still the source of inspiration. Its best wines still achieve a remarkable degree of elegance and balance that many others can only dream of.

Not all Burgundy is like that. The region stretches from chilly Chablis in the north to the edge of Beaujolais in the warm south, a distance of 125 miles (200 km). Only a small fraction of that distance is occupied by white vines. After Chablis there is a gap of nearly 70 miles (112 km) before Meursault and Puligny-Montrachet in the Côte d'Or, a short hop southwards from there to the Côte Chalonnaise, and then another break of some 15 miles (24 km) before reaching the Mâconnais.

Buying Burgundy is as fraught with danger as buying a second-hand car. It is not so much the make of car that matters as the man who sells it to you. If he is reputable, you could walk away with a bargain, a

READING LABELS

● The term *grand cru* applies to particular vineyards, such as Bâtard-Montrachet (in the village of Puligny-Montrachet) or Les Criots (in Chassagne-Montrachet); each of these has its own *appellation* independently of the village.

● The term *premier cru* covers other vineyards, for example Les Perrières (in the village of Meursault) or Les Pucelles and Clavoillon (in Puligny-Montrachet); these wines are usually labelled with both village and vineyard name but, if made from several *premier cru* vineyards, they may simply be labelled with the name of the village, plus *premier cru.*

● Other wines from within the village boundary are able to use the village *appellation* only, though a specific vineyard may still be mentioned on the label.

● Other vineyards will have a more general *appellation* such as Hautes Côtes de Beaune or Bourgogne Grande Ordinaire. These less specific ACs cover a wider area, obscuring fine differences but making less expensive wines.

genuine low-mileage Ford that won't give a moment's trouble; if he is not, then you might end up with an expensive and duff Mercedes that spends more time in the garage than on the road.

So it is with Burgundy. The makes or names, the *appellations*, offer the nearest we can get to a cast-iron warranty that the wine does come from where it says – the village of Puligny-Montrachet for example. But there are lots of Puligny-Montrachets, not all equally good. It is the man who made it, the *négociant* who blended it, or the merchant who stocks it, that we need to get to know.

The practical complexity arises from a few simple principles. Foremost among these is the AC system which, as throughout France, varies in degree of specificity. The best vineyards, designated *grands crus*, can produce sublime wines, depending on the producer. *Premier cru* does not refer, as in the Médoc, to the top wines but to the second tier. These are, or again can be, brilliant and exciting wines.

Village wines come from vineyards within a village boundary and may either be from a single plot of land, or a blend of wines from several. Regional *appellations*, such as Hautes-Côtes de Beaune, cross village boundaries and may, as in the case of Bourgogne Blanc AC, extend to whole regions.

By itself, the *appellation* system is fairly straightforward. But it is complicated by an inheritance system which, by dividing the estate equally between all children, has progressivly segmented the whole of Burgundy into smaller and smaller plots. This could mean that a grower now has, say, one row of vines in each of four vineyards in Puligny-Montrachet, and a couple each in two vineyards in Meursault. His options are to make and bottle the wine from each vineyard separately; to make two village wines by combining the separate vineyards within each; to make a generic white Burgundy; or sell it all to a *négociant* who will combine it with the wines of other growers.

And there is no simple way for the consumer to tell which is best.

THE BURGUNDY TASTE The one thing all the top wines do have in common, though, is the grape variety. Chardonnay's international stardom has confirmed two things. First, its adaptability to different conditions: pale, light and refreshing in Alto Adige for instance, and golden, unctuous and rich in Australia's Hunter Valley. Although not reaching such extremes in Burgundy, it does help to explain differences between the leaner style of Chablis and the intensity and complexity of Montrachet.

The second thing that Chardonnay's missionary work has brought home is that there is still nowhere quite like Burgundy for elegance, for sheer class at the top of the range. It still produces wines that are balanced, complete, integrated, with acidity restraining any natural exuberance. It is still the model that most New World producers have in their head when they plant their first Chardonnay vines. If you want to taste the best Chardonnay in the world, this is where you come, chequebook in hand, to join the queue.

BEGIN WITH THE COTE D'OR There is no point mucking about with Mâcon if we really want to take a swing at the big Burgundy taste. We could start with Chablis, but it can be a bit lean. By all means keep Mâcon and Chalon for everyday drinking, and by all means revel in taut, elegant Chablis at every opportunity, but sooner or later we have to face the Big One. It will cost us more money than most wines but we have to experience it: so screw up the courage, plunge in and begin with the Côte d'Or (see **Côte d'Or**).

OTHER BURGUNDY Wouldn't it be nice if there was somewhere rather like the Côte d'Or and Chablis without the superstars, just making simple, enjoyable wines from Chardonnay that most people can afford. That should be what happens further south in Mâcon and the Côte Chalonnaise. When Côte d'Or prices began to get out of hand, we went there because it seemed sane and calm by comparison. Nobody would claim that Mâconnais and Côte Chalonnaise wines even begin to measure up to what the Côte d'Or can do, but that doesn't matter provided they are well made, clean, fresh with a bit of fruit and quite cheap. Unfortunately, they are becoming expensive. Nobody expects the wine to be given away, but when compared to others for value they often leave you wondering whether they're worth it (see **Mâcon, Côte Chalonnaise**).

If Mâconnais and Côte Chalonnaise prices horrify you, there are always the regional *appellations*. Grapes for Bourgogne Blanc can be grown as far apart as Chablis and Beaujolais, and it is extremely variable stuff. Some, from conscientious growers, is surplus Chardonnay aged in oak that can be as good as some other people's Meursault; some contains Pinot Blanc and Pinot Gris, and may be very ordinary.

The producer's name is paramount for Bourgogne Blanc, and the best ones [★★/■■→■■■] include:

Buxy Co-operative	Jaffelin
Côche-Dury	Javillier
Drouhin	Jobard
Faiveley	Labouré-Roi
Jadot	

Another general AC, Bourgogne Grande Ordinaire is not in the slightest bit *grande* but is terribly *ordinaire*. Unless your luck has completely run out there should be something, somewhere that is better to drink than this.

Bourgogne Aligoté is an *appellation* covering Burgundy from Chablis in the north to Mâcon in the south. The wine can be more than a curiosity, but only just. Tart, sharp, lemony, tangy and unripe-tasting, it is made from the Aligoté grape, grown mostly on the poorer Burgundian sites (see **Aligoté**).

Burgundy's sparkling wine, Crémant de Bourgogne, is made from Pinot Noir and Chardonnay, as in Champagne, plus Pinot Blanc and Aligoté. They can come from anywhere between the northerly Yonne and Mâcon. Low yields and extended ageing help to keep quality up; the wines are invariably dry; and the style can be full and quite soft without being fat or flabby.

The best producers of Crémant de Bourgogne [★★/■■→■■■] include André Bonhomme and Cave de Lugny.

WHERE NEXT? For a comparison with great Burgundy, go to the best Australian and California Chardonnays (see **South Australia, Victoria, Western Australia, Napa Valley, Sonoma**).

It is in the middling price and quality levels that much of the competition has come lately. Whenever Chardonnays are gathered together for comparative tastings, it is the New World that sweeps the board for value. Switching grape varieties, **Entre-Deux-Mers** has improved tremendously; there is plenty of it, and it is not greedily priced. **Alsace** can eat most of them for breakfast.

CALIFORNIA

This sun-drenched centre of the American wine universe suffers from what media people might descibe as an "image problem". As with Italy, some people's perceptions of the wine are rooted either in hearsay or in experience of only the most basic and dreary examples. In Italy, this might mean a watery, over-priced Frascati; in California, it would probably mean a cheap jug wine from the hot Central Valley. Such wines are not particularly unpleasant, merely dull, although some Central Valley producers (such as Gallo) are able to maintain a consistently reasonable standard at a low price and turn out some good varietals too.

And in fact the true taste of California is quite the opposite of dull. The wines tend to have almost too much flavour for a palate used to European subtleties. With such a wonderful climate, the grapes are normally gathered at peak ripeness. There is also no substance in the view of California as home to the additive industry; overall winemakers here probably use fewer additives than their European counterparts. Of course the wines are "engineered" a little, otherwise the whites would be like those made back in the 1950s – high in alcohol, slightly sweet and unstable unless pasteurized.

California's image as the principal purveyor of make-believe generic wines is, however, partly true. The so-called generic market is very important in the US, and a vast amount of passable wine is sold as Chablis, Sauternes or even Dry Sauternes to a thirsty American public. Together with the much-misused Champagne, these names are an almost deliberate nose-thumbing exercise by California producers. Until the 1970s they exported virtually no wine at all: for a California winery, "export" meant sending the wine on a train to New York. California wines were, in the main, for Californians; certainly the finest wines were consumed within a bare 50-mile radius of the winery.

Today, generic wine is frequently still sold under a brand name in California, but by the time it has reached Europe "Chablis" will have metamorphosed into something more innocuous such as "California white wine". More interesting wines are labelled varietally as "Chardonnay", "Riesling" and so on.

Noble varieties such as Chardonnay, Riesling or even Sauvignon are capable of standing alone, and frequently do in California, but a degree of blending adds complexity to lesser varieties. Some white grapes grown in California have unfamiliar names like Emerald Riesling or Gray Riesling, but, unfamiliar though they may be, it is important to remember that they are all (like those grown in Europe) from the *vitis vinifera* family, and not from native American vines such as *vitis labrusca*; the latter, although hardly suitable for winemaking, crops up in some other producing regions such as New York State.

Other grapes have trick names such as Johannisberg Riesling (which is used to distinguish the true Riesling of the Rhine from other contenders) or Fumé Blanc, which is Sauvignon Blanc in marketing man's disguise, usually (but not always) with a short spell in oak to earn its Fumé stripe. Undisputed queen of the vines is Chardonnay, with price tags to match.

THE CALIFORNIA TASTE Forceful flavour and early drinkability are key features of California fine wine, and this is why many have conquered all at blind tastings in Europe. Winemakers are proud of their assertive wines and use high technology to extract the fullest flavour from their grapes. However they are gradually widening the range of styles, reducing alcohol levels and modifying taste to a more acceptable lightness.

Most generic wines from wineries such as Gallo, Paul Masson, Inglenook, Almaden are produced from grapes grown south of San Francisco away from the famed Napa and Sonoma valleys. In the giant agricultural heartland of California, the Central Valley, all types of crops flourish. Thousands of acres of Thompson Seedless grapes are grown for the table and blending into table wines. This variety, like Ugni Blanc (see **Trebbiano**) is widely used for a bland reliable base wine to which is added Semillon and Chenin Blanc as well as Colombard. The resulting blend has an agreeable fruity nose with a hint of honey from the Chenin and melon from the Colombard.

At the next quality level, look for assertive grapey flavour rarely found in European wines. The California Riesling flavour, for example, is far richer and spicier than any found along the Rhine in Germany; late harvest and *Botrytis* versions can be good and very sweet. Many of the wines of all varieties smell like flowers in full bloom, with a hint of pollen and honey.

Fumé Blanc or Sauvignon Blanc may well be grassy and fresh, but the generally warm climate does not encourage this; some are oaked, some are not. In comparison with those from the Loire or New Zealand, California's Sauvignons are less pungent and powerful, but they do go rather better with food.

Chardonnay has a heavy, buttery scent with hints of wet wool in the aroma. Some of the finer wines, labelled with variety and vineyard name, are aged in wood casks to add to the flavour. The Californians tend to import European oak to give an authentic taste, rather than use native American woods. But it is worth remembering that in Burgundy the oak gives tannin, structure and ageability; here it is more often a mere flavour accessory.

In general, California does like to keep in step with fashion, so changes in style are inevitable. Chardonnay, for example, has recently been forsaking the riper, more exotic fruits in favour of greater restraint, barrel-fermentation and the like. If we want predictable wines we should buy Masson and Gallo brands; if we are prepared to be adventurous we should drink the more individual wines with a grape, a region and a year on the label.

CHOOSING CALIFORNIA WINES Most of the best-known wine regions of California, such as Napa Valley, Sonoma and Carneros, lie to the north of San Francisco, and some of the state's very best wine is indeed grown here (see **Napa Valley**, **Sonoma**). But the regions south of the city are just as worthy of attention and often less expensive.

Santa Clara is home to some well-known wineries such as Almaden and Paul Masson [★→★★/■■], which blend grapes from north and south to make commercial, agreeable wines at reasonable cost. Old Italian family wineries such as Guglielmo and San Martin [★→★★/■■] produce good table wines and some excellent dessert wines such as Moscato Amabile. Mirassou Vineyards [★★/■■], which has been active since 1854, produces wines of consistent quality, including varietals as well as a blend of Gewürztraminer, Pinot Blanc and Riesling known as Fleuri Blanc.

To the south of Santa Clara, Monterey's cool climate produces some excellent flavoursome varietals and blends, both dry and sweet (see **Monterey**). Further to the south, in the cool maritime-affected climate near San Luis Obispo, Edna Valley Vineyards [★★/■■■] makes a good Chardonnay.

Santa Barbara, like Monterey, was not a grape-growing zone until the late 1960s brought expansion and a search for quality. This coastal region of the hot Central Valley is cooled by ocean fog, and is thus able to grow delicate varieties such as Chardonnay. The most important winery here is Firestone [★★/■■], whose best whites are Riesling and Gewürztraminer with a subtle and not too "vegetal" flavour. The late harvest Riesling is sweeter and very drinkable. Prices tend to be mid-range rather than "boutique". The other large producer is Zaca Mesa [★★/■■], which makes a good Sauvignon, full-flavoured yet fresh.

Then there is the Central Valley, which runs north to south through the heart of California. Two-thirds of the state's wine production has its origin here. It is immensely hot but immensely fertile for all crops, including grapes. The heat is a problem though and many hybrid grapes have been developed to overcome the flavours of "raisin" and "tar" which excess exposure to heat can give a wine.

This is California at its most high-tech, with giant wineries resembling refineries and huge fleets of tankers transporting the grapes under gas to the presses. Much of the wine is generic and sold in large containers or "jugs". The wines benefit from simple, cool-temperature fermentation. If they are not always distinguished, at least they are fresh, pleasant and drinkable.

Good Central Valley producers [★→★★/■■→■■■] include:

Cribari	*Gallo*
Delicato	*Inglenook Navalle*
Franzia Bros	*Papagni*

Quady also makes an interesting sweet wine from Orange Muscat called Essensia [★★/■■■], designed for drinking with puddings.

CALIFORNIA WINE AND FOOD California whites have the personality to enhance most food, though some may seem a little too bumptious. Experiment by combining a Sauvignon Blanc with garlic or barbecued chicken, a light Chardonnay with grilled snapper or a weighty one with oyster stew.

WHERE NEXT? Search out the Old World prototypes of California styles – **Burgundy** for Chardonnay, the **Loire** and **Bordeaux** for Sauvignon Blanc, **Germany** for Riesling. And see what Washington (see **United States**) and **Oregon** do with the same grapes.

CANADA

The Canadians have been trumpeting the success of their improved wine industry of late. It is based in British Columbia, where you need to visit a provincial liquor store to buy alcohol at all, and in Ontario on the opposite coast.

In British Columbia, Claremont [★/■■] makes some reasonable Gewürztraminer, Pinot Blanc and Chenin Blanc. Other wineries here concentrate on sweetish white wines made from Okanagan Riesling (no relation of the Rhine variety).

Ontario, like New York State, favours hybrids due to the harsh climate. Charal [★/■■] produces a Seyval Blanc and the large producer André [★/■■] makes a range of hybrids. Much better are the wines of Inniskillin [★★/■■→■■■], a "serious" winery producing Riesling, Chardonnay and Gewürztraminer, which shows how Canadian wines might improve in the future.

Other good Canadian producers [★→★★/■■] include Bright's and Château des Charmes.

WHERE NEXT? Cross the frontier to Washington (see **United States**) or **New York State** for similar wines, and look to **England** for another variation on the hybrid theme: Seyval Blanc is the fashionable grape there now.

CAVA

Spain's sparkling wine industry dates from the 19th century, when Champagne was enjoying a world-wide boom. The reason for Cava's existence, then and now, revolves largely around price. Demand for *méthode champenoise* wines is high, but Champagne's price puts it out of reach for many of us.

Nobody could accuse the generally sound, but a little pedestrian Cava wines of being too zippy and bitingly fresh. The flavours are broad, full and sometimes fat, although they are becoming livelier by degrees. The Macabeo grape has the fruit, Xarel-lo provides much needed acidity and structure, while the refined Parellada polishes the hard edges and adds aroma. As inexpensive but well-made sparklers, big, flavoursome Cava wines can give a lot of pleasure.

Codorníu [★★/■■] (which started the whole business off in 1872) and Freixenet [★★/■■] are the two largest producers, and among the top few for quality. Segura Viudas [★★/■■], a Freixenet subsidiary, is reckoned to be the best; other good names [★★/■■→■■■] include Parxet, Mont Marçal and Mestres. The styles run from non-*dosage* Brut de Brut through to Dulce or Doux wines, but the majority are dry to medium-dry.

The most recent development is a move towards Chardonnay. Raimat, a subsidiary of Codorníu, has produced the first, extremely successful 100% Chardonnay [★★/■■].

WHERE NEXT? For equivalent value in the fizzy world, there is only one direction to go: down-under. So try an Aussie sparkler from Yalumba, Seaview or Seppelt Great Western (see **Barossa Valley**).

CHABLIS

First off, Chablis comes from Chablis. That may sound obvious, but vast quantities of wine labelled "Chablis" have never been near the place. It is a small village beside a small river, the Serein, in some green, hilly countryside in northern France, between Paris and Dijon.

Spanish Chablis, California Chablis, South American Chablis, whatever else they may be, are not Chablis. It is a nice name, you can hear them thinking in Spain, California and South America: short and pronounceable – let's use it. They did, and watched, spellbound, as the stuff positively ran out of the shops. Not surprisingly this got up the noses of real Chablis producers. I mean, suppose the Chablisiens started calling their wines "Napa Valley" or some such: that wouldn't be fair would it? Well, just for devilment, someone has. Let us hope the message strikes home.

THE CHABLIS TASTE As we might expect of Chardonnay in a northern climate, there is an apple-crisp freshness to Chablis. It is greeny-gold, appetizing, bone-dry, lean, in some years slightly tart, in others creamier and softer, but it never develops the rich, full, fat, tropical fruit style that Chardonnay does in warmer climates. Chablis has a bright, glinting, cutting edge that keeps it refreshing, keeps the taste keen and lively, and brings you back for more and more sips.

There is also a mineral component, attributed to the Kimmeridgian limestone soil, and often described as steely or flinty, which seems to give the wine backbone. Grape and soil together produce a feeling of tautness in the wine, with the tension of a coiled spring. Chablis isn't a laid-back, relaxed sort of wine; it is rather on edge, as if restlessly looking at its watch and wondering if it shouldn't be on its way.

All this you can get from stainless steel, and many producers stop there; for them that is the essence of Chablis. It can be drunk with pleasure at two years but will keep its zing for as many as five. However, when the wine is fuller, either in a good year or when it comes from lower yields in the *premier* and *grand cru* vineyards, then oak-ageing is an option. These wines are bigger, more concentrated, and taste as if the apples have had vanilla cream poured over them, with a sprinkling of lightly toasted nuts on top. They will require longer before being ready to drink, and will last longer once they are.

CHOOSING CHABLIS Because of its popularity, there has been pressure on Chablis to expand. Most of the outlying land that was Petit Chablis has now been incorporated into Chablis proper. This straight AC Chablis, which accounts for over half the production, is the basic but usually good wine whose appley zing we can rely on.

Premier cru, next up the scale, has been making conversions faster than a television evangelist. Land that was formerly plain Chablis has, not always with justification, joined the ranks of the famous *premiers crus*. For the moment it is probably safer to stick to the originals – Côte de Léchet, Fourchaume, Mont de Milieu, Montée de Tonnerre, Montmain and Vaillons are among the best – always remembering that the producer's name is paramount.

Grand cru Chablis is really a cut above the rest: bigger, richer, more intense and characterful, with more finesse about it. Seven vineyards qualify for *grand cru* status: Les Clos, Valmur, Vaudésir, Les Preuses, Grenouilles, Blanchot and Bougros. It is these wines that benefit most from oak-ageing and are correspondingly longer-lived. They are best drunk at five to ten years, when they develop the complexity of apples, nuts, butter, toast, spice and cream.

The best producers [★★→★★★/■■→■■■] include:

La Chablisienne Co-operative	Michel
Dauvissat	Raveneau
Drouhin	Simmonet-Febvre
Fèvre	Testut
Laroche	Vocoret

The best vintages for Chablis include 1988, 87, 86, 85, 83, 81 and 78.

CHABLIS AND FOOD Fresh, flinty Chablis with oysters is a horse-and-carriage partnership, as is lobster, as long as the sauce isn't too rich. The fuller, fatter Chablis are needed if buttery sauces come into the dish, and also work well with poultry.

WHERE NEXT? Ignore other "Chablis" from around the world; instead try Chardonnay wines from **New Zealand** and California's **Sonoma**, from northern **Italy** and from **Spain**; you will find that no-one else makes anything quite like Chablis. For a different taste look east to **Alsace** and its Sylvaners.

CHAMPAGNE

Champagne is an AC wine produced in northern France – and no other part of France, and certainly no other country – from three grape varieties: white Chardonnay, and the black grapes Pinot Noir and Pinot Meunier. The first two are the classic grapes of Burgundy 150 miles (240 km) to the south. Up here, though, in Champagne's rolling, featureless wheatfields, they are rather out of their depth: the still wine they make is pinched and mean because of the high acidity. But that crisp northern acidity is exactly what makes sparkling wine so exciting. It has to have that incisive cut, otherwise it can seem fat, heavy and dull, hardly the ideal aperitif. The well-drained chalk soils on which the grapes are planted are responsible for the delicate flavours and thus for the overall quality.

Reims and Epernay are the centres of production, separated by the valley of the River Marne (planted mostly with black grapes) and the Montagne de Reims where Pinot Noir does especially well. South of Epernay the Côte des Blancs is devoted almost entirely to Chardonnay. Sixty miles (100 km) away to the south-east in the Aube, most of the grapes are black. It may seem strange that such an aristocratic wine as Champagne should be a blend not only of grape varieties, but of wines from far-flung vineyards. But that, in fact, is one of the main reasons for its aristocracy.

The blending of component wines is one of the top jobs in any Champagne house. It determines the house style and, in the case of non-vintage wines, must be consistent from batch to batch and year to year, evening out the vagaries of vintage variation. It is perfectly possible to make a wine from just one grape variety – Blanc de Blancs, from Chardonnay only, is distinguished by its lightness, fruit and elegance, while Blanc de Noirs is generally fuller, richer and firmer – but blending produces a balance of flavour, freshness, body and fruit, together with the finesse that is one of Champagne's hallmarks. In some top Champagnes there may be as many as 50 different components, from different years, grapes and vineyards.

Drinkers are divided over their preferred style of Champagne. It can vary from pale lemon to deep golden; from a green, stinging freshness overlaid with baker's yeast, to a mellow, biscuitty richness; from a light, young Champagne that might open the batting before lunch, to a mature and gentle evening's entertainment; from white to pink; from bitingly bone dry to rich, sweet and creamy.

THE MÉTHODE CHAMPENOISE Of all the ways to put sparkle into wine, *méthode champenoise* is the most sophisticated. It works by repeating the process of fermentation, but in bottle. The aim of most fermentation in the wine business is to produce alcohol; carbon dioxide is a by-product that escapes into the air. With fizz the aim of the secondary fermentation is to produce carbon dioxide and hang on to it; the extra alcohol is incidental.

Wine is made in the normal way and fermented to dryness. Before bottling, yeast and sugar are stirred in. This gets to work producing both carbon dioxide and alcohol. Since the wine is in bottle there is nowhere for the gas to escape, so it dissolves in the wine. By varying the quantity of sugar added, a wine can be made fully sparkling, or semi-sparkling as in *crémant* Champagne.

There is a snag, though. The dead yeast cells and spent nutrients fall to the bottom of the bottle and form a sediment. Nobody wants to drink this gunge, so it has to be removed. One way is to empty the wine from hundreds of bottles into a tank, filter it, and then return clear wine to the bottles – by the so-called transfer method (or *cuve close*). What makes *méthode champenoise* unique is that the secondary fermentation takes place in the very same bottle that we buy, and the sediment is removed in a rather ingenious way.

The bottles are gradually shifted from a horizontal position to upside-down vertical. The sediment therefore collects in the neck of the bottle. By a skilled but boring process of *remuage* ("riddling"), the bottles are twisted and turned by hand in wooden desks to catch the sediment. Short cuts include automatic riddling, whereby hundreds of bottles are loaded into boxes or *giropalettes* and twisted at the same time, either by a gentle manual shove or by computer. Many producers of *méthode champenoise* wines around the world, and many producers in Champagne itself, do it this way, although some stick with traditional *remuage* for their special *cuvées*.

Recently, Moët & Chandon has been experimenting with small pellets or *boules*, in which yeasts are finely enmeshed in a porous coating that allows them access to the liquid, but which is tight enough to prevent them escaping. This way 20 or 30 fairly heavy *boules* can do the job; all it needs is a flick of the wrist to get them to sink to the neck, cutting several weeks' work down to a few seconds.

Once the sediment has collected on the base of the cork, the neck of the bottle is frozen in cold brine, the bottle turned right-way-up and the cork removed. The plug of sediment and frozen wine, about an inch long, shoots out. The wine has been "disgorged", and only a little is lost because low temperature has reduced the pressure. The bottle is topped up straight away and the customary cylindrical cork is tapped in, which swells to a mushroom shape by the time we remove it.

The time the wine spends on its yeast lees is not wasted, since it adds a rich creaminess and a depth of flavour. The better Champagnes (including vintage wines) spend longer on the lees than plain NV wines, and some make a point of remaining there for several years.

CHAMPAGNE STYLES

When Champagne is disgorged, the plug of sediment that pops out leaves the bottle less than full, and in need of a top-up. This largely consists of wine and a little sugar. The amount of sugar decides the style of the finished Champagne:

- *Extra brut* is sometimes seen; this has no added sugar.
- *Brut* is what most people think of as Champagne; with less than 15 grams of sugar per litre, the style is bitingly dry.
- *Extra sec* (extra dry) is fractionally less dry than *brut.*
- *Sec* (dry) is less dry again; some people can detect sweetness.
- *Demi-sec* (semi-dry), with 30-50 grams of sugar per litre, is distinctly sweet in style.
- *Doux* (rich or sweet) Champagne is very sweet.

All Champagne is made this way, as are most of the world's best sparklers (see **Sparkling Wines**), since it produces smaller bubbles and a finer mousse than other techniques. Other winemakers around the world are free to use this method, although the term *méthode champenoise* is due to be phased out within the EEC.

CHOOSING CHAMPAGNE Non-vintage (NV), which accounts for something like 85% of all Champagne, should be perfectly drinkable straight off the shelf. Vintage Champagne is made in particularly ripe and fine years, using only the best grapes. It is a more individual wine than NV, generally richer and fuller, less consistent because it should express the character of that particular vintage. Although some lighter wines (Blanc de Blancs) may be ready sooner, ten years is about the age to drink a vintage, by which time it is creamy and soft; some wines will last longer, but if kept too long they begin to fizzle out.

Luxury *cuvées* are a treat if money is no object. The best way to soften the blow is to drink a bottle first and then pay for it since, with a clear head, prices can seem outrageous. Recently disgorged (RD) wines, having spent longer than usual on the lees, do develop an intriguing depth of flavour. *Crémant* wines have less pressure than normal; they are "creamier" and softer as the name implies.

READING LABELS

A code in very small print on the label enables us to see how a particular bottle has been produced:
- NM = *Négociant Manipulant* (Champagne house)
- CM = *Coopérative de Manipulation* (co-operative)
- RM = *Récoltant Manipulant* (grower producing Champagne from his own grapes)
- RC = *Récoltant-Coopérateur* (grower selling Champagne from a co-operative)
- SR = *Société de Récoltant* (company formed by growers from the same family)
- MA = *Marque d'Acheteur* (wine merchant buyer's own label)

Champagne-making is dominated by the large houses or *grandes marques*. Krug [★★★/■■] is *the* great Champagne. (Some people consider Rolls Royce to be the Krug of cars.) A family-owned company making no more than half a million bottles a year, whose NV is the equivalent of most other people's luxury *cuvée*, it is one of the most complex Champagnes, with 40 or 50 different wines from eight to ten different vintages. Both this and its vintage wines are among the longest-lived Champagnes.

Bollinger [★★→★★★/■■■], which produces a rich style, has that great rarity, a patch of pre-phylloxera vines from which it produces its Vieilles Vignes *cuvée*; it also makes a much respected RD style which is kept on the lees for up to ten years.

Roederer's [★★→★★★/■■■] Brut Premier is one of the best and most consistent NVs on the market: smooth, perfectly blended and properly aged. Luxury *cuvée* Cristal, in a clear glass bottle, was developed for the Tsars and is now popular in the Far East.

Taittinger [★★→★★★/■■■] is another family-owned company whose best wine is the delicate-tasting Blanc de Blancs Comtes de Champagne; this is by no means cheap, but it is one of the best pure Chardonnay Champagnes.

Among the other best Champagne producers [★★→★★★/■■■] are the following houses:

Billion	Moët & Chandon
le Brun	Mumm
Canard-Duchêne	Perrier-Jouët
Deutz	Piper-Heidsieck
Duval Leroy	Pol Roger
Fliniaux	Pommery
Gratien	Ruinart
Henriot	Salon
Jacquesson	Selosse
Laurent-Perrier	Veuve Clicquot

CHAMPAGNE AND FOOD Many connoisseurs have indulged in a fine-tuning exercise, and matched different styles of Champagne to every course of a banquet, but Champagne is such a mood-lifter that it goes as well with fish and chips as with wedding cake. It is probably best to keep it away from heavy meat and game, and closer to oysters and smoked salmon.

WHERE NEXT? The wine world is full of people trying to make a competitor to Champagne. So far, the closest contenders have been Crémants de Loire (see **Loire**), Chardonnay-based Crémants de Bourgogne (see **Burgundy**), New World wines such as Australia's Petaluma (see **Adelaide Hills**) and the various California fizzes (see **Sparkling Wines**). Many are made by offshoots of Champagne companies, so you would think the taste might be similar. It isn't.

CHARDONNAY

Chardonnay is not the world's most widely planted white grape variety; that honour goes to Spain's lowly Airén. It may not even be the world's best white variety; Riesling would take up that challenge. But by golly, if the Burgundians, who started the whole Chardonnay craze, had one franc for every time anybody talked about it, planted it, or drank a bottle of it, they would be so rich they would be able to give their Puligny-Montrachet away free.

It is the complete opposite of Burgundy's great black grape. While Pinot Noir is fussy, finicky and fickle to grow, Chardonnay is easy, accommodating, malleable. Perhaps its only disadvantage, from a grower's point of view, is that it buds early, making it rather nail-biting for growers in cool climates where late frosts are common; but the vine nevertheless manages to withstand the cold winters of Champagne and Chablis.

The grape ripens early, has good sugar (and therefore alcohol) levels, and good acidity providing it is picked as soon as it is ready. It also has good "extract", that is to say those solid and substantial components that give flavour, body and texture to a wine.

THE CHARDONNAY TASTE Given such sound raw material it is difficult to make a poor wine from Chardonnay, although it does take skill, and the right circumstances of soil and climate, to make a great one. Perhaps the appeal to winemakers is its very elasticity and flexibility. Chardonnay does not dictate terms: it is equally happy in cool Chablis or warm California; it doesn't mind whether it is fermented in oak or stainless steel; it can be almost inconsequentially light and dapper, or built like a battleship. The winemaker can stamp his authority on it and make a distinctively individual wine; biddable Chardonnay will respond.

The Chardonnay style is so variable that there is hardly a common thread to be found, beyond the fact that we can rely on it to produce something tasty and classy nine times out of ten.

The lightest wines are usually made in cool-climate regions such as north-east Italy, New Zealand and Oregon from high yields, and these Chardonnays can be appealing. But there is much more to Chardonnay than this simple and direct appeal. One of the great marriages in the wine world is between Chardonnay and oak. When yields are relatively low, when the extract, acidity and alcohol pool their resources, then Chardonnay has the power to stand up to ageing in oak barrels; it can cope with and absorb the tannin and oak flavours, giving it the chance to mature into a beautifully rich and complex wine.

The marriage takes time to settle down, though, and if the wines are drunk too young their component parts can seem rather obvious and gauche. In fact even when they do settle down, after five or ten years, it can sometimes seem as if the flavours are separate, as if the oak has somehow been added to the wine, rather than being an integral part of it; and that does not just apply to those New World wines where oak chips or blocks actually are added, like a wooden *bouquet garni*.

Best results are often achieved by fermenting, and not just maturing, the wine in oak barrel, so that it tastes like a single, complete, integrated unit. In many cases only a proportion of the wine will be treated in this way, so as to keep the oak subtle rather than too blindingly obvious. The aim is for balance. Some bottles, particularly from California and Australia, will use either front or back label to indicate that the wine has been barrel-fermented.

Nowadays there is a whole discipline of barrel technology; you can probably get a degree in it. Not just the country, but the forest from which the wood came is important: grain varies in tightness, thus controlling the amount of contact beween air and wine, quite apart from the actual flavour the wood imparts. Many producers, notably Mondavi in California, have also experimented with variables such as the degree of charring or toasting of the barrel. The staves are assembled over a fire, and greater charring can lead to stronger, smokier, toastier flavours in the wine.

As part of their search for ways of making better wine, many Chardonnay producers are also allowing the skins and juice of the crushed grapes to stay in contact for a short while before running off the juice for fermentation. This "skintact" time helps to bump up the flavour.

Then, after the fermentation is over and all the dead yeast cells, sludge and gunk have fallen to the bottom of the cask or tank, some leave the wine for a short period before racking it off. This can help to produce a slightly fuller and creamier texture in the wine, as well as extending the length of flavour.

BEGIN WITH AUSTRALIA OR CALIFORNIA Few would dispute that the very best Chardonnays come from Burgundy: especially from Meursault and Puligny-Monrachet in the Côte d'Or, and from Chablis. It is here that the steeliness, the hard, unyielding rigidity of the wine is apparent. Here too the big, smooth, rich, fat, oily butteriness. Rarely are these characteristics overdone; they are sometimes underdone, in which case the wine can disappoint, but in the best examples they have an integrity, a harmony, a finesse and a subtlety which makes them complete in a way no other Chardonnays have matched (see **Burgundy**, **Côte d'Or**, **Chablis**, **Mâcon**, **Côte Chalonnaise**).

There is a snag though: the price. What we need as a starting point is a wine that will give us an unmistakable wallop of good Chardonnay flavour but not cost the earth. And that is precisely where Australian Chardonnays have fitted into the drinking repertoire. Big bold smells were delivered straight to our nose with assurance and confidence; full-frontal flavours hit so hard that we barely noticed the cost, which in any case was very reasonable. People who might never dream of buying white Burgundy ordinarily have had whole new worlds of taste opened up to them.

For those on a tight budget there have been blends made from the cheapest fruit the winemaker could find. They may not have been show-stoppers, but they were as fresh as an April shower and stole a march on Mâcon and its ilk. At the top end of the scale, Australia learns more with every vintage. It is amazing to think that Chardonnay was virtually unknown in Australia before 1970, and in that short time the wines have come to challenge all but the world's greatest. They are richly buttery and succulent from Coonawarra; enormous, ripe, spicy and pineappley from the Hunter Valley; clean, vibrant and lemony from Padthaway; decisive, sharp, and clean-cut from the Margaret River; elegantly European from the Yarra Valley, and so on (see **Coonawarra**, **Hunter Valley**, **Margaret River**, **Yarra Valley**, **Victoria** and **Australia**).

In California, big bold flavours and high alcohol opened the varietal innings, and helped to grab attention. You simply cannot ignore a ripe, fat, juicy Chardonnay oozing squelchy fruit juice and dripping with butter. Put it next to a white Burgundy of the same age, say two years old, and the apologetic Burgundy might just was well be a rather insignificant Muscadet for all the impression it makes. But come back a few years later and look what's happened. The Californian Chardonnay has melted away like an ice lolly in the sun, while the Burgundy is still firm, refreshing, tasty, well balanced; even the flavour of the oak lolly-stick has integrated well.

California returned to the drawing board and began to tone down the rather obvious melon and pineapple flavours, to use lightly toasty oak with some subtlety, to winkle out cooler growing regions, and to make wines with more interest and staying power. This was partly in response to a related Californian obsession, food: the state's matching accessory, the handbag to go with the shoes.

Wine should not overpower the splendidly diverse and generally light food, but complement it. Instead of putting their Chardonnay *cuvées* up against a Burgundy, producers chose abalone, squab or tuna steak instead. They would take samples home from the laboratory and decide on the final *cuvée* at the dinner table. Although they are not static, this is roughly where Californian Chardonnays stand at the moment. If the wines just happen to be getting closer to the Burgundian model, then it is a sign of California's increasing maturity (see **California**, **Napa Valley** and **Sonoma**).

OTHER CHARDONNAYS If all this were laid out on a "Snakes and Ladders" board, we should then climb a ladder to Burgundy for more elegance and complexity. It would be as high as we could go. Then we would have to slide down a snake to wines from Mâcon, to the less expensive (often branded) wines from the New World, to Alto Adige, or to relatively new regions that show promise such as America's Pacific North-West. We are coming down in terms of intensity and concentration of flavour, although the wines are often perfectly well made in their own way.

Alto Adige and Friuli-Venezia Giulia produce ultra-light, crisp, clean, apple-tart wines – some so stretched that you might be hard-pressed to believe they were made from Chardonnay at all. Indeed there has been a slight identity problem in the past. Confusion with Pinot Bianco grapes (see **Pinot Blanc**) has been such that even growers could not tell which was which in their own vineyard. Most of the confusion has now been resolved, and the best stainless steel fermented wines have a mountain purity that convinces you this is the source from which all other Chardonnays flow (see **Alto Adige** and **Friuli-Venezia Giulia**).

Similarly fresh-faced, simple and direct Chardonnays are produced in other cool climates such as New Zealand and Oregon. These styles of Chardonnay are best drunk young, within two to three years, to savour the freshness, but Chardonnay does have a remarkable capacity to age, so there is no need to panic (see **Oregon**, **New Zealand**).

Below these in quality we can enjoy wines which, although trying hard, have not quite managed to capture the essence of Chardonnay – decent drinks rather than wines typical of the grape. Bulgaria's versions, for example, can be decent for the price (see **Bulgaria**).

CHARDONNAY AND FOOD Few varietals contribute as much pleasure to food: whether it be an opening glass of simple, fruity Aussie Chardonnay with a seafood starter or a rich Meursault with lobster or turbot, Chardonnay rarely lets down a meal.

WHERE NEXT? **Riesling** is as underrated as Chardonnay is over-hyped: just as interesting, just as various. Semillon from Australia's **Hunter Valley**, given bottle age, can be a match for Chardonnay in weight and interest.

CHENIN BLANC

Chenin Blanc is the Jekyll and Hyde of white grapes, the ugly cygnet that can turn into a magnificent swan. And anyone whose experience has been restricted to the ugly cygnets of the Chenin Blanc repertoire could be forgiven for challenging its claim to be a "major" grape variety. Made into a range of styles from dry to sweet, its wines can also vary in quality from the delicious to the downright charmless.

In France's Loire Valley Chenin Blanc produces some of the country's greatest sweet wines. And not only that. Considering the work that goes into making them, their concentration and their longevity, they are substantially undervalued.

THE CHENIN BLANC TASTE The grape's distinguishing character-istic is a searing streak of acidity, which contributes both to its longevity and to its downfall. Acidity is not only a great preserver; it also gives mature wines a spring in their step, a sprightliness without which they would simply loll around looking fat and tired. While acidity is important for dry wines, the zip and crackle it gives to sweet wines is absolutely essential if they are not to become mere luscious bonbons. Chenin Blanc shares this trait with Riesling, and it is the raciness of sweet wines made from these grapes that accounts for their appeal.

But there is a dark side to this hyperacidity. In its less elegant manifestations, young Chenin Blanc that is dry or even medium-dry can be as much fun as having your teeth drilled. At its best, young Chenin Blanc is lightly floral and sweetly perfumed, has good weight and body, and is reminiscent of melons, apples, quinces and wet hay or wool. But when it is picked before the grapes have had a chance to ripen properly and fermented with little or no skin contact, there is almost no fruit to back up the screaming acidity. The apple taste turns sour. If sucking a lemon doesn't satisfy your craving for acidity, then some of these Chenin Blancs will.

Part of the problem is that, even when Chenin Blanc is made decently, its varietal character does not have the definition of, for example, Sauvignon Blanc – a neighbour that performs embarrassingly well along the Loire in Touraine, Sancerre and Pouilly. Trying to smell Chenin Blanc can be like listening to music with cotton wool in your ears: its smell is fuzzy, muffled, indistinct.

An increasing tendency with still wines is to blend Chenin with some Chardonnay or Sauvignon Blanc, which gives them a pronounced and welcome lift of fruit. This is happening in the wide-ranging Anjou AC, in the VDQS Coteaux du Vendômois and, most successfully, in the Saumur Blanc from the Cave Coopérative des Vignerons de Saumur at St-Cyr-en-Bourg.

This lack of well-defined "primary" grape and fruit aromas is what makes the "secondary" aromas so important. These are the complex smells that transmute and develop in bottle: the reward for keeping the right wine the right length of time. Dry Chenin Blanc becomes nutty; sweet Chenin Blanc becomes first apricotty and then delightfully honeyed.

But it takes time. Decades. Chenin Blanc is not a grape for beginners. The best wines need cellaring for 20, 30 years or more, requiring remarkable patience.

BEGIN WITH THE LOIRE Few people are prepared to wait 30 years to discover whether or not they like Chenin. So the best approach is to go straight out and buy the best, most venerable bottle you can find. The place to start is the Loire, which produces a range of styles from very sweet to very dry.

In the valley of the tributary River Layon which joins the Loire downstream of Angers, winemakers concentrate on the production of sweet wines. Their devotion is rewarded by some serious rivals to Sauternes (see **Coteaux du Layon**). Dry Chenin Blanc is made consistently well in pockets throughout Anjou and Touraine. The *appellations* of Savennières and Jasnières are tiny, consequently their wines are expensive and hard to find but worth the hunt (see **Loire** and **Anjou**).

OTHER CHENIN BLANCS Chenin Blanc may sometimes seem a bit rocky on home territory, but it completely goes to pieces when it travels. We have grown used to New World countries breezing into Europe, picking up a grape variety, and running off with prizes for outclassing the original. Chenin Blanc is one grape that has so far eluded their magic.

In South Africa Chenin Blanc goes under the name Steen, and is that country's most widely planted variety. Clean, modern, fresh, but often rather ordinary wines constitute the bulk of the country's output (see **South Africa**).

The picture is even less enthralling in California. What on earth possesses such an otherwise exciting region to populate over 20% of its white wine vineyards with Chenin Blanc? Any country that prides itself on a varietal approach should either coax more varietal character from it, or re-plant with something less boring (see **California**).

Argentina and Chile also make everyday Chenins, while Australia turns out some as crisp and green as a Granny Smith. Is there, one wonders, a white grape variety that will not do well in New Zealand? Acidity levels are well up to Loire standards and there is a purity about the wines that is rarely achieved elsewhere. If there is anywhere to challenge the Loire's supremacy, it is New Zealand (see **Australia** and **New Zealand**).

CHENIN BLANC AND FOOD The richer styles of Chenin make a wonderful drink by themselves, but fresh fruit is the natural accompaniment for these, either as a snack or at the end of a meal. Otherwise, the generally high acidity of the drier versions can be a bonus with food: dry Chenin refreshes the palate and will stand up to the more demanding accoutrements such as a light vinaigrette or a sorrel sauce. The slight sweetness of a medium-dry Chenin also helps to balance that quality in shellfish such as lobster and scallops.

WHERE NEXT? If you like the rasping acidity of young, dry or medium-dry Chenin Blanc there is little else to do but buy another bottle. If it is the richer, sweeter, more mature style that appeals, then **Rieslings** of *Auslese* quality and above (and their late harvest or *Botrytis*-affected New World equivalents) make an interesting comparison. If acidity in the sweet wines is too much, then the **Sémillon** wines of **Sauternes & Barsac** (and their New World equivalents) will solve that problem.

CHILE

Chile has been the success story of the late 1980s. Its white wines have come like a bolt from the blue to astonish tasters who thought that Chile only made Cabernet Sauvignon, and rather heavy, harsh Cabernet Sauvignon at that.

Like California, the vineyards are blessed by their situation. The central valley zone is the finest by far and the Maipo Valley probably the Napa of Chile. The most successful white grape is Riesling, but Sauvignon Blanc and Semillon do well, and Chenin Blanc is also grown. The climate is a little too dry for good Chardonnay.

The characteristic taste of Chilean white wines is earthy and forceful, yet quite soft, slightly oily and "green".

Good Chilean producers [★★/■■→■■■] include:

Canepa	San Pedro
Concha y Toro	Santa Rita
Cousino Macul	Undurraga

Of these, Canepa is noted for its Sémillon; and Concha y Toro, long famous for its Cabernet, now has experimental plantings of Gewürztraminer and Chardonnay. Miguel Torres of Spain (see **Penedès**) also has a winery in Chile, and uses the latest cold fermentation techniques to improve the quality of its white wines [★★/■■→■■■].

WHERE NEXT? **Argentina** takes a more Italian approach to white wine. **New Zealand** is Chile's most direct wine neighbour, and **Spain**, with its language links reinforced by Torres, has some interesting wines in **Penedès** and **Rioja**.

CHINA

Wine grapes have been grown here in a desultory fashion for some 90 years, but so far the mainland Chinese have shown a marked lack of enthusiasm for grape wine, preferring the rice variety which undoubtedly goes well with their food. However Remy Martin invested in the industry during the 1980s to produce whites such as the bland and fruitless Dynasty [★/■■], very close in flavour really to rice wine, and other table wines made with the Muscat Hamburg and the local Dragon Eye. Now Italian Riesling and Chardonnay have been planted and the Hua Dong winery is known for its experimental plantings.

WHERE NEXT? Absolutely anywhere: spin the wheel.

CLARE

South Australia's most northerly vine-growing region is out on a limb some 60 miles (96 km) north of Adelaide and quite hot. Some Chardonnay, Semillon and Sauvignon is grown but the star white variety is Rhine Riesling, which produces big, spicy, intensely flavoured wines.

Clare Rhine Rieslings stop short of hefty lusciousness on account of the crisp citrussy acidity, and many manage to achieve an attractive delicate fragrance. It is strange that this variety, flaunted as the ultimate cool-climate quality grape in Germany, should outshine others in such an apparently hostile climate. But it does. And it makes some very good, slightly raisiny *Botrytis*-affected wines too.

Wineries in the Barossa Valley and elsewhere use Clare Riesling, but among the successful locally-based wineries are the Stanley Wine Company [★★→★★★/■■], whose Spring Gully and Bin 7 Rieslings can be good to excellent, and the stylish, exciting Tim Knappstein Enterprise wines [★★→★★★/■■], including a Rhine Riesling and a Fumé Blanc.

These producers are followed [★→★★/■■] by:

Jim Barry	*Mitchells*
Fareham Estate	*Pike's Polish Hill River Estate*
Jeffrey Grosset	*Watervale Cellars*
Mount Horrocks	

WHERE NEXT? Try **New Zealand** for Sauvignon Blancs of a similar inspiration, **Germany** for the originals of the Clare Rieslings, and the **Loire** for the cool-climate prototypes.

COLOMBARD

In France this grape variety has traditionally been confined to the ignominious fate of a distiller's grape. It may be all right for Cognac and Armagnac, went the thinking, but it would be very infra-dig in a wine. The floweriness is all right, but the high acidity brings tears to your eyes. Then it went to California and it was talent-spotted, picked out from the back row of the chorus and thrust into a leading role. And by leading, I mean leading: it is the state's most widely planted white grape variety (see **California**).

Just as a Hollywood star takes to new Cadillacs, so Colombard has taken to being seen in expensive new oak. It might work, although some have been rather overdone. It is probably best to enjoy the fresh style while it is young, and drink the most recent vintage.

Meanwhile back in France, spirit sales were not what they used to be. Lots of Colombard and Ugni Blanc (Trebbiano) grapes began looking for another career, and they found it in the delightful Vin de Pays des Côtes de Gascogne (see **Côtes de Gascogne**). This is the sort of wine that everybody wants. It is crunchily crisp as a Cox's pippin, lemony fresh, dry, zingily lively, the sort of wine you start slurping while you cook, or drinking as an aperitif, and just carry on while you're eating or until there are no more bottles left.

WHERE NEXT? **Sauvignon Blanc**, and **Chardonnay** from a region like **Alto Adige**, do a similar sort of thing and with a bit more style. But not at this price.

CONDRIEU & CHATEAU-GRILLET

The tiny vineyards of Condrieu and Château-Grillet, some 20 miles (32 km) up-river from Hermitage produce the northern Rhône's other great white wine style. These wines are made from the rare

Viognier, a rather disease-prone grape which oxidizes easily and yields barely 20 hectolitres per hectare.

The prime position of Condrieu's vines, overlooking the river and facing the sun, doubtless contributes to the fragrant peachy, apricotty flavour of the wines and the rich oily texture spread over a distinctly dry and earthy base. Low acidity prevents them ageing well, so they are best drunk at about three years. The best Condrieu producers [★★★/■■] include:

Pierre Dumazet	*Jean Pinchon*
Paul Multier, du Rozay	*Georges Vernay*

The region's other wine is even rarer. Château-Grillet is a small single-estate AC of only 7.5 acres (3 ha), making a more intense and complex wine, still infused with peaches and apricots but with a slightly warmer honey richness and a musky quality about it.

The wine will age for longer than Condrieu, having spent 18 months in oak: so drink at about eight to ten years. But beware – rare grape, singular taste, small AC, tiny yield, only 16,000 unusual Rhine-style bottles a year for the whole world. What does it sound like to you? Exactly. It is *très* snob, costs a fortune, and we are paying for its rarity as much as for the taste. There is only one producer [★★★/■■■].

WHERE NEXT? Viognier is grown nowhere else, if we exclude a tiny patch in California. See if an aged **Anjou** Chenin fits, or try an oaky Sémillon with bottle-age or a Rhine Riesling from **Australia**.

COONAWARRA

South Australia's great rectangular patch of dirt some 8 miles (12 km) by 2 miles (3 km) majors in red wines, but the white wine boom of the 1970s persuaded some companies to shift the emphasis a little, and a few excellent whites are produced, principally from Chardonnay, with Riesling in tow.

The sea, only some 50 miles (80 km) away, helps to keep the region cool, deflecting the style away from the heavy and overblown excesses of some warmer regions. Chardonnays nevertheless have big, rich, opulent, succulent fruit, and are often medium-toasty and buttery. They are usually soft in youth, but juicy from their moderate acidity, very more-ish, and benefit from bottle age: many are still going strong at 6-8 years. Alcohol can be up to 13%, and oak fermentation helps the style enormously. They are way out of the light citrus mould and well into ripe melon, even figs and liquorice.

The best Chardonnay producers [★★→★★★/■■] include:

Hollick	*Rouge Homme*
Mildara, Jamieson's Run	*Wynns*

Riesling wines are light, with good fruit, but rarely special.

Padthaway is Coonawara's annexe, some 50 miles (80 km) to the north on similar *terra rossa* soil with a very similar climate. It produces some very good whites, in fact many of them have the edge on Coonawarra thanks to their more contemporary, appetizing style. Most Padthaway fruit is crushed, drained straight into a chilled and insulated tanker, and carted off to a winery miles away, perhaps in the Barossa Valley. Not all of it appears under a regional Padthaway label; much is blended with juice from elsewhere.

Chardonnays have clean and zippy fruit yet full-blooded flavour; they are fresh, well balanced, and intended for drinking fairly young, generally at two to four years old. Sauvignon Blanc is impressive: clean, fresh, vibrant, lemony, off-dry, not too green or sappy.

Yields are generally good, and prices reasonable, so Padthaway makes a good-value starting point for South Australia's modern mid-range styles. Producers [★★→★★★/■■] include:

Hardy, Siegersdorf	*Seppelt*
Hardy Collection	*Wynns*
Lindemans	

WHERE NEXT? **Western Australia** takes a similarly controlled approach to white wines; compare the Chardonnays. Go back to **Sancerre** for the Sauvignon starting-point, or over to **New Zealand**.

CORSICA

Corsica was planted with many new vineyards following Algerian independence, but it missed a great opportunity to plant something decent. Given Ugni Blanc – usually considered fit for distilling rather than winemaking on the mainland, and rarely distinguished in its Italian guise as Trebbiano – together with the equally humble Vermentino, plus a bit of Malvasia, Corsica is looking up at a considerable hurdle before it even starts to pick and press the grapes.

So no chance of a silk purse here. Much Corsican wine is ordinary in the extreme. There are seven regions within the general Vin de Corse AC, few of them very exciting; the best producers [★→★★/■→■■] are Domaine de Torraccia and SICA de Figari. Ajaccio has an ace up its sleeve in the form of Domaine Peraldi, which has very definitely woken up to what is going on in the world. These are fresh, clean, modern wines which are beginning to show that Corsica has a future.

However, as over much of southern France, innovation on any sort of scale is not taking place within ACs but as a result of the freedom to experiment provided by *vins de pays*. Corsica's producers of Vin de Pays de l'Ile de Beauté are taking advantage of this by planting Chardonnay and other varieties, which lowers the hurdle and gives them a sporting chance of vaulting over it.

WHERE NEXT? **Provence** and **Tuscany** are the twin neighbouring influences, and nearby **Sardinia** a more distant relation. Take a look at **Vins de Pays** and Midi offerings such as La Clape (see **Coteaux du Languedoc**) for wines made under similar conditions.

COTE CHALONNAISE

The limestone outcrops of the Côte de Beaune (see **Côte d'Or**) re-appear haphazardly in the Côte Chalonnaise, and it is on these that white grapes thrive best. Montagny and Rully have them in greater abundance than, for example, Mercurey and Givry, and hence produce rather more white wine. Other geographical and climatic characteristics (altitude and cool temperatures) combine to make the wines of the Côte Chalonnaise less ripe and round than those of Meursault and Puligny; they have much less definition and know-where-I'm-going flavour.

Rully is light and fresh, with a softish, slightly fuzzy edge and a whiff of herbs. Montagny is an all-white AC but, given the amount of practice they obviously get, we should expect something a bit less apologetic, something with a bit more drive and fruit. Sometimes it is like trying to eat a Golden Delicious apple with a mouth full of cotton wool. Mercurey is an improving white AC.

Oak has to be used very carefully with all of these; leave the wine in barrel ten minutes too long and it could easily overbalance. But when this is properly judged the wines can be exactly what we are looking for: something that really feels like Burgundy in the mouth but not in the pocket. *Premier cru* means very little: in Montagny the wines have 11.5% alcohol, that's all it means. Crazy. The wines are best drunk at around two to four years. The Buxy Co-operative [★★/■■→■■■] is one of the best producers, along with [★★/■■→■■■]:

Broisset	*Jadot*
Chanzy	*Jaffelin*
Cogny	*Juillot*
Delorme	*Latour*
Drouhin	*Moillard*

Côte Chalonnaise whites go well with delicately flavoured food and most fish, particularly poached salmon and turbot.

WHERE NEXT? Contrast with **Chablis**: same grape, a few score miles north, but different soil. And see the new Chardonnays of the Ardèche and similar southern French areas for a challenge.

COTE D'OR

The heart of white Burgundy (apart from the major coronary artery at Chablis) is the Côte d'Or, a thin strip of hillside running south from Dijon for some 40 miles (65 km), made up of the Côte de Nuits in the north and the Côte de Beaune in the south. Both *côtes* produce red wines, but white wines are concentrated in the Côte de Beaune. Minuscule amounts of white are made in the Côte de Nuits to the north, and are not commercially significant

The best vineyards, where fine differences in soil and drainage interact with microclimatic blips and foibles to produce incomparable wines, are designated *grands crus* (see **Burgundy**). All the *grands crus* are in the Côte de Beaune. These wines can be sublime, although they are not always so; it depends how determined the producer is to make them sing.

THE COTE D'OR TASTE This is archetypal, copybook Chardonnay – model Chardonnay for the world: well-bred, well-proportioned, graceful, elegantly dressed. It is not thin and overcropped, not heavy and gawky, but balanced; there is buttery richness, but the wines are not greasy and fat; there is restraint, but the wines are not pinched and tart; there is juiciness, but the wines are not mere thirstquenchers. Fruit and oak harmonize into whole wines which are greater than the sum of their parts. This is, after all, where Chardonnay calls home.

BEGIN WITH MEURSAULT Meursault is, on the whole, consistently good, a rare thing in Burgundy. And it doesn't usually charge the highest prices. While it may not provoke elaborate, gushing and fanciful praise like the very top Côte d'Or wines, it does show us unequivocally what it is that makes Burgundy so special.

This is where Chardonnay shows its buttery richness, and where it marries perfectly with oak. Meursault is dry but not as lean and taut as Chablis further north; it fills out into a more ample, well-built shape. It is rarely fat or overweight, but has enough flesh to accommodate all the flavours of peaches and cream, of buttered toast sprinkled with cinnamon, of nuts and honey, on which it seems to gorge itself.

The best Meursault is succulent, balanced, undeniably aristocratic, and ages remarkably gracefully, usually at its best between five and ten years. It is very close to many people's idea of what white wine drinking is all about. Meursault-Blagny (from a tiny hamlet straddling the boundary with Puligny-Montrachet) is slightly leaner, less generous, but still top quality.

There are no *grands crus* in Meursault but it hardly matters because the *premiers crus* say it all anyway. Even simple village wine can be good, but it is worth saving up for a *premier cru* from a good producer to see what all the fuss is about. The best producers [★★ → ★★★ / ■ ■ ■] include:

Buisson	*Comtes Lafon*
Coche-Debord	*Duc de Magenta*
Coche Dury	*Jean Monnier*
Jean Germain	*Guy Roulot*

OTHER CÔTE D'OR WINES Meursault's vineyards carry on south into Puligny-Montrachet, and the style does not change abruptly as it crosses the administrative boundary. Puligny's *premiers crus* are every bit as good as Meursault's, and would make just as big a splash, were they not overwhelmed by the power and star quality of the *grands crus*: Chevalier-Montrachet, Bienvenues, Bâtard-Montrachet and Le Montrachet.

The extra bit of drainage afforded by the underlying limestone seems to push the vines into overdrive, producing ripe grapes and concentrated juice that fumbles its way around for a decade before beginning to find its feet. Then it is like Concorde. Take a *premier cru* and you think you are going fast; but when you drink a *grand cru* the throttle opens and it goes supersonic.

Just as you cannot really believe you are travelling faster than a bullet, so you wonder how a wine can be so incredibly dry and firm, yet impossibly rich and opulent at the same time. You wonder where the extra flavour comes from, and try to separate the toasty, smoky, roasted coffee flavour from the nuts and spice, and the nuts and spice from the honey and cream. But you can't, it is all one, integrated, complete, so you give up and enjoy it. You might as well, you've paid enough for it. These are among the very best white wines produced in the world.

The best and most reliable producers of Puligny-Montrachet [★★ → ★★★ / ■ ■ ■] include:

Blain-Gagnard	*Louis Latour*
Bouchard Père & Fils	*Leflaive*
Louis Jadot	*Romanée-Conti*
Comtes Lafon	*Villamont*
Marquis de Laguiche	

The Montrachet and Bâtard-Montrachet vineyards are shared with the village of Chassagne-Montrachet, which also has its very own *grand cru* Criots Bâtard Montrachet. The village boundary hardly matters, though, because *grands crus* are above such things.

Chassagne-Montrachet actually makes more red wine than white, but its *premier cru* vineyards return the temperature to normal after the excitement of sonic booms and bullets. By normal I mean very similar in style and quality to the *premiers crus* of Puligny and Meursault. For some reason the village does not have their *cachet*, so Chassagne prices may be a whisker lower and therefore worth snapping up.

The best and most reliable Chassagne-Montrachet producers [★★ → ★★★ / ■ ■ ■] include:

Blain-Gagnard	*Pierre Morey*
Génot-Boulanger	*Michel Niellon*
Jean-Noël Gagnard	*Ramonet-Prudhon*
Gagnard-Delagrange	

The other great white *grand cru*, Corton-Charlemagne, comes from the northern end of the Côte de Beaune, from the upper slopes of the hill of Corton between Aloxe-Corton and Pernand-Vergelesses. It is more reserved than its Puligny cousins, tighter, less ripe, more closed in for longer (it needs at least ten years), but with a generous pinch from the spice box. The best producers [★★★/■■■] include:

Bonneau du Martray	Olivier Leflaive
Faiveley	Louis Latour
Jadot	Tollot-Beaut

Elsewhere in the Côte de Beaune, many *appellations* operate on a very tiny scale, some turning out as few as 3,000 bottles. They can be worth seeking out for interest, curiosity, and sometimes good value. Among the best are St-Aubin and St-Romain. Good St-Aubin producers [★★/■■■] include:

Bachelet	Morey
Clerget	Prudhon
Jadot	Roux
Jaffelin	

Good St-Romain producers [★★/■■■] include:

Bazenet	Gras
Buisson	Thévenin-Monthélie

Auxey-Duresses and Pernand-Vergelesses are straightforward rather than distinguished. Good Auxey-Duresses producers [★★/■■] include Jadot, Leroy and Duc de Magenta; good Pernand-Vergelesses producers [★★/■■■] include Laleure-Piot, Pavelot and Rapet.

Other *appellations* [★→★★/■■→■■■] include: Corton, which also has Pinot Blanc and Pinot Gris (here called Pinot Beurot) grapes in the blend; Beaune, where Drouhin's Clos des Mouches [★★★/■■■] is good; Hautes-Côtes de Beaune; Ladoix-Serrigny; Santenay; and Savigny-lès-Beaune.

Best Côte d'Or vintages include 1988, 86, 83, 82, 79, 78 and 76.

COTE D'OR WINE AND FOOD Fine Côte d'Or whites deserve to be accompanied by simple, elegant dishes. Plain sole or turbot are traditional. Experiment with cheeses that are not too strong.

WHERE NEXT? These are the wines **California** and **Australia** try to match: check if they do. Within France, **Chablis** *grands crus* can be very close to Côte d'Or wines in good years.

COTEAUX DU LANGUEDOC

Languedoc is in the heart of *vin de pays* country. Vines grow like weeds, and are about as useful unless there is some way of preserving the fruit and acidity. The problem is not unique to the Midi. California's Central Valley and Australia's Murray Valley are hot spots with similar problems. It takes money (and a desire to do more than fill the wine lake) to install the proper equipment to cool-ferment and make it work. But where that message has struck home the improvements in quality have been startling. Because of the scale of investment needed, co-operatives and other large organizations have been in the forefront of the revolution.

Much of the region's best wine is red; for whites, the highlight of the Coteaux du Languedoc is the district of La Clape. A limestone massif at the mouth of the River Aude, its soil and climate are ideal for producing white grapes (which include Clairette, Malvoisie and some

Chardonnay) and, given the wines' capacity for ageing, potential is considerable. The best producers [★/■■] include:

J Boscary	Domaine de Pech-Redon
Yves Lignères	J Segura

In Faugères, another district better known for its reds, a little fresh white wine for early drinking is made by Bernard Vidal [★/■■].

The hearty, simple food of the Midi makes few demands of the region's wines. Languedoc whites do well with cod, oysters, mussels – almost all seafood – as well as onion and leek tart.

WHERE NEXT? **Provence** is close in style, perhaps a little ahead in quality. Cross the border to **Spain** for a different tradition and different grapes, but the same warmth. Look to **California** for a similar environment and often better winemaking.

COTEAUX DU LAYON

The most luscious sweet wines of the Loire, its equivalent of Sauternes, come from downstream beyond Angers, in the valley of the River Layon. The production of sweet wines, however, presents difficulties for growers. In good, ripe years (1986, 85, 83, 76, 69, 64 and 59) the grapes will be affected by *Botrytis*. As with Sémillon in Sauternes, when Chenin Blanc succumbs to *Botrytis* brought on by autumn warmth and humidity, the grapes rot and shrivel, concentrating sweetness and preserving acidity. They will make excellent rich wines for long keeping, but in tiny quantities. When conditions are unfavourable in this region – and routinely in less favoured parts of the Loire – growers have to be content with a more general late picking rather than a selective berry-by-berry collection. The result is a wine whose sweetness is less concentrated.

Within the Loire's Coteaux du Layon are two small *appellations* which are the *crème de la crème* of sweet Chenin Blanc: Quarts de Chaume [★★★/■■■] and Bonnezeaux [★★★/■■■], the latter being the richer. Compare them with Sauternes; they may not seem as luscious, although the alcohol, at around 13-14%, is about the same. That is the effect of Chenin's powerful acidity. The wines of Bonnezeaux and Quarts de Chaume are gentler, somewhere between the density and rich honey of Sauternes and the floweriness and feather lightness of, say, a Mosel *Beerenauslese*. The apricot and peach fruits are ripe, succulent and warm. They will soldier on for decades, the acidity keeping them awake when most other wines have fallen fast asleep. There is no bedtime for Bonnezeaux [joke]. Best producers [★★★/■■→■■■] include:

Baumard	l'Echarderie
la Soucherie	Gauliers

The larger AC Coteaux du Layon rarely reaches the same intensity. To continue the Bordeaux analogy, these are the equivalent of, say, Loupiac or Ste-Croix-du-Mont: sweet, but not necessarily with the same degree of *Botrytis* infection, and for that reason relatively inexpensive. Good producers [★★/■■→■■■] include Château de Plaisance and Cuvée Adrian.

These elegant dessert wines are superb with fruity puddings: pear tart, peaches and cream, baked apricots.

WHERE NEXT? Head off to the Rhine for Germany's response to similar conditions (see **Rheingau, Rheinhessen, Rheinpfalz**), or to **Sauternes & Barsac**, also for *Botrytis* wines.

COTES DE DURAS

This is the sort of easily-overlooked region that can provide pleasant surprises. Sandwiched between Entre-Deux-Mers and Bergerac, the Côtes de Duras lies just outside the Gironde *départment*. Although its wines are made from the typical Bordeaux selection of Sauvignon Blanc, Sémillon and Muscadelle, it is Sauvignon that dominates here.

This dry wine is the next-best thing on the Bordeaux fringe to Bergerac Sec. Like Bergerac, it comes on strong with the nettle and grass flavours, but is, if anything, slightly less incisive and edgy, slightly easier on the nerve endings. It needs to be drunk very young to catch its wispy freshness, but it is not expensive, and co-ops supply most of it; UNIDOR [★/■→■■] markets it under various labels.

WHERE NEXT? Try **Côtes de Gascogne, Vins de Pays** or anywhere in southern Europe where winemakers are competing for the not-too-dry market. Wines from **New Zealand**, Washington (see **United States**) and **Alto Adige** cost a little more but can be better value.

COTES DE GASCOGNE

Although a mere *vin de pays*, this wine illustrates how successfully modern winemaking, even using the most ordinary of grapes, can satisfy contemporary tastes.

The starting point is Ugni Blanc (see **Trebbiano**) and Colombard grapes, universally dismissed as being so poor, making such thin, sharp, acidic and undrinkable wine, that the only thing anybody had ever seriously thought of doing was to distill it. The *départment* is Gers in south-west France, home of *foie gras*, and the distilled spirit is Armagnac. Whatever you do, went accepted wisdom, don't drink the wine. But spirits are not as popular as they were. What should growers do with the spare grapes?

Given the ability of stainless steel and temperature-controlled fermentation to extract more fruit than was ever previously thought possible, and given slightly riper grapes, the new-style wine whooshed up on the flavourometer. "Is it made from Sauvignon Blanc?" we wonder, because we are so used to that grape's fresh grassy punch on the nose. No, from a couple of down-and-outs that nobody would have given house room before, and that now taste lightly of lemons, apples and pears. Remarkable: a wonderful vindication of *vins de pays* – a tribute to the co-operatives [★/■→■■] that churn it out so inexpensively, and to producers [★→★★/■→■■] such as:

Cassagnoles	Planterieu
Jalousie	Tariquet
Meste Duran	

Although a whisker less successful, exactly the same approach in the Cognac region has produced a very similar Vin de Pays Charentais.

These ultra-crisp, fresh wines are ideal drinking partners for cold meats and *antipasti*, fish terrines and gravlax.

WHERE NEXT? At their best, the wines of **Sicily**, **Penedès** and **Coteaux du Languedoc** can match the freshness of Gascogne wines.

COTES DE ROUSSILLON

Roussillon, situated like nearby Coteaux du Languedoc in the *vin de pays* country of south-eastern France, has been AC since 1977. The region's most distinctive sweet wines are its *vins doux naturels*, but dry wines – including *vin vert*, a sharp-tasting local speciality – are produced under the Côtes de Roussillon *appellation*.

The best producers [★→★★/■■] of dry white wine in the Côtes de Roussillon include:

Domaine de Canterrane	*Mas Péchot*
Cazes Frères	*Tresserre*
Château de Jau	

Look out also for co-operative wines [★/■■] from L'Agly, Cassagnes, Les Vignerons de Maury and others.

WHERE NEXT? Corbières, and the unusual still wines of Limoux, are nearby and similar. **Penedès** wines come from close by, a mere mountain away.

CYPRUS

The finest white wine of Cyprus is the intensely sweet Commandaria [★★/■], which sometimes compares with the Constantina of South Africa. The wine is made in a similar way to Italian *vino passito*: from pressed sun-dried grapes that reach high alcohol levels naturally, without fortification. The main grape for all Cypriot white wines is the indigenous Xynisteri.

At present there are very few good dry white table wines although the "sherries" have improved in quality. Arsinoe [★/■] is a widely available white wine which has a rather flat, dull taste, produced by Sodap, the only co-operative on the island.

Other producers [★/■→■■] include Etko/Haggipavlu, Keo (producers of Aphrodite dry white wine) and Loel, which makes a drinkable white wine from Palomino, the Spanish sherry grape.

WHERE NEXT? **Greece** has more individual, more variable wines. **Sicily** offers some good modern tastes as well as the traditional boring ones. Commandaria has its counterparts in Greek **Mavro**, Spanish **Málaga** and Sicilian **Marsala**, all of which are usually better.

ENGLAND

England's notoriously erratic climate has led many to question the value of resuming winemaking after 500 years of ale and imported claret. The country is at the far north of the wine world, and it is expecting a lot for grapes to ripen at all, even in the very south.

Yet the past 20 years has yielded some very acceptable wines – almost all white – and have shown that true quality may yet be a real possibility. The glorious summer of 1989 was the shot in the arm the English needed; if the "greenhouse effect" provides many more summers like that we may see a sustained succession of vintage years for English wine.

A bewildering variety of grapes are now grown, from the familiar Pinot Meunier and Müller-Thurgau to oddities such as Seyval Blanc, a hybrid vine capable of making rather dull wine in adverse conditions (as it does in New York State). In among these are curiosities like Bacchus, a fragrant, Muscat-like German grape, and Schönburger, a flowery, scented crossbreed of Pinot Noir and Hamburg Muscat.

Other "halfbreeds" include: Huxelrebe which has a pungent "green" taste; Kerner, which tastes like a light Rhine Riesling; and Reichensteiner, produced from French, German and Italian grape varieties to make a kind of Eurovinous Song Contest wine – bright and fruity but bland.

English producers [★→★★/■■] include:

Adgestone	Hambledon
Biddenden Vineyards	Lamberhurst Priory
Breaky Bottom	Pilton Manor
Bruisyard	Staple St Hames
Chilford Hundred	Tenterden
Chiltern Valley	Three Choirs
Carr Taylor	Wootton
Elham Valley	

Carr Taylor, winner of several awards for its wines, also makes a *méthode champenoise* sparkler.

WHERE NEXT? The Mosel is the inspiration for many English winemakers (see **Mosel-Saar-Ruwer**), but the **Loire** may be closer in style. Like English wines, Washington's lighter wines make good aperitifs (see **United States**).

ENTRE-DEUX-MERS

In 1978, when I knew even less about wine than I do now, I spent a long autumn picking grapes in Entre-Deux-Mers. The farmer, who barely scratched a living, was not in the least bit interested in making decent wine; even I, up against practical winemaking for the first time, could tell that. I thought I had just been unlucky, but in the late 1970s most Entre-Deux-Mers was like that. "It is French," the attitude seemed to be, "what more can you want?"

Entre-Deux-Mers, like Graves, has now put all that behind it. The region covers the tongue of land "between the two seas" of the Rivers Garonne and Dordogne, stretching inland to the Gironde department's boundary, as far as Côtes de Duras. The grape varieties used in the blend – Sémillon, Sauvignon Blanc and Muscadelle – are the usual Bordeaux trio for white wines.

The wines do not have the stature or weight of Graves, but they are one up on straight Bordeaux Blanc (see **Bordeaux**). They are light, apple-fresh, and generally inexpensive wines for everyday drinking. The innovation that woke them up was temperature-controlled fermentation. Ferment the grapes cool, and the fresh grassy aromas stay fresh; they don't turn to stale, damp hay like they used to.

These are unpretentious, easy-drinking wines, the bread and butter of the Bordeaux trade, and since freshness is one of their most enjoyable characteristics they should be drunk very young. A few are given a gentle twist of oak, but more to fill them out with a little creamy richness than to make a long-lived giant.

Sauvignon Blanc brings the piercing bite of acidity, and wines made only from this should be drunk as soon as possible. But one of the great qualities of Sémillon is that, while it can be as green and grassy as Sauvignon during the first year, it opens and rounds out in time, giving the wines more body. A good Entre-Deux-Mers using both grape varieties should therefore be able to last, and improve, over at least a couple of years.

The best producers here [★/■■] include:

Bonnet	Moulin-de-Launay
Launay	Thieuley
Laurétan	de Toutigeac

WHERE NEXT? Try **Graves** for the example E-D-M is always chasing, **Bergerac** for another go at the same style, **New Zealand** and **Bulgaria** for successful inroads into the same price bracket.

FRANCE

What is the best white wine in the world? A Montrachet from Burgundy, perhaps? The great Sauternes Château d'Yquem from a venerable vintage? Champagne? Whatever it is, France is where we go to look for it. There are wonderful Chardonnays from California and Australia. There are sensational Rieslings from Germany. But they never quite have the stature, the greatness, of France's best whites.

The trouble is, there is precious little of the best wine to go round: the reputations of Burgundy and Sauternes seem to be in inverse proportion to the amount of wine they produce. Champagne is more accessible, but the top *cuvées* keep themselves at arm's length by their price. Most French wine that most people drink is considerably less exalted. But it is precisely these less exalted wines – the underrated dry wines of Alsace, the astonishingly transformed light- to medium-bodied wines of Graves and Entre-Deux-Mers, the remarkable new breed of *vin de pays* – that have shown the greatest progress during the 1980s. French wines are now better than they have ever been, across the board.

France is an old wine country, almost as old as Italy, and has its share not just of dry, sweet, still, sparkling, light, medium and full-bodied wines, but also of rare grapes and unusual tastes. In the southwest, for instance, are Mauzac, Ondenc and Loin de l'Oeil, making sharp Gaillac and bland Côtes du Tarn; Manseng for Jurançon; there is Jaquère in Savoie, and Savagnin in the Jura, responsible for the sherry-like *vin jaune*. They are not the sort of grape varieties that anybody would rush off and plant in Oregon, but they are part of the richness of French life.

FRENCH WINE LAW

● French wine law works on the principle that the best wines result from the rather mystical coming together of grape variety, soil and climate. Where these are all uniquely specified, together with small print about yield and ageing, then the wine is *Appellation d'Origine Contrôlée* (AOC or, more commonly, AC). Most of the famous French wines are AC. The AC does not guarantee quality, but it does (or should) guarantee that a wine comes from where the label says it does, and be made from the correct grapes and so on. The word "Supérieur" on a label does not mean that the wine is better, just that it contains an extra degree or half a degree of alcohol.

● Below this are *Vins Délimités de Qualité Supérieur* (VDQS), with similar controls to AC but for separate regions. This category has all but disappeared as most of them have pulled their socks up and been promoted to AC.

● Less strictly controlled, *vins de pays* display distinct regional charactistics and the region of origin is always given on the label.

● *Vin de table*, the everyday plonk of the working man, can be made from more or less any grapes, grown more or less anywhere; indeed it must not be too specific about where it comes from, in order not to be confused with AC wines. This is wine at its most elemental, unoriginal and uninspiring, although the trend over recent years has been a move toward more characterful wines.

There has been ample time in which to discover that Chardonnay performs magnificently on some hillsides, in the Côte d'Or and Chablis for instance. And time, too, to become such a prisoner of tradition that it may not occur to people to try other hillsides which may, if chosen carefully, produce wine at least as good if not better than the ones already in use. France's infinite variety and constant state of flux, its ability to produce classic and everyday wines with equal panache, add up to a fascination that is unequalled anywhere.

WHERE NEXT? See the specific entries on French wine styles: **Aligoté, Alsace, Anjou, Beaumes-de-Venise, Bergerac, Blanquette-de-Limoux, Bordeaux, Burgundy, Chablis, Champagne, Condrieu & Château-Grillet, Corsica, Côte Chalonnaise, Côte d'Or, Coteaux du Languedoc, Coteaux du Layon, Côtes de Duras, Côtes de Gascogne, Côtes de Roussillon, Entre-Deux-Mers, Gaillac, Graves, Gros Plant, Hermitage, Jura, Jurançon, Loire, Mâcon, Monbazillac, Muscadet, Pineau des Charentes, Provence, Rhône, Sancerre & Pouilly-Fumé, Saumur, Sauternes & Barsac, Savoie, Touraine, Vin Doux Naturel, Vin de Pays** and **Vouvray**.

FRANKEN

Like Baden, Franken is predominantly dry wine country. Correction, it is predominantly beer country, on the edge of Bavaria, east of the Rheingau, off towards Bayreuth and Nürnberg, where the climate begins to turn severe and continental. Those who take time off from beer-drinking understandably enjoy wines of a weighty, earthy and dry disposition. Production is centred around the city of Würzburg.

Like Baden, too, Franken goes in less for the ethereal aromatic styles, and more for the full, dense, four-square kind. Both regions produce substantial wines, which come closest in Germany to that characteristic which so many Italian white wines possess, vinosity, a kind of "wine-iness" that is neither fruit nor flowers, just wine. For some reason Franken seems concerned to highlight the distinctiveness of its containers: you pour from a flat flagon or *Bocksbeutel* into a Franken *Stein*.

Some of Franken's greatest successes are with the Silvaner grape. Franconian Silvaner [★★/■■] is earthy and vegetal, sometimes a bit green and sappy, sometimes a bit smoky, but usually the wines are among the best examples of the grape anywhere. Müller-Thurgau [★★/■■→■■■] is increasing, and even it digs deeper than the superficial floweriness that characterizes it elsewhere. Riesling [★★/■■■] has difficulty ripening, but when it does, in warm sunny years, then it can be honeyed and immensely satisfying.

Regional names to look for include the villages of Iphofen (*Grosslage* Burgweg), and Castell (*Grosslage* Herrenberg), both in Bereich Steigerwald; *Grosslagen* Burg and Ewig Leben in Bereich Maindreieck; and most of all the Würzburger Stein vineyard. Good producers [★★/■■→■■■] include:

Bürgerspital	*Johann Ruck*
Fürstlich Castell'sches	*Randersacker Co-operative*
Domänenamt	*Staatlicher Hofkeller*
Juliusspital	*Hans Wirsching*
Ernst Popp	

WHERE NEXT? **Austria** has more sun to coax more sugar into the grapes, but like Franken makes dry wines. **Baden** is the nearest German equivalent.

FRASCATI

Made in the hills south of Rome, Frascati has traditionally supplied the city with dry, everyday jug wine. It combines the high-yielding, light Trebbiano with the more serious and more difficult-to-handle Malvasia. The latter's tendency to oxidize and become flabby is rescued by Trebbiano's fresh acidity.

Unfortunately, too few producers have the patience to bother with Malvasia, and innocuous Trebbiano often dominates. The less Trebbiano in the blend, the more interesting the wine. Fontana Candida [★★/■→■■] is good but Colli di Catone [★★/■→■■], made entirely from Malvasia and sold in a kinkily-shaped satinized bottle, is generally reckoned the best: it does not scream with flavour, but has a gentle, nutty quality, with considerably more body and weight than other examples.

A single vineyard version of this, Colle Gaio [★★/■■■], is the most concentrated of all. Just as Roberto Anselmi and Leonildo Pieropan have shown that Soave can be taken seriously, so Antonio Pulcini has shown that "real" Frascati is possible.

Other good producers [★→★★/■■] include:

Il Marchese	*Monteporzio*
Mastrofini	*Villa Simone*

Frascati is so easy-going that the Romans tend to drink it with anything and everything; it is best with seafood or creamy pasta.

WHERE NEXT? For lighter Italian wines, see **Trebbiano**; for more interesting wines see **Malvasia**.

FRIULI-VENEZIA GIULIA

This hilly corner of north-eastern Italy, up by the borders with Austria and Yugoslavia, has undergone something of a viticultural revolution over the last 20 years and now produces some of the country's best white wines – most notably in the neighbouring zones of Grave del Friuli, Colli Orientali del Friuli and Collio.

CHOOSING FRIULI WINES Grave del Friuli, like its Bordelais cousin Graves, is so-called because of the region's soil conditions, where gravel predominates. In places the earth is rich and alluvial, and these areas produce everyday wines. When gravel does become visible there is a chance of finding some really fine stuff, which can also represent quite a bargain.

The white varieties allowed by DOC in Grave del Friuli include Tocai, Pinot Bianco (see **Pinot Blanc**), Pinot Grigio (see **Pinot Gris**) and Verduzzo. This last is a local variety which makes dry wines something like a Soave but with a little more bitterness in the finish. Producers to look for in Grave del Friuli [★★/■■] include:

Azienda Agricola	*Fratelli Pighin*
Kechler Co-op	*A A Plozner Co-op*
Duca Badoglio	

The nearby districts of Colli Orientali del Friuli and Collio produce wines said to have a spicy "Hungarian" quality. The traditional grape varieties grown are the same as for Grave del Friuli and reliable examples come from the co-operative – Cantina Sociale Cooperative del Friuli Orientali [★★/■■], which uses the Molin di Ponte trademark. The nutty, oily wines produced from Tocai are particularly good; the best producers [★★/■■→■■■] include Abbazia di Rosazzo and Schiopetto.

A number of producers have also begun to experiment with white blends of foreign varieties, with some outstanding results [★★→★★★/ ■■■], among them: Jermann's Vintage Tunina (a blend of Pinot Bianco, Chardonnay, Sauvignon Blanc and Picolit); Schiopetto's Blanc di Rosis (made from Pinot Bianco, Sauvignon Blanc, Tocai and Malvasia); and Gravner's Vino Gradberg (made from Malvasia, Prosecco, Ribolla and Pagadebit).

A curiosity of the region is the dessert wine Picolit, made from the grape of that name. At its best the flavour is a heady mix of pears, walnuts and honey, with a bitter tinge to the finish – not so far removed from Hungarian Tokay. The wine goes best with blue cheeses such as Gorgonzola. Reliable Picolit producers [★★/■■■] include:

Conti de Maniago	*Al Rusignul*
Rocca Bernarda	*Luigi Valle*

An excellent – and cheaper – alternative to Picolit is the sweet *amabile* Verduzzo or Verduzzo di Ramandolo produced in Colli Orientali from the same grape that makes dry wines in Grave del Friuli. Good producers of this subtle, fruity wine [★★/■■] include:

Abbazio di Rosazzo	*Ronchi di Fornaz*
Giovanni Dri	*Volpe Pasini*
Felluga	

FRIULI WINE AND FOOD In general, Friuli wines make interesting foils to food. Tocai goes well with crabmeat and paper-thin *prosciutto*; sweet Verduzzo is ideal with apple strudel.

WHERE NEXT? Range across northern Italy to **Alto Adige**, which offers an Alpine variant with a German flavour. Try **Tuscany** for a more southern wine, Piedmont for more sophistication (see **Gavi**). Slovenia in **Yugoslavia** has some good wines, but hides them beneath oceans of ordinary plonk.

GAILLAC

Gaillac's grapes probably pre-date the Romans, and some of their names seem to be descended from a lost language: Mauzac, Ondenc, and the out-of-sight Loin de L'Oeil. The tastes range from sharp and tangy to pinched, austere and aggressive, like green, under-ripe apples soaked in lemon juice; riper grapes and sweeter wines give off an aroma of cider. Perhaps that is why they take so well to being fizzed up.

Three different kinds of sparklers are made. Gaillac is best known for its faintly spritzy *pétillant* or *perlé* wines, which traditionally owe their prickle to the small amount of carbon dioxide produced by the malolactic fermentation. But fully sparkling *mousseux*, a semi-sweet *méthode champenoise* wine, is the classiest, and there is some tank method *brut* and *demi-sec*. Between them Mauzac, Muscadelle, Sauvignon, Sémillon, Ondenc and the unusual Loin de L'Oeil provide perfume, lift, spice and appley bite. The co-op [★→★★★/■→■■] makes the lion's share. Other good producers [★/■→■■] include Jean Cros, Labastide-de-Lévis and Domaine de Labarthe.

WHERE NEXT? The drier **Vinho Verde** wines have a similarly sharp attack and light prickle. **Muscadet** has a family resemblance. Acidity levels can compare with **Chenin Blanc**, so try dry sparkling Chenin Blanc-based wines from the Loire (see **Anjou**, **Saumur**, **Touraine**).

GAVI

From around the Langhe, Roeri and Alto Monferrato hills of southern Piedmont – an area renowned for the chunky red wines of Barolo and Barbaresco – comes an unusual trio of light white wine styles: Gavi, Arneis and Favorita.

Gavi, the best-known of the three, is made from Cortese – a light, acidic grape, fairly low in alcohol. A good deal of everyday wine is simply bottled under the grape name or as "Cortese di Gavi". The wines of Gavi DOC are a little better: still crisp with an attractive oily richness but no great injection of flavour. If they were half the price they would be a bargain.

La Scolca's Gavi dei Gavi [★★/■■] is reckoned the best; other good examples [★★/■■] include Bergaglio's Rovereto di Gavi, Deltetto and Tenuta San Pietro.

The Arneis grape makes a delightful wine for drinking young: medium- to full-bodied, rich in texture, with good crisp acidity during the first year or so. It occupies that part of the flavour spectrum inhabited by ripe apples, pears, quince and lightly roasted nuts, and has a gentle, sensuous, smoky quality that gives it depth. It does not shout with noisy varietal flavour, nor scream with aromatic pungency, but then few Italian wines do; it is a gentle, contemplative wine of some distinction and class.

Reliable producers of Arneis [★★/■■] include:

Castello di Neive	Malvirà, Damonte
Deltetto	Voerzio
Giacosa	

Another grape that is coming on in leaps and bounds after years of neglect is Favorita. It makes a pale, lightweight, delicate but beautifully perfumed wine more reminiscent of Germany than Italy.

Good producers of Favorita [★★/■■ → ■■] include:

Cavallotto	Malvirà, Damonte
Deltetto	Voerzio
Franco-Fiorina	

The white wines of Piedmont come into their own as aperitifs, but they can also make generous food partners. Gavi dei Gavi served with fresh egg noodles, Parmesan and Piemontese truffles makes a sumptuous treat.

WHERE NEXT? Chenin Blanc; northern Rhône wines (see **Condrieu & Château-Grillet**); and other Italians from **Friuli-Venezia Giulia** and **Tuscany**

GERMANY

Germany's wine laws seem to have been organized all wrong for most of us. The country has produced great oceans of anonymous wine, a lot of which (in the past at any rate) did not even originate in Germany; in their favour, these wines at least had names that the consumer could recognize. Side by side, Germany has made some outstanding wines, but most of us have never experienced them because we simply haven't known what to ask for.

EEC regulations laid down in 1971 sought to impose some semblance of order on the German system, but what Germany does not seem to have taken on board is that most people cannot be bothered to work out the difference between, for example, an *Einzellage*, a *Grosslage*, a *Bereich* and an *Anbaugebiet*. Here we are knocking on the door, dying for a drink, and all we get is the oenological equivalent of a tax handbook thrown at us before we can place an order. In the end we will take anything, even Liebfraumilch and Niersteiner Gutes Domtal.

Germany has 11 wine-producing regions, or *Anbaugebieten*: Ahr, Hessische-Bergstrasse, Mittelrhein, Mosel-Saar-Ruwer, Nahe, Rheingau, Rheinhessen, Rheinpfalz, Franken, Baden and Württemberg. These are divided into districts (*Bereiche*), such as Bernkastel in Mosel-Saar-Ruwer, and Nierstein in Rheinhessen. A further subdivision into 150-odd *Grosslagen* describes vineyards that are grouped together by a supposed similarity of style, such as Gutes Domtal. Smallest of the sub-divisions are the 2,600 *Einzellagen*, or individual vineyards, which together make up *Grosslagen*.

The system is absolutely wonderful, from the grape's point of view: no question, you know exactly where you are, your place in the scheme of things is precisely ordained. But if you happen to be a drinker it is a right old mess. It is a production-led system, when it should be consumer-led. Fortunately some producers have recognized the problem. They make good, modern wines, increasingly dry, and give them simple no-nonsense labels: what could be easier to order than Riesling Dry?

Until well into this century, the only sweet wines available were those made from mature grapes that produced enough sugar to be naturally sweet: *Auslesen* and *Beerenauslesen*, sometimes affected by *Botrytis*. If on the other hand the must-weight (the amount of sugar in the grapes) was high enough to make a *Spätlese*, but the wine was fully fermented, then the end-result would be a dry wine with a reasonable amount of body.

GERMAN WINE LAW

Germany's top wine grade is *Qualitätswein mit Prädikat* (QmP), which relates to one of six categories of ripeness, and means that the grapes were made into wine without any further addition of sugar:

● *Kabinett*: made from fully ripe grapes;

● *Spätlese*: made from late-picked and therefore riper grapes;

● *Auslese*: made from specially selected bunches of particularly ripe (sometimes nobly rotten) grapes;

● *Beerenauslese*: made from individually selected, extra-ripe and nobly rotten grapes;

● *Trockenbeerenauslese*: made from dried, specially selected single grapes infected with noble rot;

● *Eiswein*: made from fully ripe grapes that have been left on the vine until they freeze. The ice crystals remain in the grape during pressing, thereby concentrating the sugars in the juice that remains.

The next grade down, *Qualitätswein bestimmter Anbaugebiete* (QbA), must come from one of the 11 designated wine-producing regions and be made from must of a certain minimum weight. All *Qualitätswein* is subject to official testing.

Deutscher Tafelwein (DTW) is made from a blend of grapes with added sugar to give a semblance of ripeness. The "*Deutscher*" means the grapes must be grown in Germany; plain *Tafelwein* can come from anywhere in the EEC. *Landwein*, the equivalent of French *vin de pays*, is a cut above *Tafelwein*, introduced in 1982 for wines of distinct regional character.

When technology enabled sweet grape juice to be stabilized so that it would not start to ferment of its own accord, it was found that a small amount of this *süssreserve* added to a dry wine would round it out, providing a short-cut to the sweeter, richer styles of wine. But its usefulness in balancing high acidity and filling out some of the thinner wines soon made it as common as salt in a kitchen. Without it there would not be the vast quantities of medium-sweet, characterless wine for which Germany is now infamous.

Dryness is now sweeping Germany, and one consequence of this is that we can at last taste the wine itself, and even the grape varieties in their pristine form, now that the sugar no longer obscures their flavour. This in turn is leading to a greater emphasis on single varietals. Riesling is indisputably noble, but Silvaner and Ruländer (Pinot Gris) can be good with food, while Gewürztraminer is distinctive and powerfully aromatic.

One of the main problems with very dry German wines, though, is that their exposed natural acidity can seem rather tart, lacking the harmony of a good Riesling *Auslese* whose rich sweetness balances the racy acidity. If the sweetness is removed (or not added) some of the lesser wines can appear pretty scrawny. Dry (*trocken*) wines of low must-weight (QbA wines for example) can screech and squawk rather than sing. *Halbtrocken* are softer with a little more body, so most people find them easier to drink.

Ideally the body and weight should come from the wine itself. *Spätlese trocken* wines are therefore perhaps the best introduction to the genre, while *Kabinett trocken* wines can give the simplest and purest expression of the grape.

Even some of the crosses are palatable. Müller-Thurgau, which accounts for a third of all grapes grown in Germany, is uncomplicated, if lacking in character. Kerner, a crossing of Riesling with the red Trollinger (Schiava Grossa), is particularly successful. It tastes more like Riesling than most other imitative attempts, with a clean, green leafy edge that matures well. Scheurebe, an earlier and more conventional crossing of Silvaner with Riesling, performs well when it achieves high must-weights, making good *Auslese* and *Beerenauslese* wines.

You could do worse than to start with Mosel-Saar-Ruwer, where Rieslings are full yet light, fresh and delicate. Mosel wines end up in a slender green bottle; Rhine wines, often referred to as "hock", come in a brown bottle. The English word derives from the town of Hochheim in the Rheingau, although it can be applied to the other rich, fruity Rhine Rieslings from Rheinhessen and Rheinpfalz. Situated between the Mosel and the Rhine, and reflecting this in taste, is Nahe. More substantial dry wines appear in Baden and Franken.

Wines from Germany's other growing regions are seen less often outside the country. Mittelrhein is the place to go for a Rheinfahrt and see the picture-postcard castles clamped to craggy Wagnerian cliffs high above the Rhine Gorge; between Bingen (on the edge of the Rheingau) and Koblenz (where the Mosel joins the Rhine) Riesling from the slatey slopes is crisp and firm. Most Ahr wine is red, but what little white there is can be good; the best producer is the Staatliche Weinbaudomäne. Hessische Bergstrasse is a warm region off the Rhine near Heidelberg: the best producer is the Staatsweingut Bergstrasse, and there are good Rieslings in Württemberg.

WHERE NEXT? See the specific entries on German wine styles: **Baden, Franken, Liebfraumilch, Mosel-Saar-Ruwer, Nahe, Rheingau, Rheinhessen, Rheinpfalz** and **Sekt**.

GEWURZTRAMINER

This grape variety, wherever it is grown, makes some of the world's most powerfully aromatic wine. It thrives in cool climates, and is most closely identified with Alsace, along France's north-eastern border with Germany. The prefix *gewürz-* means spice in German, and the related Traminer grape is believed to have originated in the village of Tramin in Italy's Südtirol (see **Alto Adige**).

Nearly all Gewürztraminer is dry. Sweet versions are produced by picking the grapes late in the season, when their natural sugar content has increased, and even sweeter versions from *Botrytis*-affected grapes that have shrivelled and dried on the vine. These sweet wines are intensely flavoursome but can be rather flabby, as Gewürztraminer loses acidity quickly once it ripens. A cool growing season is necessary to produce good acidity in the grapes, so it performs best when hugging the edges of wine-growing regions or higher ground – hence its success in parts of Germany and Austria, Italy's Alto Adige and New Zealand.

THE GEWURZTRAMINER TASTE Gewürztraminer is popular among amateur tasters, with good reason. You overhear buffs talking about "varietal character" in a wine, and it means absolutely nothing. Then you taste Gewürztraminer and suddenly it all makes sense. You never quite forget that first revelation.

Although its flowery aroma can resemble that of Muscat, Gewürztraminer is most easily recognizable by its distinct smell of fresh lychee. Intense and powerfully pungent, it is considered a "spicy" wine: no particular spice, just a general impression helped a little, perhaps, by the name. A high alcoholic degree is another characteristic.

Given all these elements – intense smell and taste, high alcohol, sometimes low acidity – making it becomes a juggling act for the producer. Balance is crucial. When it works well, when the flavour is restrained, even subdued, and given definition by acidity, it can be a delight. Sometimes, though, it is pushed over the top to become, as Jancis Robinson has it, "the blowsy village wench who catches the attention of the tourists".

An overpowering smell and taste, coupled with a flabbiness, sometimes oiliness, can produce drinking fatigue: after the first joyous glass you become so fed up with the battering that you may not reach the end of the bottle. Some regard this as a virtue: if a single glass satisfies, a bottle will go a long way.

BEGIN WITH ALSACE Alsace is the best place to start. Co-operatives here are extremely reliable. Their wines (sometimes under an importer's own label) will often be less expensive than a producer's but quite sound. If this modest level appeals, consider an individual producer and a "better" year for greater concentration and character. If you are still in the game, raise the ante by trying a more expensive *Vendange tardive* wine (see **Alsace**).

OTHER GEWURZTRAMINERS *Vendange tardive* wines from Alsace, although extremely rich, are still dry, whereas *Spätlesen* and *Auslesen* from Germany and Austria – and particularly the *Botrytis*-affected *Beerenauslesen* and *Trockenbeerenauslesen* – can be as sweet as they are rich. It is unfortunate that some producers feel obliged to make these late-picked, high "must-weight" wines, which are equated with quality in the Germanic scheme of things, when a fresher, lighter wine might be both cheaper and more appropriate (see **Germany** and **Austria**).

If on the other hand Alsatian Gewürztraminer already seems too powerful, Alto Adige offers a lighter version. Wines labelled Traminer will be even more delicate (see **Alto Adige**).

Australia makes some palatable Gewürztraminers, but for crisp, zingy freshness, where else would you look but New Zealand, especially the South Island (see **Australia** and **New Zealand**)?

GEWURZTRAMINER AND FOOD Gewürztraminer needs strong, rich flavours to balance it. Oily fish, in particular smoked mackerel or smoked salmon, match that character in the wine. Its generalized spiciness also takes well to oriental food, cheese or lovage soup. Overall, it is a wine to experiment with. The powerful flavour and sometimes high alcohol combine to give an impression of weight, allowing it to take on rich casseroles.

WHERE NEXT? Riesling from **Alsace** and elsewhere can taste uncannily like Gewürz at times. For the penetrating taste, try a dry **Alsace** Muscat, Muscat Ottonel from **Austria** or a dry Muscat from João Pires (see **Portugal**).

GISBORNE

While Gisborne is thought of as the high-yielding grape basket of New Zealand's North Island, Hawkes Bay, just over 100 miles (160 km) further south on the same east coast, is considered the quality region. That may be generally true, but it oversimplifies the case.

Gisborne, wetter than Hawkes Bay, is a region of mass-production. Although much of the wine is extremely ordinary, it is at least decently made. Sometimes the varietal flavours are a bit off-centre, but mostly they are bold and err towards exotic and tropical fruits. But there are treasures here too, from particularly well endowed vineyard sites, and Chardonnays can be as good as any.

Among the best wines from Gisborne are Villa Maria's Sauvignon Blancs and Chardonnays [★★★/■■■]; this producer seems to have a magic touch, whatever the source of the fruit. Other good producers [★★/■■■] of Gisborne Chardonnay include:

Nobilo, Dixon Vineyard	*Matua Valley, Judd Estate*
Delegats	*Matia Valley, Egan Estate*

Millton Vineyard [★→★★/■■■], in addition to a big, rich, tropical-style, barrel-fermented Chardonnay, also makes an excellent barrel-fermented Chenin Blanc, and a good Late Harvest Rhine Riesling, while Matawhero's forte is Gewürztraminer [★★/■■], backed up with good Chardonnay and a Sauvignon/Semillon blend.

Gisborne Chardonnays can have a slightly acidic undertone which, combined with their fruity character, makes them an excellent match for the more robust fish dishes; try them with turbot, smoked trout or grilled salmon.

WHERE NEXT? Compare Gisborne's Sauvignon Blancs with those of **Marlborough**, and its Chardonnays with those of **Tasmania**, **Margaret River** and the **Yarra Valley**.

GRAVES

Or perhaps we should say Return From The Graves – which many properties have done over the last decade. How the *appellation* was allowed to fall into the awful state it did heaven knows, but at the beginning of the 1980s Graves was a byword for some of the most cack-handed white winemaking imaginable.

Graves stretches south from the suburbs of Bordeaux in a wide swathe of land occupying the south bank of the Garonne as far as Langon. It was, until recently, a predominantly white wine region, but these were so poor that something had to happen. Two things did: production switched largely to red, while the remaining white wine producers pulled their socks up.

The wines of Pessac-Léognan, a superior kind of Graves that gained its own AC in 1987, dominate the northern end, while plain Graves encloses the famous sweet ACs of Sauternes and Barsac (see **Sauternes & Barsac**) and the less-famous sweet AC of Cérons at the southern end.

THE GRAVES TASTE When you consider the raw materials – Sémillon and Sauvignon Blanc – the depths to which Graves had sunk become even more embarrassing. Just look what they can do Down-Under with these: mature, rich, honeyed but dry Semillons from the Hunter Valley; sensational Sauvignon Blancs from Marlborough in New Zealand's South Island; simple, crisp and snappy wines when the two varieties are combined.

Fortunately Graves has improved out of all recognition. The bland, slightly sweet and either oxidized or heavily sulphured wines of the 1970s have slunk away in shame; in their place is a new breed of properly made wines that are clean, fruity, crisply refreshing, yet with the kind of substance and stylishness that France is so good at. They are among France's best dry whites.

Sémillon provides the substance, the slightly honeyed apricot fruit and kernelly nuttiness, and the ability to improve in bottle, while Sauvignon contributes the grassy freshness and lively cut that makes them attractive to drink young. Proportions vary from wine to wine; most are at their best between two and four years, so it is best not to keep them too long unless you have good reason to believe that the wine has been made to last. Some are matured, or better still fermented, in oak, and have a full, creamy vanilla-like texture and a lick of spice.

CHOOSING GRAVES The well-drained gravelly soil that gave the region its name is concentrated in Pessac-Léognan, while Graves now has more sandy and clay-like soils. This seems to make less of a difference to whites than to reds, so good wines are produced in both ACs. Graves Supérieures, at 12%, has an extra degree of alcohol compared to straight Graves, but it is also generally made sweet. While Cérons is an *appellation* for sweet wines (see **Bordeaux**), dry whites made within its boundary take the Graves AC.

The best Graves properties [★★→★★★/■■■] include:

Cabannieux	Magence
Clos Floridène	Malartic-la-Gravière
Constantin	Pontac-Monplaisir
Couhins-Lurton	Rahoul
Domaine de Chevalier	Respide-Médeville
Domaine de la Grave	Rochemorin
de Fieuzal	Roquetaillade-la-Grange
Haut-Brion	St-Pierre
La Garence	Smith-Haut-Lafitte
Laville-Haut-Brion	La Tour-Martillac
La Louvière	

The best vintages for dry Graves wines include 1988, 87, 86, 85, 83, 82 and 81.

GRAVES AND FOOD Clean, crisp Graves wines deserve good food. Try them with veal, roast chicken, salmon baked with herbs or a cream sauce, or scallops.

WHERE NEXT? Try Australian blends of Sauvignon Blanc and Sémillon, especially those from **Western Australia**, or other French blends such as Château La Jaubertie from **Bergerac**.

GREECE

Many people's experience of Greek wine is limited to retsina (see **Retsina**), but the country's sweet Malvasias and Muscats were among the treasures of the ancient Mediterranean.

One of the best is Muscat of Samos [★/■■]. Made from Muscat à Petits Grains, it is a rich, luscious, honeyed yet finely balanced after-dinner treat. Other Muscats with varying degrees of sweetness [★/■■] include those of Rhodes and Lemnos, and those from Rion and Patras in the Peloponnese. The island of Santorini produces a full-bodied, dry and quite alcoholic white, together with a sweet wine made from partially dried grapes [★/■].

Greece also makes some ordinary dry white table wine, such as Demestica from Achaia Clauss [★/■], but most white wine is rather flabby and oxidized.

On the island of Cephalonia, however, Nicholas Cosmetatos makes attractive, fresh and crisp dry whites from local Robola and Tsaoussi grapes under the Gentilini label [★★/■■]; cool fermentation and cautious use of oak help enormously. This could be the style of Greek wines of the future, but the country still has a long way to go.

Carras, under the Côtes du Meliton label [★→★★/■■], makes whites of a more international style from native varieties blended with Sauvignon and Ugni Blanc: acceptable but unexciting.

WHERE NEXT? **Portugal** is progressing far faster, as is Greece's northern neighbour **Bulgaria**. No-one else makes Retsina, although a heavily-oaked white **Rioja** is half-way towards it.

GROS PLANT

This second wine of the Muscadet region is produced around the mouth of the River Loire. Gros Plant du Pays Nantais, to give it its full title, is often made by the same producers as Muscadet from their plantings of the Gros Plant or Folle Blanche grape.

Gros Plant is enjoyed throughout northern France whenever anyone has a plate of shellfish and needs a refreshing wine to glug with it, although it is seldom seen farther afield. Perhaps the sour-apple tartness puts people off. Besides being perfect with oysters, mussels and clams, the acidity of Gros Plant will cut the richer, oilier, more opulent fish dishes well.

Gros Plant is refreshing purely on account of its high acidity and rarely has the class of Muscadet, although a few producers are experimenting with bottling *sur lie*. Always look for the previous year's vintage; the French get through such a lot of it that it doesn't hang around – and it's not meant to. Producers [★★/■■] include:

Bernard Baffreau	*André-Michel Brégeon*
Serge Batard	*Jacques Guindon*
Albert Bescombes	

WHERE NEXT? Those familiar with the Atlantic seaboard will note a family resemblance to **Vinho Verde**, which on home ground in Portugal's Minho province can bring tears to your eyes.

HAWKE'S BAY

This rapidly-expanding region on New Zealand's North Island has more sunshine than Gisborne to the north and, although Müller-Thurgau is the most widely planted variety, its greatest successes have been with red wines. Highest quality among whites is provided by Chardonnay, and there are good Sauvignon Blancs too.

The Hawkes Bay style is decidedly different from Marlborough on South Island: bigger, fatter, fleshier, riper. There is less of the taut, green gooseberry style, more of the juicy, mellow, yellow melon fullness, with a creamy butteriness in some of the Chardonnays, yet they stop short of the generous pungent spiciness of tropical mango and passion fruit. Some people prefer the more straightforward, quieter, drinkable style of Hawkes Bay to the attention-seeking wines of Marlborough, and the better wines have a raciness and elegance that sets them apart from most Gisborne wines.

Vidal [★★→★★★/■■■] is one of the top producers, dividing its wines between Private Bin and superior Reserve labels. Its barrel-fermented Chardonnay Reserve, which can get up to 13% alcohol, has rich and powerful toasty and buttery flavours. Babich [★★→★★★/■■→■■■] is another excellent winery, and its Irongate Chardonnay is especially good. Other good producers [★★/■■→■■■] include:

Cooks	Ngatarawa
Delegats	Te Mata
Mission	

Hawke's Bay Sauvignon Blancs, with their slightly restrained style, make perfect aperitifs. They are also good partners for vegetable dishes and quiches.

WHERE NEXT? Try **Marlborough** for the local contrast, the **Loire** for the starting-point, and **Alsace** for a stylistic parallel.

HERMITAGE

The northern Rhône, unlike the Côtes-du-Rhône and Châteauneuf-du-Pape to the south (see **Rhône**) produces high-quality white wines in some quantity – most notably at Hermitage, famous for the great red wines produced on the hill of that name, above the town of Tain. Remarkably, a quarter of all Hermitage is white, and this is definitely a wine to keep. Roussanne and Marsanne are the grapes.

Drink the wine young and you wonder what the fuss is about: it seems a rather full and fat wine, reluctant to display its surly offering of windfall apples and peaches. But keep it a decade, preferably two, and it becomes oily-rich – not olive oil but the oil squeezed from almonds or hazelnuts – with the smell of roasting almonds cutting through it. There is still a peachiness about the wine, but now the peaches have cream poured over them. Surprisingly, enough acidity has come from somewhere to keep the whole thing alive. Did I say two decades? No worries. The best will keep for four, five or six.

The best producers of Hermitage [★★→★★★/■■■] include:

M Chapoutier	Grippat
J L Chave	Guigal
Jules Fayolle	Paul Jaboulet Aîné
Delas Frères	Henri Sorrel

The best recent vintages for white Hermitage include 1988, 87 and 86.

The weight of Hermitage will partner rich dishes including game, but venerable old bottles are best left unobscured by other flavours.

WHERE NEXT? White **Châteauneuf-du-Pape** is comparable. Aged **Hunter Valley** Semillon is the southern hemisphere's equivalent.

HUNGARY

Apart from Tokay, Hungary's white wines are distinctly underwhelming. There is lots of Olasz Riesling [★/■], made from the Welsch or Italian Riesling, rather than Germany's aristocratic grape variety. It is light, medium-dryish, a bland blend not a million miles in taste from its namesake in Yugoslavia. Most is made in the Great Plain south of Budapest, but slightly better wine comes from Mt Badacsonyi [★/■], where the indigenous Szürkebarát (a variant of Pinot Gris) and Kéknyelü grapes produce wine with more of a Hungarian stamp.

Hungary's other native grape varieties – Furmint, Hárslevelü, Leányka and Ezerjo – make light but interestingly honeyed drinking after a decade. Unfortunately, nobody keeps them that long. Western input (later picking for more body and character, longer skin contact) should soon bump up the fruit and improve quality without losing the Magyar magic.

WHERE NEXT? **Austria** for the same tradition, better expressed; **Yugoslavia** for similar wines

HUNTER VALLEY

If the Hunter Valley did not already have a long history of winemaking, going back to the 1820s, it is doubtful whether anybody would turn to it today and think "What a wonderful place to grow grapes!" It is too hot. Reds you might just get away with. But whites? Forget it.

Fortunately some of the best things in life happen as a result of ignoring well-intentioned advice, one of them being Hunter Valley Semillon. It was called Hunter Riesling in the old days. Now it is properly called Semillon, the same grape that goes into luscious Sauternes, dry Graves, and some very fresh Sauvignon-like wines in France's south-west. But Hunter Semillon tastes like none of these.

THE HUNTER VALLEY SEMILLON TASTE Taste it young and you wonder what the fuss is about: a light, lemony, fresh but undistinguished wine that you might swig as an aperitif, or gulp to chase down a barbied prawn, then forget about before you were on to the ice-cream. No big deal.

But taste it again at 15 or 20 years and the transformation is astounding. It has broadened out into a rich and oily wine, waxy like honeycomb fresh from a hive, but quite dry, still remarkably fresh, and so toasty it seems like it has spent months in oak. We have come to associate these buttery, toasty, oaky flavours so closely with Chardonnay, and with oak barrels, that we wonder at first if it is barrel-fermented Chardonnay. In fact it has never been near a barrel. All the ageing has been done in bottle. You begin to suspect sleight of hand. Where has all this flavour and depth and complexity come from? It is like a conjurer's empty hat that turns out to be full of white rabbits.

CHOOSING HUNTER VALLEY SEMILLON There are very few mature Semillons on the market, and they are by no means cheap. Lindemans occasionally lets slip a few bottles of Classic Release [★★★/■■■] at about 20 or 25 years old which are the genuine article. Rothbury Estate [★★★/■■ → ■■■] has also produced some excellent

71

mature Semillons. Otherwise we either have to ferret around in forgotten corners of old wine shops, wave a discreet hanky at an auction, or buy a young wine such as Lindemans 1988 Bin 7255, or Rothbury Estate Hunter Valley Semillon 1988. And then sit on them.

That is all very well, we say, but we do not want to wait 20 years. We want our Semillon now and we want it reasonably priced. In response to this, there is short-cut Semillon: oaked and ready for drinking almost as soon as it comes off the shelf. These can be fine – they are just not made from the best fruit, and they lack the haunting complexity and subtlety of the real bottle-aged McCoy.

McWilliams [★★/■■■] offers a kind of half-way house, releasing one at about five years old, although it benefits enormously if it can be kept for another five; and at 20 years old it can be astonishing. McWilliams is beginning to use some oak to try and shorten the waiting time. Inheritance [★★/■■■] is for drinking young.

Other good Semillon producers [★★→★★★/■■→■■■] include:

Brokenwood	*Saxonvale*
Peterson	*Simon Whitlam*
Rosemount, Show Reserve	*Tyrrell*

OTHER HUNTER VALLEY WINES Chardonnay is another Hunter success, perhaps better known because it is more accessible. It is improving all the time, thanks to greater reliance on barrel fermentation, and on "yeast-lees contact".

Pure Hunter Chardonnays are typically a deep, buttercup-golden yellow, rich and ripe, with pineappley fruit. They are spiked with varying degrees of oak, and are mostly full and rather fat. Succulent buttered toast, a pinch of cinnamon, and a couple of vanilla pods are common flavour characteristics, usually assembled within a large and generous framework.

Tyrrell's Vat 47 [★★/■■■] is a big, bold, and classic example of the Hunter Chardonnay style. Rothbury Estate Reserve Chardonnay [★★→★★★/■■], barrel-fermented, is rich, buttery and spicy, wonderfully drinkable even at two or three years. There is no need to keep these wines for 20 years. Their early drinkability, combined with superlative class and quality, and such broad and generous fruit, are the sort of things that tempt drinkers away from Burgundy in droves. Especially when you compare the price.

Peterson's Chardonnay [★★→★★★/■■■] is also top-notch, and with rather more fruit and less of the pervading oak that intrudes in some Hunter Chardonnays. Rosemount's range of Chardonnays, including the moderately rich and very decent Show Reserve [★★/■■→■■■], the spicy-oaky Giant's Creek [★★/■■■] and the immensely big, opulent Roxburgh Vineyard [★★★/■■■], show what the Upper Hunter Valley can do.

Other good Chardonnays [★★→★★★/■■→■■■] are made by:

Evans Family	*McWilliams*
Hungerford Hill	*Saxonvale*
Lake's Folly	*Simon Whitlam*

Wyndham Estate's Chardonnays [★★/■■] include Bin 222, attractively buttery for drinking off the shelf, and Oak Cask Chardonnay, spicier and longer-lived by a year or two. Wyndham also makes an exceptionally good Late Harvest Rhine Riesling [★★/■■].

In addition, there are Semillon/Chardonnay blends [★★/■■], mostly for early drinking, made by McWilliam's (Hanwood), Lindemans and Rothbury Estate. Other Hunter Valley wineries to note are Murray Robson and Tulloch [★★/■■].

Other wineries in the Upper Hunter and in Mudgee to the south-west [★★/■■ → ■■■] include:

Amberton	*Hollydene Estate*
Arrowfield	*Huntington Estate*
Botobolar	*Montrose*
Craigmoor	

HUNTER VALLEY SEMILLON AND FOOD These are wines built for drinking with food. Try them with sole fillets or with prawns and dill or, best of all, with grilled oysters.

WHERE NEXT? Try Mudgee (see **New South Wales**) or fly back to France for a **Hermitage**, a **Graves** or a dry white from a **Sauternes** producer to try beside a Semillon; compare **Côte d'Or** wines with the Chardonnays. Look to California for equally serious whites (see **Napa Valley** and **Sonoma**).

ITALY

One of Italy's problems as a wine-producing country is that drinkers fail to take its wines seriously. In view of the fact that output often far exceeds that of France, and given the hundreds and hundreds of wines made, it seems a shame that so many consumers still dismiss most of them as mere "vino". If only wine had another name in Italy. Those straw-covered carafes of blessed memory have much to answer for.

Much wine goes either abroad for blending or into simple *vino da tavola* for local consumption. Of some 7 billion litres made each year, only about 12% is DOC. But many non-DOC wines are eminently drinkable, perfect accompaniments to *risotto* or seafood.

Wine is to Italy what tea is to Britain. The only difference is that the Brits have to import tea-leaves while the Italians are fortunate to inhabit a land where almost any grape variety has to be restrained from over-achieving. Most prolific of all is Trebbiano, which has the dubious distinction of being the most productive white vine in the world. Most wines made with Trebbiano are equivalent to a typical teabag – a daily drink rather than a gastronomic experience. Yet even this dull grape may rise to undreamed-of heights and take on a positively "Lapsang Souchong" pizazz when vinified with new technology to produce wines like Galestro from Tuscany or delicate Lugana from the shores of Lake Garda. Trebbiano responds well to high-tech treatment, turning from a flabby, dull wine to a crisp drinkable one such as Sicilian Corvo with ease.

Given the vast number of white grape varieties in Italy, there should be an enormous range of varied and interesting wines. But they often cover a narrower range of styles than we might expect. A certain blandness seems inherent. This may be because most wines are meant to be drunk with food; it is as if they are told to shut up and not interfere with the conversation. They might be asked to partner simple vegetable dishes, salty-spicy anchovy-flavoured dishes, meats and sauces, mountains of tomatoes, umpteen cheeses and what have you. If all the wines had strong personalities, most mealtimes would be taken up with arguments and end in tears.

Another thing that is often asked of white wines is that they should be refreshing. In Trentino-Alto Adige acidity is not a problem, but in many other places in Italy it can be, or certainly was before stainless steel came along. Other ways of freshening or livening up the wines

ITALIAN WINE LAW

● The DOC system, introduced in the mid-1960s, is an attempt to impose some sort of order on thousands of individualists. All wines fall into one of three categories, the first of which is *vino da tavola* (table wine), covering all wines outside named quality areas – as well as the (often fine) wines of those individualists who refuse to tow the legislators' line.

● *Denominazione di Origine Controllata* (DOC) is the next step up, meaning a wine produced in a named area to specified methods of production: there are 220 DOCs.

● The peak of vinous perfection should be *Denominazione di Origine Controllata e Garantita* (DOCG), of which there are six red and only one white, Albana di Romagna. The DOCGs supposedly conform to even stricter controls than the DOCs, but the promotion of Albana to this elevated status raised doubts about the validity of the "guarantee".

● As a further refinement, some of the DOC regions have a restricted Classico area which usually – not always – signifies the best wines the region has to offer. A wine labelled "Superiore" is generally one with slightly higher natural alcohol, although it too may refer to the area of production. "Riserva" applies to higher quality wines of a DOC or DOCG that have been aged for longer than usual; "Riserva Speciale" implies even longer ageing.

developed. A slight bitterness helps, or a slight prickle on the tongue. So many wines are made with a prickle of carbon dioxide that it would be unwieldy to list them all.

Some of the more striking wines are made from Muscat and Malvasia, both used for dessert wines throughout Italy. The floral pungency of the grapes is often intensified by drying until they resemble sultanas; they are then vinifyied as a rich syrupy "pudding wine". This includes Vin Santo and Recioto styles and some, such as the Sicilian Moscato di Pantelleria, may well have the classic note of bitterness at the finish to balance the sweetness. Other sweet wines are made from rarer grapes, such as Maculan's Torcolato from the Veneto, a rich, honeyed blend of Tocai and Vespaiola.

It is best to begin with a simple, straightforward DOC wine such as Soave, Frascati or Verdicchio: not the industrial versions, but one from a good producer, since DOC by itself is not a reliable guide to quality. The north is well stocked with clean, dry wines: light and mountain-fresh from Trentino-Alto Adige; up-to-date and varied from Friuli-Venezia Giulia and parts of the Veneto; both serious (Gavi) and frivolous (Asti) from Piedmont.

On the whole, Italian co-operatives (*cantine sociali*) are well ahead of the game, thanks to investment in technology. The wines may not be exciting, but they are generally sounder than, say, those from their Iberian cousins. Individual producers pride themselves on their individuality. There are definitely some regal wines to be had – but, as the princess remarked, you may have to kiss a lot of frogs before you come across a prince.

WHERE NEXT? See the specific entries on Italian wine styles: **Albana di Romagna, Alto Adige, Asti Spumante, Frascati, Friuli-Venezia Giulia, Gavi, Marsala, Oltrepò Pavese, Orvieto, Piave, Sardinia, Sicily, Soave, Tuscany, Verdicchio** and **Vin Santo**.

JURA

Out of the Jura, south of Alsace in eastern France, come The Wines That Time Forgot. The Jura hills rise towards the Alps of Savoie to the south, and produce a wide range of wines including sparklers, the peculiar *vin jaune* and the rare *vin de paille*. Côtes du Jura is the all-embracing AC, within which are Arbois, L'Etoile and the diminutive Château-Chalon.

The main grape is Savagnin, which makes a weird-tasting wine totally out of step with everything else that France produces. The small grapes ripen late and develop powerful, earthy and strange flavours, a bit like stale nuts kept too long in a jar. Ordinary Savagnin wines can taste uncomfortably close to some of the *vitis labrusca* wines made in New York State. The other variety, however, is Chardonnay, in one of its light, mountain-fresh moods. With a lot of Chardonnay and a little Savagnin, the drink is considerably improved.

But the speciality is *vin jaune*, France's answer to *fino* sherry. Left in the barrel for at least six years, the wine develops a surface mould of *flor* which protects it from the air, allowing a very gentle oxidation. Unlike sherry, the wine is not fortified, and *vin jaune* is a long way from the lively, tangy, yeasty bite of a recently-bottled *fino*. It is closer to a curious blend of old fruit and barrels with a strong smell of damp hay, and leaves a lingering impression that you are a time traveller who has wandered back one century too many.

The tiny AC of Château-Chalon makes the best, that is to say the most characterful, *vin jaune*, but the style is common throughout the region. It is bottled in dumpy *clavelins* and will last for decades. The rare, expensive and traditional *vin de paille* is made by drying grapes in racks, rather like Recioto di Soave or Vin Santo in Italy.

Henri Maire seems to dominate the region with a pink *vin gris* [★/■■] and a less than thrilling sparkler called *vin fou* [★/■■]. Among the other best producers [★→★★/■■] are Jean Bourdy, Château d'Arlay and the Pupillin Co-operative.

WHERE NEXT? Taste a real *fino* or *manzanilla* from Jerez (see **Sherry**), or a **Montilla** *fino*. If the oddball flavours of Savagnin appeal, try wines made from other quirky grapes for the fun of it (see **Gaillac**, **Jurançon** and **Savoie**).

Also try any **Loire** wine made from Chenin Blanc, or a Rhône wine made from either Viognier (see **Condrieu & Château-Grillet**), or Roussanne and Marsanne (see **Hermitage**).

JURANÇON

This corner of south-west France in the foothills of the Pyrenees is famous for its sweet *moelleux* wine, produced around the town of Pau – and so it should be.

Jurançon Sec, made from the Gros Manseng grape, is the region's dry "insurance" wine, and an extremely decent one at that: medium-bodied, off-dry, rounded, with the smell of apricots (fruit, kernel and all) and good length of flavour. Grapes for dry wines, harvested relatively early in the season, are less subject to worsening weather conditions; dry wine is thus less risky to make. It guarantees a steady income while grapes for sweeter wines are concentrating their sugar, going mouldy from *Botrytis* or just rotten from damp.

Jurançon Moelleux, the real joy, is made from the smaller-berried Petit Manseng, which gives a more concentrated flavour and more body. Yields, as with Monbazillac, are higher than in Sauternes and Barsac, so it is never as unctuously rich as they are; and acidity is high, so it has a clean refreshing streak running right through. But Jurançon Moelleux is one of the under-appreciated glories of the south-west: deliciously, appetizingly honeyed, and ripe and exotic with the taste of mangoes sprinkled with cinnamon.

The best producers [★★/■■] for both sweet and dry wines include:

Cauhapé	*Guirouilh*
Caves Vinicoles de Gan	*Château Jolys*
Jean Chigé	

WHERE NEXT? Jurançon's acidity gives it more of an affinity with the sweet Chenin Blanc-based wines of the **Loire** than anywhere. See how you get on with **Vouvray**.

LIEBFRAUMILCH

At a time when Germany had 30,000 different named wines – as it did before the 1971 Wine Law reduced this to a more manageable 2,500 – it was easy to see the attraction of one, just one, that wine drinkers outside the country could pronounce, and which they could recognize when they saw it again.

The name of this famous (or perhaps infamous) wine, which amounts to a good half of its appeal, derives from the Liebfrauenstift-Kirchenstück vineyard near Worms, but there is no longer any connection between the two. Liebfraumilch long ago took on a life of its own. It is a QbA wine, which means that the grapes (or 85% of them at any rate) must come from within a single *Anbaugebiet* or designated wine region.

Four such regions are permitted to make it: Rheinhessen, Rheinpfalz, Rheingau and Nahe. Very little is made in Nahe or Rheingau, although Rheingau Liebfraumilch is considered the best. Rheinhessen and Rheinpfalz have the open rolling country that is necessary for high-volume production.

At best, Liebfraumilch is light, flowery, sweetish, and "of pleasant character" as the law insists it must be. There is no harsh acid to worry about, no withering tannin, no austere dryness. There are no complicated nuances of taste – indeed there is often very little taste at all – and no need to wonder whether or not it is ready to drink yet. All you have to remember is to cool the wine. It could not be simpler. It is like a tricycle: this is where you begin.

The driest that Liebfraumilch can be is *halbtrocken* and most are much sweeter than that. The light, flowery aroma comes from the grape varieties used. In theory any variety sanctioned for QbA wines is permissible, providing that at least half the blend is made from one or more of the following: Riesling, Silvaner, Müller-Thurgau, Kerner. In practice, Riesling is too valuable, and is reserved for higher quality wines. Müller-Thurgau, on the other hand, obliges with a high yield and just enough scent to persuade you that somebody might have waved a bunch of flowers in the vicinity of the wine before it was bottled.

Like mother's milk, Liebfraumilch comes attractively packaged and tides you over until you cut your teeth on real food. But where would we all be without it? If drinking had to begin with young claret, or Valpolicella Amarone, 99% of us might not come back for a second glass. Liebfraumilch is the honey that lures many of us into the wine world. Once there, we stay for entirely different reasons.

It is high-volume business. There are no small-scale growers beavering away to make just a few cases of de luxe Liebfraumilch, so the biggest brands such as Blue Nun [★/■] or Crown of Crowns [★/■→■■] are among the best. Other palatable wines [★/■] include:

Hans Christof	*Goldener Oktober*
Deinhard	*Madonna Valckenberg*

WHERE NEXT? To begin with, stay with the sweetness level. Tasting dry, or even medium-dry wines can be something of a shock unless they are taken with food; other medium-sweet wines will cushion the blow, while offering some variety of flavour. Although Liebfraumilch is a QbA wine, some *Deutsche Tafelweine* are slightly more exciting. Other QbA wines (providing they do not specify *trocken* or *halbtrocken*) will also provide variety, and should possess a little more style (see **Germany**).

If lightness appeals, consider the Mosel for feathery-light wines and crisp apple freshness (see **Mosel-Saar-Ruwer**). If you want a little more weight, try other wines from **Rheinhessen** and **Rheinpfalz**, or even the **Rheingau** though these may be slightly more expensive.

If there is money to spare, it is worth exploring some of the richer, fuller, sweeter styles of QmP wines: *Kabinett*, *Spätlese* or even *Auslese*. For more aroma, try a **Muscat** or **Gewürztraminer** wine.

LIQUEUR MUSCAT & TOKAY

Some of Australia's most distinctive wines come from hot, dry north-east Victoria, close to the Murray River around Corowa and Rutherglen. This is "sticky" country. Conditions favour high sugar levels in the grapes, and sweet, fortified wines have long been a traditional product of this rather hostile environment. As late as 1960, something like 70% of the wine that Australians drank was fortified. There is no end of "sherry" and "port" produced, but Liqueur Muscat and Liqueur Tokay are genuine originals, not copies of European styles.

Production is small, but then so is consumption. Fortified wines may not be as fashionable as they were, but these wines are so chock-full of flavours that they just have to be tasted.

A fanciful recipe for these wines might read: "take one bottle each of port, sherry and Madeira, a jar of treacle, a pint of *espresso* coffee and a pound of chocolate caramels. Mix well and leave under a corrugated tin roof in the hot sun for a few years, topping up as necessary until it becomes really concentrated". But in fact, they are made from grapes.

The grape for Liqueur Muscat is the Muscat à Petits Grains Rouges, similar to the grape that makes Asti Spumante and Muscat de Beaumes-de-Venise, but here called Brown Muscat. The wines are fortified to stop fermentation and retain the natural sweetness (like port), and then aged in wood in a form of *solera* system (like sherry), but the high evaporation rate under the baking sun (in which they are cooked like Madeira) keeps them much more treacly than any other wines.

They are generally a dark chestnut or mahogany colour, and while there may be little flavour of Muscat, there is a lot of dense, sweet, sticky, raisiny, liquorous intensity of the kind in which you could stand a drawer full of spoons, as well as the taste of dates, syrup of figs and chocolate raisins. Despite all this they retain an essential freshness.

Liqueur Tokays are less often seen, which is a great pity because they are even better. The grape is Muscadelle, which plays a small part in some Bordeaux wines, and the style has nothing to do with either the

Tokay (Pinot Gris) grape of Alsace or with Hungarian Tokay. The flavours fan out into an amazing range: toffee, chocolate, caramel, butterscotch, honey, marmalade, roasted and burnt coffee, Tia Maria liqueur, and, believe it or not, green olives and fish oil.

Buy the most venerable wine you can afford in order to get the richest and most complex flavours, though it may be better to begin with a younger, less expensive version to acclimatize your mouth gradually. The family-sized producers of the region are specialists and have been for generations. The best [★★/■■] include:

Baileys	*Chambers Rosewood*
Brown Brothers	*Morris*
Campbells	*Stanton & Killeen*

Liqueur Muscats are not so much something to drink with food as food in themselves. Christmas cake, chocolate – indeed any very rich, sweet pudding that is too much for most other wines – is worth trying with them.

WHERE NEXT? These wines are unique. The only other drinks, apart from liqueurs, that come within a hundred miles of the style are dark, sweet **Sherry**, **Málaga**, rich Malmsey **Madeira** and **Port**.

LOIRE

The River Loire runs for 635 miles (1,020 km) from the heart of France into the Atlantic. White wines here constitute over 86% of total production. Apart from Muscadet and Gros Plant, they are made chiefly from Chenin Blanc and Sauvignon Blanc. Chenin Blanc is planted in among the châteaux of the central Loire. In Anjou, it makes dry Anjou, Saumur Blanc and Savennières, and the wonderful sweet wines of Coteaux du Layon, Quarts de Chaume and Bonnezeaux (see **Anjou**, **Saumur**, **Coteaux du Layon**); and in Touraine it produces, among others, Vouvray and Montlouis (see **Vouvray**). Its high acidity also makes it perfect material for the Loire's sparkling industry.

CHOOSING LOIRE WINES Chenin Blanc performs best when fully ripe, but the Loire is not the best place to ripen any grape, let alone Chenin, with any regularity. So the dry wines tend to be green, tart, pinched and acerbic more often than they should. An increasing tendency with still wines is to blend Chenin with some Chardonnay and Sauvignon, which gives them a pronounced and welcome lift of fruit. This is happening in the wide-ranging Anjou AC (see **Anjou**) and in the VDQS Coteaux du Vendômois [★/■■]. Although the VDQS of Thouarsais [★/■■] sticks to Chenin Blanc, its white wines can be grassily fresh.

The Loire's other white grape, Sauvignon Blanc, extends its territory upstream. Until New Zealand came on the scene the Loire virtually had the crisp, nettley, grassy Sauvignon Blanc market sewn up. In cool regions such as this it combines nettles, gooseberries, elderflower, blackcurrant leaves and a waft of asparagus in a wonderfully peacock-like aromatic display, and is as dry as a bar after the rugby team's been in. It is best-known with its Sancerre or Pouilly-Fumé hats on; other wines in this part of the region based on Sauvignon Blanc include Menetou-Salon, Reuilly and the under-valued Quincy. Coteaux du Giennois is a VDQS with promise. But the best-value wine is probably from back down in château country near Tours (see **Sancerre & Pouilly-Fumé**, **Touraine**).

Although not strictly in the Loire, the wines of Haut-Poitou have nowhere else to go. They are out on a limb near Poitiers, and doing very nicely thank you. Although only a VDQS Haut-Poitou is not in the least apologetic. It produces as crisp and starched a Sauvignon as any in France; if it zings once it zings a dozen times. Chardonnay is excellent from here too, thanks to the Haut-Poitou Co-op [★★/■→■■].

Apart from the sparkling wines of Saumur and Vouvray (see **Saumur**, **Vouvray**), there is also a creamier, gentler, half-pressure sparkler called Crémant de Loire. This may include Cabernet Franc, Chardonnay or other grape varieties in the blend, and can be made over a wide region from Touraine to Anjou, but its wines are of consistently high quality; the best producers [★★/■■→■■■] include Gratien & Meyer, Caves de la Loire and Domaine Richou.

The Loire is a place to dawdle and explore. There are several small *appellations*, mostly crisp and green and dry, but made from some quirky and unusual grapes. Among them, and always worth a try for curiosity, are Cheverny VDQS (some of it made from the Romorantin grape, unique to Cheverny); Coteaux d'Ancenis (especially the wines made from Malvoisie, Alsace's Pinot Gris); Pouilly-sur-Loire (the same Pouilly where Fumé is made, but this is from the less-than-inspiring Chasselas grape), St-Pourçain VDQS (which uses the Tressalier grape), and Vin de l'Orléanais VDQS (made from Pinot Blanc and Chardonnay).

Finally the Vin de Pays du Jardin de la France wines are not all as pretty as the name. It is difficult to generalize since it is one of the biggest *vin de pays* in France, but prices are so reasonable that we can afford to give them the benefit of the doubt.

LOIRE WINE AND FOOD Loire wines, in their classic, crisp, dry form, are superb fish wines, and come into their own served with smoked haddock, smoked eel, herring, mackerel or trout.

WHERE NEXT? **New Zealand** is the obvious choice: Sauvignon has adapted superbly here. Washington could be a contender soon (see **United States**). **Alto Adige** whites offer similar freshness; Mosel whites move into sweeter territory (see **Mosel-Saar-Ruwer**).

MACON

In Mâcon the warmer climate brings out something riper and fuller in the wines than in the neighbouring Côte Chalonnaise; they can develop a bit of juicy richness. Mâcon-Villages holds out more promise than either basic Mâcon, or Mâcon Supérieur, whose only superiority is alcoholic (it clocks up 11%). Mâcon-Villages applies to 43 villages, the best of which can substitute their name after the hyphen instead of the generalized "villages", as in Mâcon-Lugny or Mâcon-Clessé for example.

This is co-operative country, and good ones [★★/■■→■■■] include those at Chardonnay (from where the grape could well have originated), Clessé, Lugny, Prissé, St-Gengoux and Viré.

Pouilly-Fuissé is the star of the Mâconnais when it is made well, but sadly most of it isn't. Stick to a good producer such as Noblet [★★/■■■] or one of the following [★★/■■■]:

Corsin	*Labouré Roi*
Duboeuf	*Vincent*

St-Véran can be more reliable and quite a bit cheaper. Good clean winemaking and fresh, ripe Chardonnay fruit make this an example for other ACs to follow. They are decent wines with no pretensions to greatness, and no illusions about what they are worth. Good producers [★★/■■] include:

Corsin	Loron
Duboeuf	Mommessin
Louis Jadot	Prissé Co-operative
Louis Latour	Vincent

Pouilly-Loché [★★/■■■] and Pouilly-Vinzelles [★★/■■■] are reasonable alternatives, as is Beaujolais Blanc [★★/■■■] which is also made from Chardonnay.

These white Burgundies are versatile partners for all kinds of food. Classic combinations include snails, sole, turbot and *andouillettes*.

WHERE NEXT? Wines from the nearby **Côte Chalonnaise** share the same character and can be cheaper. **California** Chardonnays, at the less expensive, non-oaked, end of the spectrum, are comparable. **Alsace** Pinot Blanc is a less-hackneyed alternative, while northern Italy provides different Chardonnays in much the same price band (see **Alto Adige, Friuli-Venezia Giulia**).

MADEIRA

Most fortified wines seem to operate on two levels. There is the genuine, flavoursome, brilliant original, and there are the mass-market cheap compromises that trade on the name without giving much idea of why the drink is so special. It happens with sherry and Montilla from Spain, and with port and Madeira from Portugal.

To compound the error, we get the idea that because the mass-produced drinks are cheap, the expensive ones must be a rip-off. Nonsense. It is completely the reverse. The apparently expensive drinks can be sensationally good value – a 20-year-old fortified wine, perhaps, for less than the price of a two-year-old claret that you can't drink for 20 years – while the cheap ones are usually the rip-off because they deny us the opportunity to experience the gloriously deep, long-lasting flavours that we should be tasting.

THE MADEIRA TASTE Madeira was originally an accident. Casks of wine from the Atlantic island, 300 miles (483 km) off the African coast, were traded around the world. The wine became somewhat "cooked" after it had crossed the Equator a couple of times, but instead of tasting foul it was discovered to be rather nice. Eventually it was shipped back and forth deliberately in order to achieve the right amount of cooking, before being returned home and then sold to customers in northern Europe.

But what a palaver, and how much easier if the barrels could be heated on the island; which of course they now are, in an *estufa* or heated room, warmed by hot water pipes. After fermentation and fortification (which takes place at different stages depending on the style: the earlier it is done, the sweeter the wine will be) they spend a minimum of 90 days, which in practice can run to six months or even a year, at 95-104°F (35-40°C). Then the barrels are left to mature until they are ready: five years, ten, 20, 50, 100 – how long can you wait? Longer maturation produces more interesting flavours.

Traditionally there are four basic styles of Madeira, ranging from the driest, Sercial, through Verdelho and Bual to Malmsey, the sweetest. The names refer to the grape varieties used in each.

Sercial produces a pale, rather sharp and tangy wine that needs around ten years in barrel to knock the edges off; there is sometimes a light attractive cheesy whiff, like a mature parmesan. Despite the dryness, and the acidity that keeps them fresh, there can still be a chocolate richness about them.

Verdelho is medium-dry with more colour and body, and a more pronounced nuttiness and cheesiness, with great depth of flavour and a lively streak of cleansing acidity.

Bual is medium-sweet, darker still, often with a greeny tinge at the edge, fuller-flavoured, rounded, supple, with a feel of chocolate caramel and a distinctively oxidized smell; you can begin to see where the term "madeirized" comes from to describe wines that have had long exposure to the air.

Malmsey (made from the Malvasia Candida grape, the same that makes Frascati) is the richest and sweetest, with a whiff of burnt caramel. It has a velvety texture but, like all Madeiras, is never cloying because of the balancing acidity.

Terrantez and Bastardo are two other grape varieties, hardly used now, but venerable bottles may occasionally turn up at auction.

CHOOSING MADEIRA The youngest style sold, Reserve, is five years old. Special Reserve is ten years old and Extra Reserve is 15. In all cases the age refers to the youngest component in the blend. Vintage Madeira, only made in exceptional years, must spend at least 20 years in cask before being released.

The best producers [★★→★★★/■■→■■■] include:

Blandy	*Leacocks*
Cossart Gordon	*Rutherford & Miles*

A five-year-old Reserve or ten-year-old Special Reserve from one of these is the best place to begin. Pick the style according to sweetness preferred, but consider Verdelho or Bual as a starting point.

Other good producers [★★→★★★/■■→■■■] include:

Barbeito	*Pereira d'Oliveira*
Borges	*Shortridge Lawton*
Henriques & Henriques	

A word about keeping Madeira, especially the better bottles, is in order. It is one of the few wines that lasts longer than the cork. Store a bottle on its side for half a century and the cork will begin to crumble, so unless the wine is to be drunk straight away it is a good idea to keep it standing upright. Secondly, the cooking and lengthy maturation make Madeira virtually indestructible. Keep it as long as you like before opening, and once opened it will last very happily for months.

All the above concerns real Madeira, the top-level stuff. But there is the shadowy bottom layer which, sadly, accounts for the majority of Madeira sold. For various reasons, principally to do with the vine louse *phylloxera* which virtually destroyed the vineyards during the 19th century, only a small proportion of the vines planted are Sercial, Verdelho, Bual or Malmsey. Most are Tinta Negra Mole, a black, jack-of-all-trades grape that can make wines vaguely similar to each style but far less distinguished. They are all right for cooking.

EEC regulations insist that 85% of the wine in the bottle must be made from the grape variety named on the label. This poses particular problems for Madeira as Sercial, Verdelho, Bual and Malmsey are essential style references as much as varietal designations. From 1992 onwards, Tinta Negra Mole wines will have to drop "Sercial", "Verdelho" or whatever from the label and devise some other stylistic description, or possibly just call themselves Tinta Negra Mole. Stranger things have caught on.

MADEIRA AND FOOD Madeira is not a natural food partner. Verdelho and Bual, though, make distinctive first course drinks, especially with soup. Malmsey is a satisfying after-dinner drink and goes well with cakes; try it also with Norwegian *gjetost* cheese.

WHERE NEXT? Marsala, Málaga, Sherry, Montilla, Australian **Liqueur Muscat & Tokay**

MALAGA

This sweet, fortified wine has been progressively elbowed out of its prominent 19th-century role as favourite tipple of the British and Russian Empires. Torremolinos is just up the road, so it is more profitable to build hotels along the coast than to grow grapes. And tastes have changed. Who wants to drink dense, sweet, sticky wines any more?

Well, me for one. Perhaps not every day, but life would be poorer without a glass of it now and again.

There are several styles of Málaga, nearly all sweet, ranging in alcohol from 15 to 20% and made principally from the grapes that provide the sweetening for sherry: Pedro Ximénez and Moscatel. They go through a *solera* system rather like that used for sherry, so they are blends, not vintage wines. They are raisiny, toffee-like and treacly at their luscious best, sometimes with smells of roasting coffee and nuts.

The best place to begin is with Scholtz Hermanos's Solera 1885 [★★★/■■]. The date refers to when the *solera* was first laid down; in theory there should be an incy-wincy fraction of 1885 in there somewhere, a tiny fraction more of 1886, and so on. The effect of all this is to add to the wine's complexity.

One of the best styles is Lagrima, made from only the free-run juice. Others wear their style on their sleeve: Dulce Negro is sweet and black. So is treacle.

Other good producers [★★→★★★/■■] include Larios, Perez Teixera and Hijos de Antonio Barceló.

WHERE NEXT? Sweet *oloroso* **Sherry, Port, Madeira**, sweet **Marsala**, Australian **Liqueur Muscat & Tokay**

MALVASIA

This vine, known throughout the ancient world, still produces some impressive sweet wines, and in drier form is blended with Trebbiano to make the popular Frascati. Malvasia can be confusing because it has many different strains; some wines with similar names, like Malvoisie from the Loire and Switzerland (which is, in fact, Pinot Gris), are not made from any of them. (To complicate matters further, Malvoisie *is* used as a synonym for Malvasia in some other parts of France.) There are also dozens of wines, especially in southern Europe, that contain a proportion of Malvasia, but too little for it to have much of a discernible effect on the taste.

THE MALVASIA TASTE Malvasia makes deep-coloured, full-bodied, strongly scented wines with a flavour that is sometimes nutty, sometimes musky, sometimes reminiscent of apricots, but they oxidize easily and can seem flabby. Sadly, the grape's popularity is declining. This is partly because its blending partners are easier to handle or have higher yields, and partly because New World attempts to make sweet wines have used higher-profile grape varieties such as Riesling and Sémillon.

BEGIN WITH SWEET WINES The sweet, honeyed, gingery-spicy Malvasia delle Lipari, made on the Lipari Islands north of Sicily, is a relic of ancient times (see **Sicily**). Tuscan Vin Santo, one of the great sweet wines of the world, is the most accessible form of sweet Malvasia (see **Vin Santo**).

Malmsey, the sweetest style of Madeira, was originally made from Malvasia, but since phylloxera ravaged the vineyards in the 19th century much Madeira has been made from the general purpose Tinta Negra Mole variety (see **Madeira**).

OTHER MALVASIAS Some dry Malvasias are made in Tuscany and in the Emilia-Romagna DOCs of Colli di Parma and Colli Piacentini, where they can also be sweet and/or *frizzante*. But the grape's most common appearance is in a blend with Trebbiano as Rome's traditional quaffing wine, Frascati (see **Frascati**), and in Est! Est!! Est!!! [★/■→■■]. Other Latium dry Malvasia-based wines include Marino [★/■■], Velletri [★/■→■■]. In Tuscany, Trebbiano-based Galestro appreciates the Malvasia influence (see **Tuscany**). Wherever these grapes meet, Trebbiano's freshness balances Malvasia's potential flabbiness, but it is Malvasia that provides the interest.

Other Malvasia wines include Lanzarote Malvasia [★/■→■■] from the Canaries and Toro [★/■] from north-western Spain. Some white Riojas also include Malvasia, and dry white port is made from it.

MALVASIA AND FOOD Sweet Malvasias are for drinking either with pudding or instead of it. Vin Santo could, at a pinch, act as an aperitif; Malmsey on the other hand is too rich to come anywhere but at the end of a meal; biscuits, cake or nuts are the best accompaniment.

WHERE NEXT? Vernaccia di San Gimignano (see **Tuscany**) is a dry alternative to the Malvasia grape.

LA MANCHA

What a place! Enormous. Vast. A high plateau slap bang in the middle of Spain, sprawling away to the south and east of Madrid. And how it sprawls. The main white grape variety is Airén, the world's most widely planted grape variety. That is not because growers in other countries have been falling over themselves to plant it – you won't find it anywhere else in Europe or the New World – but simply because La Mancha is so big.

The harsh, arid climate produces only tiny yields, so Airén makes barely a third of the wine it is capable of producing. And until quite recently it tasted, to all who had not been raised on it, flat, oxidized and alcoholic, one of the least attractive wines you could wish (or not wish) to come across.

Things have not changed completely, but new, fresh wines are being made alongside the old. Early picking conserves more acidity in the grape; stainless steel and temperature control retain it in the bottle. Provided we drink it soon after it is made, we should benefit from the improvements. Light, soft, easy-drinking whites with a little fruit but no great distinction are what we get for the money. And the money is another reason for drinking it: La Mancha wines are not expensive.

The best producers [★/■→■■] include:

Bodegas Julian Santos Aguado	Campo Nuestra Padre Jesus del Perdón
Campo Nuestra Señora de Manjavacas	Rodriguez y Berger
	Vinicola de Castilla

Although not in La Mancha, good wines [★/■→■■] are produced over to the east in Valencia and Utiel-Requena from the Merseguera grape by Bodegas Schenk, Valsangiacomo and Vinival

Drink these simple wines with simple food: mild patés and cheeses, or with *mojete*, a traditional Spanish vegetable dish.

WHERE NEXT? Try **Portugal** for another set of approaches to the same latitude, **Navarra** for fresher, more vivid Spanish whites, **Sardinia** for oddballs with Spanish bloodlines.

MARGARET RIVER

This is Western Australia's star wine-producing region, 175 miles (280 km) south of Perth. It is a born-again district that, despite being hot, windy, and arid, produces wines as good as any in the country. Planted towards the end of the last century, it very nearly died but was revived, appropriately by a doctor, in the late 1960s.

The region's image is helped by the general policy of producers not to make "cask" wines, but to concentrate on classic grape varieties and to aim straight for high quality. The white varieties that do best are Chardonnay, Semillon and Sauvignon Blanc, and oak is a feature that runs through many of them.

Margaret River does manage to extract a lot of "varietal flavour" from its grapes. Chardonnays are made in a generally rich and buttery style, and often fermented in oak, but they are not short on acidity which gives them a good, sharp definition. The attraction of Chardonnays here is their classic fullness of flavour, with toasty oak and vanilla, spicy pepper and cinnamon, and a generous pineappley ripeness, yet without any hint of the overblown too-tropical fruit that so often afflicts hot-climate Chardonnays. Semillon combines a light lemony freshness with a waxy, oily richness in a textbook example of how the variety should taste. Margaret River Sauvignons can have a gentle smokiness and a serious, rather restrained feel, which gives them a great sense of balance. Above all they have tons of flavour.

Semillon/Sauvignon blends vary from green leafy to rather tropical mango, but most are well-made and enjoyable. They have an intense and pungent aroma, with the green leafiness dominating when the wines are young; there is nothing apologetic about the style, these are positive, forceful flavours.

There is a feeling, common to all these Margaret River varietals, that the wines are purposeful, as if they know just how they ought to taste and are jolly well going to stick to it. Nothing seems to happen by accident. It is all straight to the point, resolute, decisive, full of drive and vigour.

The best Margaret River producers [★★→★★★/■■■] include:

Cape Mentelle	*Leeuwin Estate*
Cullens	*Moss Wood*

After these come the following [★→★★/■■→■■■]:

Ashbrook	*Pierro*
Cape Clairault	*Redgate*
Chateau Xanadu	*Vasse Felix*
Happ's Vineyard	

WHERE NEXT? Try **South Australia** for the more traditional approach to Australian winemaking, **New Zealand** for a competing modernist, Washington (see **United States**) for comparable wines from an equally new area. Head back to **Sancerre & Pouilly-Fumé** for the Sauvignons.

MARLBOROUGH

Marlborough, the prime spot on New Zealand's South Island, must have clocked up the fastest rise in viticultural history. Nothing much happened until the firm of Montana arrived in 1973. Now Marlborough is New Zealand's third-largest wine region after Gisborne and Hawkes Bay, and still climbing.

The region is at the north end of the island. It has well-drained gravelly soil, lots of sun, and a long, slow, dry growing season and ripening period. It is perfectly endowed to make white wines.

THE MARLBOROUGH TASTE The single most distinctive taste associated with Marlborough – and, indeed New Zealand – is that of Sauvignon Blanc. During the 1980s, Marlborough Sauvignon stepped onto the world wine stage and began to sing at the top of its voice. The world listened in amazement. Screamingly pungent, razor-edged, leafy-green pure Sauvignon flavours burst forth with an intensity unmatched elsewhere.

It is so distinctive, so pure and definitive, so authoritative, that for many people it constitutes the finest expression of the grape that the planet has so far achieved. And that means it can outstrip France's Sancerre and Pouilly-Fumé, which were the traditional, and until recently unchallenged, masters of the grape.

Marlborough Sauvignon has intense, clean-as-a-whistle fruit, tasting as green as the island looks. It is rarely a tart, sharp, aggressive green, but more usually has the smell and taste of nettles, of blackcurrant leaves and gooseberries, occasionally of asparagus or green peppers. Fairly high acidity gives the wines good attack and keeps them as fresh as a field of daisies. There is a taut, steely quality about them, reminiscent of Chablis. The only time they come unstuck is when the grassy asparagus becomes pronounced in older bottles.

Because Sauvignon's typical burst of powerful aroma can subside after 12-18 months in bottle, and because, even here, it does not have quite the body that it seems to need, a little Semillon is usually blended in. It is this blending that creates the harmony. For pure zippety-doo-dah Sauvignon freshness, these wines are best drunk within a year to 18 months; but they will round out and tone down for a year or two after that as the Semillon begins to take control.

BEGIN WITH SAUVIGNON BLANC The acknowledged star performer is Cloudy Bay [★★★/■■■] owned by David Hohnen of Cape Mentelle in Western Australia (see **Margaret River**). Like Eton, you have to put your name down for this well in advance in order to qualify for a few precious bottles. And the place has only been up and running since the mid-1980s. It is a classic, benchmark taste that all wine drinkers should experience.

Montana [★→★★★/■■] is New Zealand's largest wine company, making everyday staples such as the teutonic Müller-Thurgau-based Blenheimer, a sort of antipodean Liebfraumilch. But it makes extremely good Sauvignon at half the price of Cloudy Bay. (It is also getting into fizz in a big way with the Champagne firm of Deutz).

Corbans's Stoneleigh Vineyard [★★★/■■■] also makes an excellent Sauvignon; in fact some of Cloudy Bay's grapes have come from the same vineyard. The other top producer of the Marlborough region is Hunter's [★★/■■■].

OTHER MARLBOROUGH WINES But there is more to Marlborough than Sauvignon Blanc. Chardonnay does extremely well here, some would say even better than Sauvignon. It is early days yet, and there is stiffer competition from around the world, but some excellent wines have come from the above producers, with good ones also from Te Whare Ra and Merlen [★/■■→■■■].

Rhine Riesling benefits enormously from the long slow growing season; late-picked versions, in ridiculously short supply, can be sensational. Montana makes one [★/■■]. Gewürztraminer is wonderfully underplayed, with good acidity and a delicate aroma that give it remarkable finesse. Even Müller-Thurgau can develop the sort of character that is usually only hinted at elsewhere.

MARLBOROUGH WINE AND FOOD Marlborough Sauvignons have crispness and bite to cut through foods that might overwhelm other wines. They go well with vegetarian food, Caesar salads and shellfish, and amazingly well with blue and goat's cheeses.

WHERE NEXT? Hawke's Bay is the competing New Zealand region. Try Sancerre & Pouilly-Fumé to see if they have regained their lead in the Sauvignon stakes.

MARSALA

This sweet fortified wine is named after the port of Marsala in Sicily, where it is made, and is a rough Italian approximation to sherry, much of it rather inferior. The wine style was "invented" in 1773 by an English wine merchant called John Woodhouse, who reasoned that the white wines of the area would travel better if they were fortified, adding some two gallons of alcohol to every hundred-gallon barrel of wine. The resulting wine achieved an early success when Admiral Nelson ordered large quantities for his Mediterranean-based fleet.

Like Madeira, much Marsala is destined for culinary use, especially in *zabaglione*, a deliciously frothy custard. And much of it deserves no finer fate. The best Marsala, though, does have something of the depth of flavour of an *amontillado* or *oloroso* sherry, which makes it a pleasant aperitif or an unusual accompaniment to powerful cheeses.

The grapes used are the local Grillo, Cataratto and Inzolia, which are allowed to shrivel on the vine before picking until they look almost raisin-like. After fermentation the wine has some 12-14° alcohol which is augmented by adding two syrups: *sifone* (made from a blend of dried grapes and wine alcohol) and *cotto* (made from grapes which have been "cooked" down to a caramelized syrup). Together they give Marsala its pungent flavours and slightly rubbery taste. Look for wines labelled Superiore (aged for at least two years) or Vergine (aged for a minimum of five). Vergine is unsweetened and often aged in barrel. With ten years' ageing it is labelled Riserva or Stravecchio.

The best producer is de Bartoli, whose Superiores [★★/■■■] are a rich, toffee-and-nut 20-year-old and a delicate, friskily fresh younger wine called La Miccia. But his most interesting wines are not, for some intractable Italian reason, allowed to be called Marsala. In fact, they are made in the old, dry, pre-Woodhouse style, achieving alcohol levels of around 17% quite naturally. Vecchio Samperi [★★/■■■], bottled at ten, 20 and 30 years old, develops wonderfully concentrated flavours of nuts and caramel. A fresher, younger, but still perfumed version [★★/■■] is called Josephine Doré.

Other good producers of Marsala [★★/■■] include Florio (which is controlled by Cinzano) and C Pellegrino.

WHERE NEXT? Málaga, Sherry and many other Mediterranean wines are equivalents. Other oddities like Greek Mavro (see **Greece**) and Tuscan **Vin Santo** survive from ancient times.

MONBAZILLAC

Monbazillac is a sweet country cousin of Sauternes, based like it on the Sémillon grape. It has exactly the same problems as Ste Croix-du-Mont, Loupiac, Cadillac and Cérons, the immediate neighbours of Sauternes. To make real *Botrytis* wine is risky and expensive. Even Sauternes has a job convincing people to pay a realistic price, so what chance does Monbazillac stand?

When it is made properly, the wine is richly honeyed, with a trace of liquorice and a shade less bite than Sauternes, and can last a decade or two, in rare cases four or five. More often, however, commercial reality means that few producers wait to see whether or not *Botrytis* will strike. Most wine is simply sweetish, haunted by the pale ghost of honey but lacking the rich, sticky, oozing nectar itself. These are best drunk within about five years.

Most wine is made by the large co-operative group UNIDOR, which owns the picturesque Château de Monbazillac [★★/ ■■]. Other good châteaux [★→★★/ ■■] include:

La Borderie	*La Jaubertie*
Le Caillou	*Septy*
Le Fage	*Treuil-de-Nailhac*

WHERE NEXT? Loupiac and Ste-Croix-du-Mont (see **Bordeaux**) are nearby equivalents, as are some of the lesser wines of **Sauternes & Barsac**. Elsewhere, Chenin Blanc wines from the **Loire** and *Auslesen* from Germany's **Rheingau** offer the same degree of sweetness, with perhaps more acidity.

MONTEREY

When California's Silicon Valley was advancing southward during the 1960s, winemakers looking for alternative vineyard sites discovered Monterey. The region had never before been used for growing grapes as the climate was thought too cool and breezy for the vine. This very coolness has been the making of Monterey. Its grapes have a fullness of flavour that can be comparable to Alsace, and late picking is often possible due to the length of the growing season.

Plantings were pioneered here by Mirassou Vineyards, Paul Masson and Wente [★★/ ■■→ ■■■], the latter renowned for its Gray Riesling. These wineries were followed in 1973 by Monterey Vineyards [★★/ ■■], which has been instrumental in promoting the region and produces excellent fruity Gewürztraminer, Riesling, Chardonnay, and Sauvignon Blanc. The special ''Thanksgiving'' Riesling has good ageing capacity. Many of the wines made in the region are *Botrytis*-affected, and Monterey Vineyards makes a highly-regarded Sauternes-style wine from Semillon and Sauvignon Blanc.

In the hills above Monterey is the small vineyard of Chalone [★★★/ ■■■], renowned for its high-quality Chardonnay, often compared to white Burgundy. The wine adds a smoky fragrance to its big, buttery constitution; Pinot Blanc is promising too.

South of Monterey, near the town of Greenfield, is the Jekel Vineyard [★★/ ■■→ ■■■], which has successfully produced and marketed a range of top varietals world-wide. Jekel's Chardonnay and Riesling are highly rated, with a ripe full flavour but none of the excess heaviness for which California is sometimes criticized.

WHERE NEXT? Elsewhere in California, **Sonoma** attempts the same delicacy, as does the Santa Ynez Valley of Santa Barbara county. Or go north to Washington (see **United States**). **New Zealand's** winemakers have the same priorities of freshness and fruit flavour.

MONTILLA-MORILES

Montilla is a bit like sherry but not as expensive: that seems to be the general view. But it has been playing the role of cheap sherry substitute for so long that it has almost convinced itself there is no more to life than that. Why should we want a cheap substitute for sherry when the real thing is such good value anyway? Cheap sherry is already a substitute for real sherry, and a poor one at that, so even cheaper Montilla is even less of a bargain. In any case, Montilla is subtly different from sherry; the good ones are worth drinking for their own sake.

Montilla is made inland, just south of Cordoba, around the villages of Montilla and Moriles. The hot sun brings natural alcohol levels up to around 14-15%, so, unlike sherry, it does not always need to be fortified. The principal grape variety is Pedro Ximénes, which is often used to make thick, rich sweet wines in Jerez and Málaga. It does that here too, but also makes the light, straight *finos* or dry Montillas, and the *amontillados* or medium Montillas.

Finos are produced by the action of *flor*, just like sherry, and a limited *solera* system operates. The overall effect is generally of a simpler, blander, slightly fatter product, without the tangy, zesty bite of *fino* sherry, or quite the depth of nuttiness of a good *amontillado* sherry. This is not necessarily a criticism, because there are times when the gentler effect of Montilla may be more appropriate.

In the UK market, Montilla cannot use the sherry terms *fino*, *amontillado* and *oloroso*; instead, they are labelled Pale, Medium or Cream. In other markets, including the USA, the Spanish terms apply, despite opposition from the Jerezanos who believe they have a divine right to use them. Since the very term *amontillado* means "in the style of Montilla", this fortunately cuts no ice.

The real gems of Montilla are the dry *olorosos*, which are deep, nutty, long and complex, sometimes tasting of prunes, sometimes of espresso coffee. There is also a small quantity of impenetrably dark, very rich, sweet and sticky Pedro Ximénes wines that smell like a bag of raisins or a just-baked rich fruit cake. They have a softness and intense, luscious, ripe figgy, treacly feel, backed up by great length of flavour that is unequalled in Jerez, rarely equalled in Málaga, and is perhaps closer to Australian Liqueur Muscats and Tokays.

The best producers [★→★★/■→■■] include:

Alvear	*Gracia Hermanos*
Carbonell	*Bodegas Monte Cristo*

Dry Montillas are classic aperitif wines. A bottle disappears rapidly with most hors d'oeuvres and especially *tapas*. A glass of *fino* Montilla with a bowl of Spanish olives can be very close to heaven. Montilla is also one of the best wines to drink with artichoke.

WHERE NEXT? Sherry, Málaga, Madeira, Marsala, Australian **Liqueur Muscat & Tokay**

MOROCCO

Morocco has a much smaller vineyard area than its North African neighbours to the east: its acreage is some 10% the size of Algeria's. Its standards, however, are much higher. Some of the wines have an *Appellation d'Origine Garantie* and are subject to quality control.

The central Moroccan producer is SODEVI [★/■]. The Fez/Meknes area is the top region for quality but there are few white wines; the emphasis is on *vin gris*, a very pale rosé, made from a blend of Cinsaut and Carignan grapes.

WHERE NEXT? Compare **Algeria** and **Tunisia**. Or look across the Straits to **Portugal**, where in the south of the county wines are being made in similar conditions.

MOSEL-SAAR-RUWER

Germany's Mosel calmly loops around great sweeping bends, altering the aspect of the vineyards along the river. Here, this bank of the river is perfectly exposed; just round the bend the opposite bank faces the full force of the sun. The best vineyards skip from one side to the other, producing the most thrilling wines when raking sharply up the precipitous undercut slope on the broad outside sweep of a bend, less successful on the gently flat, inside slip-off slope.

If these wines don't excite you, then very little from Germany will. But it is best to make sure of a really good one, even if that means paying a bit extra.

THE MOSEL TASTE The great appeal of Mosel wines is their harnessing of opposing forces. We can taste the struggle between richness and lightness; between racy acidity and honeyed sweetness, elegance and vitality, and between simple, brisk, appley freshness and ethereal subtlety and complexity. They have an edginess even when ripe that makes them vigorous, lively and exciting. And all this without recourse to more than nominal levels of alcohol.

To call the resulting wines "balanced" seems rather tame. The tension never eases. But after five, ten, sometimes 20 or more years in their elegant green bottle they do achieve a harmony that seems greater than the sum of the parts. The wines dig deep, mining an apparently inexhaustible seam of complexity. And they do all this because of two things: the Riesling grape, and the steep, slatey slopes the river has engineered.

CHOOSING MOSEL WINES So much of the business surrounding German wines is coldly analytical that we are in danger of seeing the wines as little more than an intellectual exercise. Finding our way around from *Einzellage* to *Grosslage* by way of *halbtrocken spätlesen* is a bit like playing three-dimensional chess against a computer: a great achievement if we can manage it, but not a lot of fun if we are honest about it. Not, say, compared to sloshing some greeny-gold, spine-tinglingly fresh and richly honeyed liquid into a big glass and drinking it.

So it is better, I think, to begin with a little passion, some emotion which, as the word suggests, will keep us moving, searching for ever better wines. If, and only if, we are struck by the glories of Mosel Riesling, then it will be worth getting out the chess pieces and mastering the difference between, say, Bereich Bernkastel and Bernkasteler-Doctor Auslese. If not, then we may as well just forget about the whole thing.

The reputation of the Mosel rests not on the familiar *Grosslage* names – the Schwarze Katz of Zell, Piesport's Michelsberg – nor on the even larger *Bereiche* such as Moseltor and Bernkastel, but on some of the smaller sites. Perhaps the style reaches its apogee in the middle Mosel, around Bernkastel. Here the ripe, succulent, sometimes appley, sometimes honeyed fruit is shot through with a bolt of tinglingly fresh and nervy acidity to produce classic Mosel Riesling in half a dozen villages. They are somehow full yet light; delicate, but charged with a remarkable energy, and leave you feeling complete but not sated; they seem to express perfectly the meeting of cold, grey, flinty slate and sun-ripe, squishy fruit.

Regional names to look for include Piesport (Goldtröpfchen rather than Michelsberg), Braunberg (Juffer vineyard), Bernkastel (the nearly vertical Doctor vineyard rises straight up from the half-timbered village), Graach, Wehlen (Sonnenuhr vineyard), Zeltingen, and Ürzig. Good producers [★★→★★★/■■] include:

Bischöflichen Weinguter	*Richter*
Friedrich-Wilhelm-	*St Johannishof*
Gymnasium	*Freiherr von Schorlemer*
Fritz Haag	*Dr Thanisch*
Reichsgraf von Kesselstatt	*Vereinigte Hospitien*
Lauerberg	*Wegeler-Deinhard*
Otto Pauly	*Zentralkellerei*
Pauly-Bergweiler	*Mosel-Saar-Ruwer*
JJ Prüm	

But. There are those who feel that the quintessential Riesling style really comes from the slatey valleys of Saar and Ruwer, which join the upper Mosel either side of the Roman town of Trier. Riesling ripens with difficulty, but, when it does, what we can taste is steely, minerally, ultra-clean and light as a feather; the pure, raw, naked grape unencumbered by trills or flounces. It may seem fragile, but the piercing, racy fruit is hard-edged and real enough.

Regional names to look for include: Ayl (Kupp vineyard), Serrig, Ockfen, Wiltingen (the best estate is Scharzhofberger), Maximin Grünhaus, Oberemmel, and the Karthäuserhofberg vineyard.

The best producers [★★→★★★/■■] include:

Bischöflichen Weinguter	*Schloss Saarstein*
Friedrich-Wilhelm-	*Freiherr von Schorlemer*
Gymnasium	*von Schubert*
Geltz-Zilliken	*Bert Simon*
Kartäuserhof	*Staatlichen Weinbaudomänen*
Reichsgraf von Kesselstatt	*Vereinigte Hospitien*
E Müller	*Heinz Wagner*
Rudolf Müller	

The best Mosel vintages include 1988, 85, 83, 79, 76 and 75.

MOSEL WINE AND FOOD These delicate wines make excellent aperitifs and go with softshell crab, avocado and veal. Or a peach.

WHERE NEXT? The **Rheingau** offers equivalent quality, but emphasizes weight and flavour rather than delicacy and finesse; the **Nahe** offers something in between. **Loire** wines display the French approach to similar cool-climate conditions. Nowhere in the New World is quite so cold and steep, but try interesting new "cool-climate" regions such as **Tasmania** and **New York State**.

MULLER-THURGAU

The world's most famous designer grape variety came off the drawing board over a century ago. The idea behind it – to improve on Nature – sounded appealing. Wine made from Riesling tastes wonderful, but the vine itself has drawbacks: it ripens late, which makes it susceptible to frosts, storms and other seasonal hazards; it is fussy about where it will grow; and yields can be low. Why not, thought a certain Dr Müller, who was born in the Swiss canton of Thurgau, cross this high-quality grape with something early-ripening and high-yielding to create a vine endowed with the best qualities of both? So far as we can tell, he picked on the rather plain Silvaner grape as a mate.

Unfortunately, the gene for quality appears to have been recessive, and the final product offers mere early-ripening abundance. Nevertheless a lot of German growers, and a lot of Liebfraumilch drinkers, are grateful for what has become a great commercial success. Müller-Thurgau is now Germany's most widely planted grape variety. It has spread east to Hungary and Czechoslovakia, south to Italy, and half way around the world to New Zealand.

THE MÜLLER-THURGAU TASTE Wines produced from Müller-Thurgau grapes make for light, soft, easy drinking. They are uncomplicated, undemanding, approachable. There is no need to delve into a big bag of evocative and recherché associations to conjure up an idea of their smell and taste. Some of them are lightly fruity, others are not; some are vaguely flowery, others are not. There is little more to it than that, and often considerably less.

Müller-Thurgau wines are invariably inoffensive – except to people who like their wine to taste of something. Given the low natural acidity, care must be taken not to oversweeten them. A little sweetness is useful, though, in covering up for lack of real definition, and most Müller-Thurgaus are consequently medium-dry. The grape can also function rather like a tailor's dummy in a shop window: it is a useful device on which to hang something colourful and interesting to attract attention. A lot of Müller-Thurgau and a little Gewürztraminer, for example, makes a very saleable commodity.

The Müller-Thurgau grape may be prolific, but it does not make durable wine. Don't keep Liebfraumilch or other Müller-Thurgau wines; they will not improve.

BEGIN WITH LIEBFRAUMILCH It is easy to be cynical about Müller-Thurgau, as many growers are, but it does happen to make the kind of wine that launches most people into their drinking careers. Liebfraumilch, the grape's most common manifestation, provides a bridge between fruit juice and soft drinks on the one hand, and "real" adult wine on the other (see **Liebfraumilch**).

OTHER MÜLLER-THURGAU WINES Because of its low natural acidity, Müller-Thurgau thrives best at the cooler extremes of the world's grape-growing regions. One country where wines rarely lack acidity is New Zealand. The grape does well here, producing over half of the country's output of wine. In its usual anonymous role, Müller-Thurgau plays a part in everyday wines such as Cooks Tolaga Bay, Nobilo's White Cloud and Montana's Blenheimer, but its real potential remains under-exploited. Kumeu River [★★/■■] and Hunter's [★★/■■■] both make "serious" dry Müller-Thurgaus, but such wines are rare (see **New Zealand**).

The alternative to cool latitude is high altitude. Tiefenbrunner's lofty Feldmarschall vineyard in Alto Adige makes a steely, firm Müller-Thurgau with a surprising amount of backbone. Pojer & Sandri's Müller-Thurgau di Faedo, also from north-east Italy, is more supple and delicate (see **Alto Adige**).

Everyday German wines are made from Müller-Thurgau in Baden and Franken. The uninformative label may say nothing more than Baden Dry, indicating a reluctance on the part of producers to embrace this grape variety in public (see **Baden, Franken**).

Surprisingly perhaps, it is Austria's second most popular grape variety after Grüner Veltliner, grows like a weed in Hungary and Czechoslovakia, makes about half of Luxembourg's production (where it is known as Rivaner), and is England's most widely planted variety.

Growers at the difficult margins of viticulture, like those in England, are often so grateful just to see some of their grapes ripen that they are unconcerned about inflicting extremely ordinary wines on us. One is reminded of the less-than-expert violin player who attempted to excuse the sounds he made on the grounds that the instrument was difficult to play. "Difficult?", grumbled a disgruntled listener, "I wish it were impossible."

MÜLLER-THURGAU AND FOOD This unassuming, flexible grape produces wine that is happy with most food. It really comes into its own as a thirstquencher. It is also a useful foil to strong-flavoured food. Try it with a curry or other spicy dishes.

WHERE NEXT? The light aromatic quality of a good Müller-Thurgau is echoed in some **Muscats**. If the aroma is altogether too gentle, then **Gewürztraminer** will provide a big leap in power. For more finesse, **Riesling** is a satisfying alternative, and the level of sweetness can be chosen to suit your palate or circumstances.

MUSCADET

This wine from the mouth of the Loire around Nantes seems to have cornered the market as the ultimate partner for seafood. It is dry, light- to medium-bodied and refreshing. Ordinary Muscadet derives this quality from its relatively high acidity, while the best has a slight prickle that performs the same function more gracefully. It is unusual in having a maximum permitted alcoholic degree of just over 12%.

Nobody is quite sure why it is called Muscadet. Its name is a synonym for the Melon de Bourgogne grape from which it is made, but where the synonym came from remains a mystery.

THE MUSCADET TASTE Muscadet's neutrality of taste and slight prickle, combined with its specific role as a wine to drink with food, make it one of the most Italian of French white wine styles.

The grape is an early ripener, which has the effect of ensuring good acidity while not allowing much flavour to develop in the skins. Rather too much Muscadet is thus merely refreshing, without a lot of character. Later picking, although slightly riskier, solves both these problems at a stroke. Good Muscadet is not particularly high in acidity, but has a ripeness of flavour that many cheaper wines lack.

CHOOSING MUSCADETS The ability to recognize two simple descriptions on the label will weigh the odds of finding a good Muscadet in the drinker's favour. First, make sure you buy Muscadet de Sèvre et Maine. This *appellation*, named after the two tributaries that join the Loire at Nantes, is the best producing region; fortunately around 85% of Muscadet comes from here. Second, look for wine that has been bottled *sur lie*. Wine left on its lees in barrel after fermentation is complete develops more flavour, complexity and body than if it is bottled straight away. This technique is widely employed in the New World, often with Chardonnay, to add dimensions to the flavour.

The effect of the technique on Muscadet is to develop a fuller, softer, creamier feel. I have lost count of the times I have given up on Muscadet, bored by thin and characterless examples, only to find my faith restored by a good *sur lie* wine. The process also gives it a slight but attractive yeasty taste, somewhat similar to that quality in Champagne, which develops its yeastiness from maturing on the lees in bottle. By the same token, a little carbon dioxide dissolves in the Muscadet, which we experience as a slight prickle on the tongue.

Muscadet from a good producer will cost a little more, but it is well worth the outlay just to experience how good the real thing can taste. The best producers [★★/■→■■] include:

Couillaud Frères	*Louis Metaireau*
Jacques Guindon	*Sauvion et Fils*
Joseph Hallereau	*Chereau-Carré*
Pierre Luneau	

Generally speaking, Muscadet is not a wine that takes to ageing; look for the most recent vintage.

MUSCADET AND FOOD Nothing could be simpler: Muscadet goes with fish, fish, and more fish. Drink it beside a tower of pink-shelled *langoustines* and crab, light grey oysters and small black winkles, preferably eaten with the sea visible from the restaurant window. In these circumstances it performs well throughout a whole meal, from aperitif to cheese.

WHERE NEXT? In Brittany, **Gros Plant** is considered an alternative in restaurants because it is usually cheaper. Ideally, though, trade up to the best Muscadet you can afford. Alternatively, try **Aligoté**, **Gaillac**, dry **Vinho Verde**, Müller-Thurgau from **Alto Adige**, or Pinot Grigio from **Friuli-Venezia Giulia**.

MUSCAT

Muscat is not so much a single grape variety as a family of varieties, ranging from yellow and pink to red, brown and black. Most Muscat wines are sweet, and many are fortified. The finest kind for winemaking is Muscat Blanc à Petits Grains, known in Italy as Moscato Bianco. Among White Muscat's triumphs are fizzy Moscato d'Asti and Asti Spumante from northern Italy, *vins doux naturels* such as Muscat de Beaumes-de-Venise and Muscat de Frontignan from southern France, and the Greek Muscat of Samos.

Other white varieties include Muscat of Alexandria, which is suited to hotter climates and makes poorer wine, and Muscat Ottonel, a high-yielding 19th-century clone, which, as a piece of biological engineering marginally outshines Dr Frankenstein's experiments.

THE MUSCAT TASTE The great appeal of Muscat is its powerful, but soft, elderflowery peachy smell, and its fresh, juicy grapiness. It is just like stuffing handfuls of sweet grapes into your mouth – which, in fact, many people do since Muscat is a widespread and popular table grape. The wine is instantly likeable, thanks to a little sweetness, and so uncomplicated that it can unsettle "serious" drinkers.

Muscat Blanc à Petits Grains, whose name specifies both the colour and size of the grapes, is the epitome of the Muscat taste. Small grapes have a higher ratio of skin to juice than big grapes, and since the aromatic components are found just under the skin, a large number of small grapes gives more flavour to the wine than a small number of large ones. By stopping the fermentation with alcohol or filtering out the yeasts before all the sugar has been converted, some unfermented grape juice is left in the wine. This accounts for both the sweetness and the fresh grapey aroma characteristic of many Muscats.

BEGIN WITH FIZZ The most straightforward, uncluttered way to enjoy Muscat is in sweet, fizzy Moscato d'Asti or Asti Spumante. Because the wine is only partially fermented, it is low in alcohol – usually around 5-6%. The unfermented grape juice that remains accounts for the sweetness. Asti provides the welcome of a St Bernard dog that puts its paws on your shoulders and licks you enthusiastically (see **Asti Spumante**).

Anyone who finds this overpowering can take comfort from a gentler, less odoriferous animal. In France, Muscat is blended with the more subdued variety Clairette to make a mid-Rhône sparkler under the Clairette de Die *appellation* (see **Rhône**). It is also a major component in one of the most successful low-alcohol wines so far produced, Pétillant de Raisin [★/■], made along the flat, sandy Mediterranean coast by Listel using "organic" methods, together with some Ugni Blanc (see **Trebbiano**) and Clairette grapes to tone down its pungency; it is not expensive.

OTHER MUSCATS At what is best described as the opposite extreme are the Australian Liqueur Muscats from Rutherglen in Victoria. These are heavy, dark, powerful, highly alcoholic, syrupy, treacley-sweet wines that have no counterpart anywhere. You can barely believe that the same light White Muscat grape could produce such a different style. Indeed it is not quite the same grape, but a close relative, Brown Muscat (see **Liqueur Muscat & Tokay**).

Muscat à Petits Grains is also the grape used to make France's best sweet *vins doux naturels*, Muscat de Beaumes-de-Venise and Muscat de Frontignan. As with Asti, it is the unfermented grape juice that provides both sweetness and the intense grapey freshness (see **Beaumes-de-Venise** and **Vins Doux Naturels**).

Because of this connection, though, Muscat à Petits Grains is also called Muscat de Frontignan, in which guise it was exported to Australia. The grape was also exported from Piedmont and is therefore sometimes called Muscat of Canelli in California.

An unusual member of the Muscat family is Fior d'Arancio. Hailing originally from Italy, it is better known in Australia and California as Orange Muscat. Brown Brothers, masters of Muscat, combine it 50/ 50 with Flora to make a luscious, but light and balanced, late-harvest wine of less than 10% alcohol (see **Victoria**). In California, Orange Muscat is a component of Quady's Essensia (see **California**).

Wines made from Muscat of Alexandria generally lack the grapiness and refinement of White Muscat. Their slightly higher alcohol, combined with raisiny flavours, make for coarser results. The strong, sweet Portuguese Moscatel de Setúbal of J M da Fonseca gets around this by macerating the wine on fresh grape skins to liven it up. A good dry Muscat is also made nearby by João Pires (see **Portugal**).

Spanish Moscatels from Málaga, Alicante and Valencia [★/■→■■] often lack finesse and can vary considerably in sweetness, but they can also be fragrant and luscious, with great length of flavour.

Until recently, Alsace was the only region where Muscat was made into dry wine. Muscat d'Alsace is crisp and clean with nutty undertones (see **Alsace**).

MUSCAT AND FOOD Muscat's powerful aroma makes it difficult to match with food, since it can be intrusive. It is really a wine for occasions. Moscato d'Asti is for when you need something simple, sweet and frothy. France's *vins doux naturels* and many late-harvest Muscats from the New World are natural pudding wines: the orange flavour of Quady's Essensia makes it one of the few wines to go marvellously with dark chocolate, and the hint of ginger is a match for lightly spicy or almond-based puddings. Muscats can also be good with fresh fruit and are well worth trying with cheese, especially blue and goat cheeses providing they are not too ripe or powerful.

WHERE NEXT? Muscat's fresh grapiness is unique, although the intense pungency of the grape variety, and something of its floweriness, can be found in **Gewürztraminer**. Although quite different in style, **Sauvignon Blanc** (especially those from **New Zealand**) can also be powerfully aromatic.

NAHE

Nahe adjoins Rheinhessen, nods across to the Rheingau (the River Nahe joins the Rhine at Bingen) and extends towards the Mosel. It is tempting to think that the wines express something of all three regions. And perhaps they do. Or at least, some of the Rieslings made by the better producers from a few vineyards do. They seem to combine the steely, minerally thrust of the Upper Mosel with the ripe, aristocratic bearing of the Rheingau, and wear an attention-seeking Rheinhessen flower in their cap. They have structure and balance and length, and that is a pretty unbeatable combination for any wine.

Village names to look for include Bad Kreuznach, Traisen, Norheim, Niederhausen, and Schlossböckelheim, although it is worth remembering that the *Bereich* (as opposed to the village) of Schlossböckelheim covers three *grosslagen*, many villages and something like 180 vineyards; while Bereich Kreuznach (as opposed to the city of Bad Kreuznach) covers nearly 150 vineyards. Much *Bereich* wine makes unspectacular and conventional drinking.

Best producers [★★→★★★/■■] include:

Ökonomierat August Anheuser	Hermann Dönnhof
Paul Anheuser	Staatsweinbaudomäne Niederhausen-
Hans Crusius	Schlossböckelheim
Schlossgut Diel	

WHERE NEXT? A subtle comparison is with Upper Mosel wines (see **Mosel-Saar-Ruwer**) and **Rheingau** wines of similar standing and vintage. Try also the less well-known **Rheinpfalz** for more weight and depth, less subtlety. Cross the Franco-German border to **Alsace** for more vinosity and dryness.

NAPA VALLEY

Napa Valley is perhaps California's best-known wine-producing region and home to dozens of "boutique" wineries, most of which make wine in the expensive category. The whole range of grape varieties is grown here. Unlike their French counterparts, Californian winemakers are not bound by *appellation* restrictions on where to plant different grape varieties; they have plenty of room for manoeuvre with their grapes and there is widespread experimentation with varieties and microclimates from year to year.

In a climate not dissimilar to that of the Gironde, the Bordeaux grapes do especially well: Sauvignon Blanc, which suffered an identity crisis before being renamed Fumé Blanc by Robert Mondavi, and Semillon. Chardonnay also yields some fine wines and Riesling often appears in late harvest versions.

As a launching pad for Napa wines, try one from the Christian Brothers, made by genuine monks to reliable standards. Apart from the dry white varieties such as Fumé Blanc [★★/■■] they make a successful, if slightly syrupy, sweet Muscat wine called Chateau La Salle [★★/■■■] which is typically old-school California.

Move up a step from these to wineries that form the backbone of the valley, producing quality wines at moderate prices. The best producers at this level [★★/■■→■■■] include:

Beaulieu	*Robert Mondavi*
Beringer	*Trefethen*
Louis Martini	

These producers make a full range of dry white varietals including Chardonnay and Chenin Blanc, with some unusual variants such as Gewürztraminer (good at Martini) and late-harvest Riesling (from Mondavi). Mondavi's Reserve wines are particularly recommended, as are the Eschol and Chardonnay produced by Trefethen.

If price is not a problem go for a fascinating "designer" name like Joseph Phelps [★★★/■■■], a millionaire-turned-vigneron from New York, who makes marvellous Chardonnay, and classic Rieslings (especially the late harvest version); or Chappellet [★★/■■■], whose Chardonnay and Riesling are good. Other notable names [★★→★★★/ ■■■] include:

Chateau Montelena	*Monticello*
Freemark Abbey	*Newton*
Heitz	*Stag's Leap Wine Cellars*
Mayacamas	

Some of California's best fizz is produced in Napa, especially by Schramsberg and Domaine Chandon, an outpost of the Champagne house Moët et Chandon. Schramsberg has an enviable reputation for *méthode champenoise*. Pinot Noir and Chardonnay are fermented in oak barrels (just like Krug), and aged on lees in the bottle for anything up to five years. Blanc de Blancs [★★★/■■■] is generally the best, offering elegant vintage wines with a slight yeastiness in youth; the pink-tinged Blanc de Noirs [★★→★★★/■■■] is bigger and fruitier.

Carneros is a small region to the south of Napa which makes excellent Chardonnay to a lighter style than Napa and Sonoma because of its cool climate. The principal wineries here [★★→★★★/ ■■■] are Carneros Creek and Acacia, the latter of which has mastered the art of making stunning Chardonnays in less than a decade. Marina Vineyard [★★★/■■■] wine is powerful, well-structured and stylish.

WHERE NEXT? Contrast Napa with neighbouring **Sonoma**, where white varieties find slightly less extreme conditions. Or range south of the Bay to **Monterey** and Santa Barbara (see **California**) where growers insist conditions are kinder still. Refer back to the **Côte d'Or** and **Germany** for (now distant) prototypes, to **New South Wales** and **Western Australia** for today's keen competitors.

NAVARRA

Rioja's neighbour is largely a producer of red and rosé wines: less than one bottle in ten from Navarra is white. Add to this the fact that most wine is made in co-operatives that are only gradually coming to terms with modern equipment, and we can see why Navarra whites have not yet hit the big-time.

Not yet. They need longer. But they are on the way up. A leading research station, plus generous local government investment, are signs of serious determination to succeed. So are the recent plantings of international grape varieties such as Riesling and Chardonnay.

Until they come on stream, the same grapes that produce white Rioja – Viura, Malvasia and Garnacha – make rather ordinary look-alikes in Navarra: fresh, light- to medium-bodied, some with a lightly flowery nose, some not. As with all wines that fail to leave a distinctive imprint by themselves, they make a good choice to drink with a wide variety of foods.

The best producers [★→★★/■■] include:

Cenalsa	*Señorio de Sarria*
Chivite	*Vinicola Navarra*

WHERE NEXT? Try **Rioja**, especially for its new-style whites; Rueda (see **Spain**); or **Portugal** where new-style wines are perhaps of a higher standard.

NEW SOUTH WALES

New South Wales, Australia's oldest wine-producing state, is renowned chiefly for the Hunter Valley, cradle of antipodean winemaking – and justly so, for this region has created the country's most distinctive white wine style, Hunter Semillon (see **Hunter Valley**). Apart from the vast Murrumbidgee Irrigation Area in the east, much of the rest of the state's wine is produced in small, isolated pockets – except, that is, for Mudgee.

Mudgee, a high plain among the hills south-west of the Hunter Valley, is kept relatively cool by its elevation. At 1500-2000 feet (460-610 metres), the grapes benefit from a long, slow growing season that produces balanced, ripe fruit flavours. This is the only Australian region to have an "appellation" for its wines, which started with the 1980 vintage. "Certified Mudgee Appellation Wine" does not claim to be better than that from elsewhere, but it does aim for a specific identity. The point is simply to make it obvious that this is one region where wines are not blended with any from outside.

Chardonnay comes up trumps here, with a creamily soft style, heaps of flavoursome fruit, and balancing acidity. Barrel-fermented wines produce a bit of toastiness; contact with the yeast lees rounds them out and gives them longer life, although they are attractive to drink straight off the shelf. Mudgee Chardonnays are more melon-like than Hunter Chardonnays, more reserved and restrained, more elegant. Some other grape varieties are also produced, but they are generally less exciting.

The best Mudgee producers [★★/■■→■■■] include Huntington Estate and Montrose which, together with Craigmoor and Amberton [★★/■■] are owned by the Hunter Valley firm of Wyndham. The highest vineyard, Botobolar [★★/■■■], runs on organic principles.

The Murrumbidgee Irrigation Area (or Riverina as the marketing people would rather call it) is the uncomfortably hot, and equivalent of Victoria's Mildura and South Australia's Riverland. Excessive heat produces high alcohol, low acidity, and coarse flavours, which has made it a traditional and successful fortified wine producing region.

Table wines are a recent phenomenon, made possible by cool temperature fermentation. McWilliams [★→★★/■■→■■■] maintains a winery here, but de Bortoli is the best-known local producer, largely on account of a hugely successful *Botrytis*-affected Semillon [★★★/■■■]. The first vintage of this (1982) was a knockout: deep golden yellow with great intensity of flavour, rich and powerful, well balanced sweetness and acidity, very close indeed to Sauternes in style, and a wine to age. Now de Bortoli makes a whole lot of variations on the theme including a Late Harvest Semillon [★★/■■], a Dry Botrytis Semillon [★★/■■], a good Show Spätlese Traminer [★★/■■■], a tropical-fruit flavoured Chardonnay from local fruit [★★/■■■], and a much more interesting and attractive, lemony buttery Chardonnay [★★/■■■] from its vineyard in the Yarra Valley.

WHERE NEXT? Try the rest of Australia for competing wines of various degrees of subtlety, and to see whether the Mudgee style stands out (see **Australia**).

NEW YORK STATE

This is an intriguing area for the wine lover, almost impossible to categorize since there are three distinct styles of winemaking. The tradition at the so-called Finger Lakes wineries is to make wine from the native American *vitis labrusca* vine (rather than the European *vitis vinifera*). These have a pungent aroma, described in wine jargon as "foxy" and familiar to connoisseurs of wine gums. In other words, the wines are an acquired taste, and exports to Europe have been virtually non-existent.

The second strand of activity here is concentrated on hybrid vines which combine the hardiness of native Americn varieties with some of the European flavour. These have also proved popular in England, which also has problems with erratic weather. Hybrids include Aurora, Rayon d'Or, Seyval-Blanc, Seyve-Villard and Vidal Blanc (the latter based on Trebbiano). The wines tend to be bland, but they are not over-acidic and are more drinkable than native varieties.

Finally, there are "real" wines as we know them, made from familiar *vinifera* varieties such as Riesling, Chardonnay and Sauvignon Blanc. Although the grapes are still often blended with hybrids for reliability, there is a move toward quality and lighter flavour.

Reliable producers [★→★★/■→■■] include:

Benmarl Wine Company	*Monarch*
Bully Hill Wine Co	*Taylor's*
Glenora	*Vinifera Wines*
Gold Seal	*Wagner Vineyard*
Great Western	*Hermann J Weimer*
Heron Hill	*Widmers*

The *vinifera* wines are said to have something of a "German" taste – light and acidic. Finest by far are those made on Long Island, where the Hargraves, owners of Long Island Vineyard [★★/■■■], make Chardonnay subtle and satisfying enough for lovers of white Burgundy.

There are also a few "serious" producers of *méthode champenoise* wines based on Chardonnay or Pinot Noir [★→★★/■■→■■■], including Knapp, Glenora and McGregor; producion is tiny.

WHERE NEXT? Head up to **Canada** or over the continent to **Oregon**. Or, in another hemisphere, try **Tasmania**, **Marlborough** and **Chile**. For the hybrid taste, go to **England**.

NEW ZEALAND

New Zealand was a buzz country during the 1980s, making some of the freshest, tastiest and most exciting white wines in the world. It has come from nowhere to centre stage in no time at all, and its potential is only beginning to be explored. It will be a buzz country throughout the 1990s and into the next millennium. To help things along, the wines have a recognizable national style, grassy and herbaceous, and this relative ease of identity simplifies the drinker's choice.

It is a curious place, climatically. The South Island sits roughly at 40-46° south of the Equator. In Europe, the equivalent latitude would encompass, say, Madrid to Lyon, from the hot central Spanish plain of La Mancha, through Rioja, Bordeaux and the extensive southern French vineyards of Corbières, Roussillon, Languedoc, Provence and the Rhône Valley as far as Beaujolais. The North Island stretches approximately between 36 and 40°, which is equivalent to the distance from Algeria and Tunisia in North Africa to the tip of southern Italy. Very Mediterranean indeed.

These European regions are mostly warm, and sometimes hot. But New Zealand isn't. Apart from Australia, 1,500 miles (2,400 km) away to the east, and Antarctica over 10,000 miles (16,000 km) to the south, there is nothing around it but sea and cold currents. So New Zealand behaves like a much cooler climate. As if the South Island were, in European terms, like Germany or northern France, only without the severe winter frosts; as if the North Island were closer in climate to Piedmont than Andalucia.

It is this that determines the choice of grape varieties and styles of wine, and helps to put New Zealand in competition with some of the world's best wine regions. The grape variety that has done most in this direction so far is Sauvignon Blanc. Pleased as they are with progress so far, many New Zealand winemakers feel that other varieties have at least as much if not more potential.

The modern revival of the industry was initially based on the apparently sound idea that since the climate was so similar to parts of Germany, then German varietals and crossings (Müller-Thurgau amongst them) would perform best. Müller-Thurgau has done remarkably well, both in terms of quality, and by delivering such enormous yields that it can out-Liebfraumilch Liebfraumilch. Riesling, especially Late Harvest and South Island versions, and Gewürztraminer, which can be delicate, even elegant, both show immense promise. But as things turned out, it was French grape varieties that really made the world sit up and take notice.

After Sauvignon Blanc, Chardonnay is the big white hope, and will be increasingly acclaimed as more and more producers get the hang of how to handle it. Maturing, and particularly fermenting, in oak is already lifting some Chardonnays to new heights. Semillon – green, grassy and Sauvignon-like at present – may find its own feet in the longer term. Chenin Blanc is mostly grown in the North Island, where it makes wines with a purity that is rarely seen outside the best examples from the Loire.

Vinously speaking, New Zealand is a child prodigy. Growers are still trying to find which varieties do best where. Marlborough Sauvignon Blanc is one big bull's eye, and some smaller vineyards are beginning to show superior quality. Examples include Nobilo's Dixon Vineyard, Babich's Irongate, Matua Valley's Judd and Egan Estates. Other producers such as Vidal and Villa Maria prefer to fire their best shot under a Reserve label, which gives them the freedom to use the best fruit they can lay their hands on.

THE NORTH ISLAND The North Island, notwithstanding the rapid development of Marlborough to the south, is still the centre of the New Zealand wine industry. Its two largest regions, Gisborne and Hawke's Bay, produce wines of considerable finesse. Auckland, in the northwest, was where the country's winemaking began. Quite a few producers are based there, but it is rather damp and humid for grape-growing, so many of them either own vineyards or buy grapes from other regions, particularly Hawke's Bay, Gisborne and Marlborough. Those wineries that do rely on local Auckland grapes tend to produce tropical-fruit styles.

The most successful of these is Kumeu River with its pineappley, toasty, butterscotchy Chardonnay [★★/■■■], and wonderfully curious Noble Dry Sauvignon [★★/■■■]. The grapes for this were infected with *Botrytis* but the wine was vinified dry, and the result is like a bowl full of apricots, peaches and passion fruit, with a jar of honey poured over. Yet it is amazingly dry, and perfect with rich fish dishes or duck parfait with raisins.

Apart from Kumeu River there is little to emerge in the way of a distinctively Auckland style, but there are many other good producers. The pride and joy of Cooks/Corbans [★→★★★/■■→■■■], the country's second-largest company, is its Stoneleigh range from Marlborough (see **Marlborough**). Among its many other lines, the straight varietal Chenins and Sauvignons, and Tolaga Bay dry white, are all best drunk young; Semillon, Gewürztraminer and Riesling (especially the excellent honeyed, *Botrytis*-affected style) will last for a little longer.

Babich, Delegats and Nobilo produce good Chardonnay, Sauvignon, Semillon and blends (see **Gisborne, Hawke's Bay**). Nobilo's whites also include a very fresh, easy-drinking Müller-Thurgau [★/■■] – one of the few New Zealand wines to be sold under a "fantasy" label, White Cloud, instead of the usual varietal label – and a Fumé Blanc with quite a bit of oak. Selaks [★→★★/■■→■■■] produces straightforward Chardonnay, Sauvignon and Semillon.

Morton Estate [★→★★/■■→■■■] is based in the Bay of Plenty, not the best source of fruit, but it is relocating and beginning to use more Hawke's Bay fruit, so its excellent wines will get even better. The white label is the basic range, black label superior. Chardonnays edge towards a rather full and buttery Burgundian style, Fumé Blancs are improving as they become fruitier, and the *méthode champenoise* wines are attractive.

Martinborough Vineyard [★★/■■→■■■] further south in Wairarapa produces tiny quantites of extremely high quality wine: Chardonnay, Sauvignon Blanc, Gewürztraminer, Riesling, and even prize-winning Müller-Thurgau. Grapes are also planted in Northland, the island's most northerly region, but wine production here is tiny and quality ordinary.

THE SOUTH ISLAND The overnight discovery and rise to fame of Marlborough has triggered great interest in the northern part of the South Island, and this region alone is now widely regarded as *the* quality region of New Zealand (see **Marlborough**).

Elsewhere on the South Island, minuscule quantities of wine are produced in Nelson near Marlborough and in Central Otago, way down in the cold south. But the area that has shown most promise apart from Marlborough is Canterbury, which is just about at the sensible southern limit of viticulture. The long cool growing season suits Riesling extremely well, but Chardonnay and Müller-Thurgau are doing well too. Weingut Seifried [★★/■■] in Nelson and St Helena [★★/■■] in Canterbury are two of the top properties.

WHERE NEXT? See the specific entries on New Zealand wine styles: **Gisborne, Hawke's Bay** and **Marlborough**.

OLTREPO PAVESE

Just north of Genoa, four Italian wine regions converge: Liguria, Piedmont, Emilia-Romagna and Lombardy. A wide range of wine is produced here under the title Oltrepò Pavese (literally "over the Po from Pavia"). The DOC wines are made on the gently rounded hills rising above the Po river valley.

Varietals for white wines include Riesling, Cortese (as used in pricey Gavi), Moscato (making *spumante* on a par with Asti Spumante) and two Pinots – the white Pinot Grigio (see **Pinot Gris**) and the red Pinot Nero (Pinot Noir).

None of the white wines of this region has a classic reputation but it is worth seeking out Clastidium, made from a blend of Pinot Nero and Pinot Grigio. This has a rich velvety style and potential to develop in bottle for eight years or more. Good producers [★→★★/■■] include A Ballabi and Casteggio.

Also in Casteggio, Frecciarossa [★★/■■] produces a dry white wine with a hint of almond in the bouquet, made from Riesling and Pinot Nero. Tenuta Pegazzera [★★/■■■] makes quality wood-aged dry whites from Pinot and Riesling grapes. Santa Maria della Versa [★→★★/■■→■■■] is a major local co-operative known for quality still and *spumante* wines.

WHERE NEXT? Friuli-Venezia Giulia has a name for whites which, though Italian, have more to do with the European mainstream, as does the **Alto Adige**. Look around Italy in general for interesting **Chardonnays**, across the Alps to **Baden** for another approach to Pinot Grigio (there called Ruländer).

OREGON

This "green" state north of California has a hundred years of winemaking history to its credit, but it is only during the past 20 years that it has burst onto the world stage.

The vineyards here are on the same latitude as Bordeaux and shrouded in coastal fog in the evenings, with enough rain to ensure quality grapes. The cool growing season makes Riesling feel at home and there are also plantings of Chardonnay, Gewürztraminer, Semillon and Sauvignon Blanc. Like Monterey in California, this is a region where *Botrytis* can flourish and many wineries make late harvest wines from Riesling.

Another grape which flourishes is Pinot Gris, bringing fruity and fragrant flavours to the wine, with good balancing acidity. The Eyrie Vineyards [★★→★★★/■■■] makes good Chardonnay and Pinot Gris, as well as an unusual Pinot Meunier.

Other good Oregon producers [★★→★★★/■■■] include:

Adelsheim Vineyard	Sokol Blosser
Hillcrest Vineyard	Tualatin
Knudsen Erath	

WHERE NEXT? Washington's wines (see **United States**) are inextricably mingled with Oregon's, but the vineyards are very different: hot and dry, with more vivid flavours in the wines. **New Zealand**, an ocean away, has much in common with Oregon. And look to the **Côte d'Or** to see if Oregon's Chardonnays have emulated Burgundy successfully yet.

ORVIETO

The town of Orvieto, and its viticulture, date back to Etruscan times. It is a place of seductive charm and, over the years, its wine has gained a fame based mostly on packaging – the picturesque *fiasco* covered in raffia which was once the standard container.

The traditional Orvieto of Italian *trattoria* fame was sweetish and golden in colour with a honey tinge to the flavour. It made agreeable if unexciting drinking as a partner for food cooked with garlic and olive oil. This *abboccato* style was achieved by adding natural grape concentrate to a dry wine, a time-consuming process which today has been largely superseded by stainless steel fermentation and all the paraphernalia of modern technology.

The modern wine, made from around 65% Trebbiano, is clean and crisp but it lacks distinctive character and has a far paler colour. The famous Chianti house of Antinori makes a top-quality Orvieto [★★/■■→■■■]. Other good Orvieto producers to look for [★★/ ■■→■■■] include:

Bertolli	*Ricasoli*
Bigi	*Ruffino*
Centrale Cantine	

Other, smaller producers who are also well thought of [★→★★/■■] include Barberani, Lemmi and Conte Vaselli.

WHERE NEXT? Some of Italy's *vini da tavola* are more exciting, more modern, more international: try Lungarotti's Chardonnays, and Tuscan Predicato wines (see **Italy, Tuscany**).

PENEDES

This is the most important of Catalonia's small clutch of wine districts in north-east Spain, just down the coast from Barcelona. Styles vary from the traditional rich, raisiny, wine of Tarragona (much of it used to celebrate communion around the world), to sparkling wines, for this is where Spain's Cava wines are produced (see **Cava**).

THE PENEDES TASTE Cava's importance to the region ensures that considerably more white grapes than black are grown, but even without that, white wine production would exceed red. Producers have to work hard, however, to extract what little flavour the native grapes can pool together. International varieties are elbowing their way in, many still on an experimental basis.

The three principal native grape varieties – Macabeo, Xarel-lo and Parellada – are not among the world's tastiest. They generally grow best in the middle Penedès, away from the hot coastal strip. Macabeo (Rioja's Viura) produces rather neutral wine, no more than vaguely aromatic. Xarel-lo is a bit coarse but scores reasonably high on acidity. Parellada, the best of the three, thrives in the cooler, higher Penedès; with temperature-controlled fermentation in stainless steel, it can turn out fresh, zingy, lightly fruity wine.

CHOOSING PENEDES WINES Most wines are a blend of all three grape varieties, but Torres' Viña Sol [★/■■] is made from Parellada only. This wine loses its freshness remarkably quickly, so it is always advisable to drink a very recent vintage.

Of the international varieties, Chardonnay is making most head-way. Jean León produces a rich, oaky, California-style one [★★/■■■], and Torres' Milmanda [★★/■■■] is full and fat. Both err towards a slightly New Worldy, tropical fruit taste. Just outside Penedès, in Costers del Segre, the go-ahead firm of Raimat [★★/■■] makes excellent Chardonnay.

Torres is particularly adept at the game of blending Spanish and international varieties. Gran Viña Sol [★★/■■] combines Parellada and Chardonnay in a lightly spicy wine with more character and a rather longer life than straight Viña Sol.

Gewürztraminer and Muscat grapes, from Torres' vineyards in the high Penedès, produce attractively aromatic wines: Viña Esmerelda [★★/■■] is a soft, easy, approachable blend of the two, smelling of elderflowers. Waltraud [★★/■■] is made entirely from Riesling. Gran Viña Sol Green Label, now called Fransola [★★/■■], balances Parellada and Sauvignon Blanc with just enough oak to make it into a serious wine.

Other good producers [★→★★/■■], most of whom use native grape varieties, include:

Cavas Hill	Marqués de Monistrol
Celler Hisenda Miret,	Mont Marçal
Viña Toña	Mas Rabassa

Outside Penedès, but still within Catalonia, some of the best fresh whites come from Marqués de Alella [★→★★/■■] in the Alella DO. The two best producers [★→★★/■■] in Tarragona and Terra Alta are Pedro Rovira and de Muller, the latter of which makes an intriguing Moscatel Seco.

PENEDES WINE AND FOOD Catalan food is distinctive and varied, seafood figuring prominently. So most Penedès wines make excellent sparring partners for fish dishes and some, such as Torres' Gran Viña Sol are versatile companions for a wider range of food.

WHERE NEXT? Contrast the assured whites of Penedès with the rather more lumbering products of Corbières north of the Pyrenees, with **Rueda** and with the ''new-style'' whites of **Rioja**.

PIAVE

The Piave River, which rises in the foothills of the Alps and emerges at the Lido di Jesolo near Venice, gives its name to the large DOC zone on either side. To the east, the research station at Conegliano does fancy things with vines which seem to work, for the wines here are known for their quality.

Prosecco is the grape variety used for both still and sparkling wines, including some *méthode champenoise*. It makes a light, dry wine with a scent of apples and almonds; definitely a wine to be consumed within a year or two of its birth. As the sparkling wine is often made by the vat method, it can offer excellent value for such a dry and agreeable style. It is also quite low in alcohol, at around 10.5%. The wine's full title is Prosecco di Conegliano-Valdobbiadene and producers to look for [★→★★/■■] include:

De Bernard	Carpene-Malvoti
Cantina Sociale di	Cantina Sociale Colli del
Valdobbiadene	Soligo

The co-operatives make a full range of sparkling and still wines. A fine *méthode champenoise* is made by Cantine Sociale La Montelliana e dei Colli Asolani [★★/■■■].

Some Pinot Grigio (see **Pinot Gris**) may be used in the making of sparkling Prosecco, and this subtle grape is also bottled under its own name by the co-operatives of Piave [★/■■]. More interesting is the DOC wine Tocai del Piave (unrelated to the Tokay of Hungary or the Tokay d'Alsace). It has a pleasant floral yet ''green'' aroma – the best [★★/■■] are from C S Colli del Soligo and Bianchi Kunkler.

Sparkling Prosecco is a delightful aperitif, but tends to be overpowered by most food; if you must eat something with it, nibble some *antipasti*.

WHERE NEXT? Contrast the other Italian fizzes from Asti (see **Asti Spumante**) and the various Chardonnay-based ones from Lombardy and Piedmont. **Friuli-Venezia Giulia** and **Alto Adige** both make still whites; the best can be ahead of Piave.

PINEAU DES CHARENTES

This is the best known of a small group of drinks officially known as *ratafias* in France, made by adding spirit to unfermented grape juice. This prevents the juice from fermenting and retains all the grape sugar as sweetness; alcohol, which derives purely from the spirit, is normally around 18%. They are usually drunk as aperitifs.

In the Cognac region, where Pineau des Charentes is made, cognac is added. Producers [★→★★/■■→■■■] include Château de Beaulon, Landreau and Jules Robin. In nearby Gascony, armagnac is used, to make floc de Gascogne; in Champagne, marc de Champagne is added. Other versions are found in Burgundy and the Jura.

WHERE NEXT? After trying the various different *ratafias*, try either straight Cognac or Muscat de **Beaumes-de-Venise**.

PINOT BLANC

Pinot Blanc wine seems to have two rôles in life: as a sound if modest food wine; and as a base for sparkling wine, particularly in Italy. It is usually made dry, though is occasionally found in sweet blends.

Like Pinot Gris, it is a mutation of the red variety Pinot Noir, although neither of these white varieties challenges the imagination of winemakers or drinkers in the way their red cousin does. It is not related to Chardonnay, although there has been, and sometimes remains, confusion between the two. Walking through vineyards in northern Italy, it is often impossible to tell which variety is which. Even the owner doesn't know. The vines were planted long before the craze for varietal purity took hold, and both sorts grow side by side.

THE PINOT BLANC TASTE It is somehow easier to understand Pinot Blanc by describing what it is *not* like. It is not an aromatic variety: a certain neutrality is common to most examples. The taste, like a featureless rock face, does not offer many hand-holds. It does not, for example, shout nettles and blackcurrant leaves like Sauvignon Blanc, nor butter and oak like mature Chardonnay.

Pinot Blanc is quite content to turn out modest, unassuming, predominantly dry wines, of light to medium body and moderate acidity. Some, from cooler regions, are appley, maybe a little steely; others are more biscuitty; some are lightly spicy; many have a gently creamy feel to them. In this respect, some of the better Pinot Blancs may stand in for some of the less ambitious Chardonnays, but on the whole Pinot Blanc is simpler and less distinctively flavoursome. It is a wine to drink young, generally within a year or two of the vintage.

This may not amount to much razzle-dazzle, but at least Pinot Blanc delivers the goods with a fair degree of reliability. It should not be dismissed simply because of its unpretentious nature. If anything, it is a victim of "varietalism". You sometimes get the feeling that Pinot Blanc has had a varietal role thrust upon it.

BEGIN WITH ITALY Pinot Blanc has been grown in parts of northern Italy (where it is called Pinot Bianco) for a century and a half, and here it makes some of the liveliest Pinot Blanc wines in the world, in many cases helped by that unmistakeable Italian trademark, a touch of spritz.

The grape performs particularly well in Alto Adige, where it can be as crisp as a pippin (see **Alto Adige**). It does well, too, in Friuli-Venezia Giulia – particularly in Colli Orientali and Collio – and in the Veneto, especially in Breganze. Most interesting are those wines where Pinot Bianco has a walk-on part. One of the best is Jermann's expensive but stunning Vintage Tunina (see **Friuli-Venezia Giulia**).

Pinot does less well over in the north-west, where it appears in the Franciacorta DOC near Lake Iseo, but picks up slightly in the Colli Bolognesi of Emilia-Romagna.

It would take a very strange grape indeed – probably square, with pips on the outside – to prevent Italians from putting a sparkle in it. Pinot Bianco is particularly well qualified. Not only spherical, but also dry and relatively odour-free, it provides a foil for northern Italy's other, better-known fizz – sweet and smelly Moscato d'Asti (see **Asti Spumante**). Pinot Bianco is one of the components in the spumantes of Franciacorta and Oltrepò Pavese, and plays a part in what is perhaps Italy's finest sparkling wine, Ferrari's Metodo Classico [★★★/■■■] from Trentino.

OTHER PINOT BLANCS In Alsace, Pinot Blanc is less highly regarded than Pinot Gris – but we need something to drink from Monday to Friday, and much Alsace Pinot Blanc is perfectly acceptable for this purpose: it is straightforward, clean, dry, light- to medium-bodied, with middling to good acidity. Some will even improve in bottle over a couple of years. As in Italy, it shows fizz potential and is the main variety in Crémant d'Alsace (see **Alsace**).

In Germany, as Weissburgunder, it is dry and medium-bodied, in contrast to Germany's predominantly light, flowery and sweetened styles. Because of the moderate acidity very high must-weights can unbalance it, rendering it rich and rather flabby (see **Germany**).

Pinot Blanc spreads eastwards through Austria, where it can make quite rich wines, into Hungary, Czechoslovakia and Yugoslavia. Some is also made in California, where it competes successfully with higher-price Chardonnay (see **Austria**, **California**).

PINOT BLANC AND FOOD Pinot Blanc wines do not distract attention from food though they rarely enhance its flavour. Alsace varieties are good with hors d'oeuvres, *choucroute*, *bisques* and even with asparagus.

WHERE NEXT? The other white Pinot, **Pinot Gris**, is an interesting next step, and more unusual; or try **Chardonnay** to see why it is supposed to be better.

PINOT GRIS

This variant of Pinot Noir is widespread throughout Europe, though it constitutes only a small proportion of wine production. Everything about it suggests inconstancy and variability: it goes under different names, can be difficult to grow, and makes different styles of wine. It is called Tokay in Alsace – but it is not the grape that makes Tokay in Hungary, nor is it Italy's Tocai, nor yet does it have anything to do with the wine Australians call Tokay. In Italy it is called Pinot Grigio, in Germany Ruländer or Grauburgunder, in Switzerland Malvoisie de Valais, and in Hungary Szürkebarát.

Usually dry, Pinot Gris wines may be deep-coloured or light and tinged with delicate pink, the berries themselves varying from pink to brown to grey to blue. It is one of the less reliable grape varieties to grow – yields can see-saw alarmingly – and is rather demanding in terms of soil and climate. But the attraction of Pinot Gris for the drinker is this very variability: it takes on a different character depending on where it is made.

THE PINOT GRIS TASTE Pinot Gris does not have a distinctive smell like Muscat or Sauvignon Blanc; it is not an aromatic variety. But it can make up for this in taste, providing that yields are kept reasonably low, because it is rich in "extract" – those components, usually derived from grape skins, that produce fullness of body and flavour in a wine.

Richness of texture, rather than finesse or subtlety, typifies Pinot Gris. Its moderate to low acidity is regarded by some as a virtue and by others as a handicap to be overcome. In most cases the wine is dry. The current fashion for Pinot Gris might have something to do with the fact that all these traits add up to a splendid partner for food.

BEGIN WITH ALSACE Pinot Gris is rightly regarded as one of the best wines of Alsace, although it accounts for only about 5% of the region's production. Here it is often rich, full-bodied, round and smooth. The texture is what appeals more than any distinctive varietal flavour, although there may be hints of smokiness in some, broad honey flavours and butteriness in others. In a laudable attempt to simplify labelling terms, the EEC has stipulated that the alternative name Tokay d'Alsace be forfeited. This has met with strong opposition in Alsace, where centuries of tradition count for more than a bureaucratic edict, but wines must now be labelled either Tokay-Pinot Gris or simply Pinot Gris (see **Alsace**).

OTHER PINOT GRIS Northern Italy's Pinot Grigio often tastes more of Italy than it does of Pinot Gris. Light- to medium-bodied, delicately perfumed, fresh, with a slightly nutty flavour and a prickle to keep it lively, it is a far cry from the heavier-handed Alsatian style. Early-picking ensures good acidity, but the grape skins barely get a chance to ripen, so the "extract" is often low. The best and broadest are made in Friuli – specifically in Collio, Colli Orientali and Grave del Friuli – and the crispest in Alto Adige (see **Friuli-Venezia Giulia, Alto Adige**).

In Germany, where it is also called Grauburgunder, Pinot Gris produces unusually full-bodied wines by German standards. They are generally soft, and the best come from Baden (see **Baden**).

Passing through France, and making an attractive Malvoisie d'Ancenis [★→★★/■■] in the Loire, Pinot Gris appears in Luxembourg and Switzerland, where very ripe grapes can produce a sweet version. Thence to Austria, Yugoslavia, Czechoslovakia, Romania and Hungary, whose late-picked, deep-coloured, honeyed Szürkebarát is one of the grape's richest manifestations (see **Hungary**).

In spite of its European success, Pinot Gris has not been taken up enthusiastically in the New World, although it is grown successfully in the north-west of America (see **Oregon**).

PINOT GRIS AND FOOD The absence of a powerfully aromatic and distinctive smell gives Pinot Gris a lot of leeway as a partner for food. It does not impose a flavour that has to be carefully matched. What does need to be matched, though, is its style and weight. Alto Adige wines make good aperitifs that can continue some way into a meal; the broader style of Friuli will take slightly more substantial foods. Alsace wines positively demand substance. In Alsace itself, this can mean anything from chicken dishes, Flammeküche and Bäckehoffe (a stew of pork, mutton and beef) to its most prestigious partner, *foie gras.*

WHERE NEXT? Pinot Grigio from **Alto Adige** and **Friuli-Venezia Giulia** can be followed up by virtually any other local varietal, since the wines all express something of their region of origin. If you develop a taste for the big, dry **Alsace** style, Alsatians would consider that you can go no further, with the possible exception of finding a **Riesling** of similar status. However, the rich butteriness that such Pinot Gris displays is reminiscent of good **Chardonnay** and **Sémillon** (preferably un-oaked) after they have been aged in bottle – but with more zip from higher acidity.

PORT

White port is a curious drink – made, one suspects, just to show that it can be done. The first duty of port, after all, is to be red. It is made from white grape varieties (Malvasia Fina and Malvasia Grossa) and comes dry to medium-sweet, medium- to full-bodied, and just as alcoholic as red port. It is made in the same way, by stopping the fermentation with alcohol, though this usually takes place later than with red port so as to produce a drier wine.

Its function, up the Douro, is to provide a brief respite between the last lingering traces of lunchtime's tawny, and the first real wine of the evening. As an aperitif, with cubes of ice, it discharges the responsibility well enough. But even the most charitable view would hardly credit it with anything like the character of sherry or Madeira. It has a slightly woolly and indistinct flavour, not shot through with a streak of tingling acidity, not bursting with the exciting flavour of a distinctive grape variety, not matured for decades into something dark and interesting. The best should be served with a twist of lemon; the rest need a sparkle to bring them to life.

The best producers [★/■■→■■■] include:

Burmester	Fonseca (Siroco)
Cockburn	Sandeman
Dow	Taylors (Chip Dry)

Try a dry white port as nature intended, or with tonic, ice and lemon. Then another. Then it will be dinner time.

WHERE NEXT? Move up to **Sherry** for more character, or try a chilled tawny port instead.

PORTUGAL

What works for Portuguese red wines should in theory work for whites: native grape varieties that no other country has ever heard of, and couldn't pronounce if it had, producing a unique range of flavours. But somehow it doesn't quite happen; the whites fall some way behind the reds. Few have the four-square fruit flavour, and they rarely develop into exciting wines as they mature.

After Vinho Verde (see **Vinho Verde**), the best known and most distinctive Portuguese white is Setúbal, a fortified wine of 15-16% alcohol whose fermentation is stopped by the addition of spirit, leaving natural grape sugar to provide the sweetness. It is made largely from the Moscatel grape, which is the Muscat of Alexandria, not the finer, more aromatic and floral Muscat à Petits Grains (see **Muscat**). The result is more liquorous and raisiny than floral.

However, J M da Fonseca & Successores [★★/■■], which makes the lion's share of Setúbal, livens up the flavour by macerating the wine on the grape skins for several months before transferring it to barrel for ageing. There are two principal versions: a vintage wine and a 20-year-old which takes the raisiny taste and makes it more intense and concentrated; this is a smoky, after-dinner wine to drink with a bowl of nuts. Both of these wines are ready for drinking as soon as they are bottled.

Among ordinary-strength table wines, Fonseca's Quinta de Camarate [★★/■■] white is a delightfully aromatic blend of Riesling and Moscatel, with a little Gewürztraminer to back them up. A dry Moscatel is also made nearby: João Pires White [★★/■→■■] is just the sort of leafy green, fresh, grapey style you would expect from an Australian let loose among the vineyards; it becomes lightly honeyed as it ages. João Pires's Catarina [★★/■■] is made largely from the Fernão Pires grape (no relation) into a rich, glyceriney, smoky, resiny wine that needs five years to mature.

The slightly minty, peppery, resiny Fernão Pires is also used in Ribatejo, where Casa Agrícola Herdeiros de Dom Luis de Margaride [★/■■] and the Almeirim Co-operative [★/■■] are the best producers. It crops up too in Torres Vedras and Alenquer in Oeste, playing second fiddle to the Vital grape; the best producers here [★/■■] include Quinta da Folgorosa, the Torres Vedras Co-op and Quinta de Abrigada.

Some of the more interesting dry table wines come from the Douro, where a mixture of native and imported varieties are used. Among the best [★→★★/■■] are Sogrape's Planalto (made chiefly from the Viosinho grape), Champalimaud's Quinta do Côtto (made from Malvasia and Avesso) and Raposeira's big buttery Chardonnay.

Dão whites can have a sharp, crisp bite to them when young, but they fill out with age into a fuller, fatter resiny style. Caves Aliança [★/■■] have a finger in the Dão pie, but the most modern wine from here is Grão Vasco [★★/■■], made by the Tazem Co-operative in conjunction with Sogrape.

In Alentejo some sound but ordinary wines are made from the Roupeiro grape. Herdade do Esporão, and Co-operatives at Reguengos, Vidigueira and Redondo are among the leading producers [★/■■]. Bairrada's reputation for whites rests equally on still and sparkling wines, the best producers [★/■■] being Caves Aliança and Luis Pato.

Bucelas, Portugal's only all-white *Região Demarcada* (or demarcated wine region) is made from the Arinto grape, which some consider to be the country's great white hope. It produces rich, medium- to full-bodied wines with a distinct and crisp lemony freshness that develops into a nutty, resinous maturity. Caves Velhas [★/■■] is the traditional producer, Quinta do Avelar [★/■■] the promising newcomer.

Portugal's sparklers compare favourably with Spanish Cava. Almost all are made by the Champagne method, though there is some gas-injected fizz. Fonseca's wines (including Lancer's) are made by the "Russian continuous" method, unique in western Europe, whereby the wine is moved slowly through a series of pressurized tanks. Bairrada is the centre of production. The fruity Maria Gomes and Arinto grapes predominate. The best examples [★★/■■] are made by Caves Aliança, Caves São João, Luis Pato, João Pires and Raposeira.

WHERE NEXT? See the specific entries on Portuguese wine styles: **Madeira**, **Port** and **Vinho Verde**.

PROVENCE

In a way, perhaps we should be glad that Provence doesn't make really good white wines. If you walk into a restaurant on the Côte d'Azur and see the prices they charge for plain ordinary whites, it doesn't bear thinking what they would charge for something special.

In fact less than 10% of Provence's output is white, most of it uninspiring, and the good stuff is confined to some very small *appellations* and properties. Perhaps the general lack of star quality owes something to the mundane grapes: Clairette and Ugni Blanc (see **Trebbiano**), with some Sémillon for luck and the local Rolle. Most wines seem, miraculously, to have escaped stainless steel and temperature-controlled fermentation, so fresh fruit flavours are conspicuous by their absence.

So although the AC Côtes de Provence covers thousands of acres, only a few of those acres produce wine worth seeking out. One of the best is Domaine Ott, whose excellent Clos Mireille [★★/■■] seems to carry the tang of salt off the sea and a whiff of the pines among which it is made. Other reliable producers [★★/■■] are:

Commanderie de Peyrassol	Maîtres Vignerons de
l'Estandon	St-Tropez
Domaine Gavoty	Richeaume
Les Hauts de St-Jean	

In Coteaux d'Aix en Provence, look for Château de Seuil [★/■■] and the good-value Château de Fonscolombe [★/■].

Château Simone [★→★★/■■■] is the only white wine producer in the 37-acre (15 ha) bijou AC Palette, and it makes an attractive herby job given the handicap of the raw materials.

Cassis is a small fishing village between Toulon and Marseille. Given the beautiful view and a plateful of fresh fish, the crisp wine can be wonderful; take them away and it can be less than wonderful. The best producer is Clos Ste-Magdelaine [★★/■■].

Anyone who collects wines made from odd grape varieties should have a bottle of Bellet in their collection. Châteaux de Crémat and de Bellet are the best producers [★/■■→■■■].

Provence wines are obvious accompaniments for anything fishy, and especially for *bouillabaisse*.

WHERE NEXT? **Vins de Pays** and the obscurer Midi *appellations* can give Provence quite a shock when it comes to well-made whites: La Clape is an example (see **Coteaux du Languedoc**).

RETSINA

Most people's experience of Greece's best-known wine is confined to holidays, when it is drunk merely out of curiosity. There is nothing else quite like it in the wine world, and so it is viewed either with suspicion – if it were any good, surely other countries would want to make a wine like it – or else with a defensive smirk, as if it might be a Greek joke perpetrated on tourists: did you hear the one about the mother-in-law and the bottle of retsina? In fact white retsina is not a bad drink, at least not as bad as many people make out.

THE RETSINA TASTE The taste is of Aleppo pine resin, originally used as a kind of internal glazing or seal for the amphorae in which the wine was stored. Although the resin's prime job was to prevent the wine from seeping out, it also minimized contact with air and thus kept the wine fresher. In time, resin was added as a matter of course, in the belief that it was the resin itself that kept wines fresh, and by then the Greeks had lived with the taste long enough to learn to enjoy it. Nowadays the resin is added during fermentation, purely for flavour.

The main asset of the resin flavour is its refreshing quality. Another resin, mastic, is used to make an Egyptian ice-cream called *dondurma kaymakli*, which is the most refreshing ice-cream in the world. And some air-fresheners are jazzed up to smell like pine. So it is not just acidity that makes wine taste fresh: a slight prickle on the tongue can do the same, as in Vinho Verde for example; a slight bitterness, as in Italy, can achieve a similar lively effect. Resin is just another, though rarer, way of livening up what might otherwise be a rather dull and slightly flabby wine from a hot country.

If the combination of wood flavour with wine strikes us as odd, then we should remember the classic partnership of Chardonnay and oak: different grape, different wood, but similar principle – except that retsina is best drunk as young as possible.

Retsina cuts through oily moussaka, mingles appetizingly with the whiff of barbecued meat, and after a nip of *ouzo* and a chunk of octopus you could be positively crying out for it. If the taste of retsina is too powerful, chill the wine; chilled retsina makes a bright and breezy thirstquencher after a day on the beach.

The best producers [★→★★/■→■■] include Attiki and Metaxas.

WHERE NEXT? If the retsina taste seems rather shocking at first, then we should acclimatize by drinking either a heavily oaked Chardonnay from **California** or **Australia**, or else a heavily wooded **Rioja** such as Lopez de Heredia's Viña Tondonia. Try also some of the more serious wines from **Greece** or **Portugal**.

RHEINGAU

For many drinkers the greatest German wines come from the 20-mile long, south-westward-flowing stretch of the River Rhine between Wiesbaden and Rüdesheim. The slope of the Rheingau vineyards, facing due south, is broader and gentler than the best sites in the Mosel. The 50th parallel, the same that touches southern England, runs through one of its most famous vineyards, Schloss Johannisberg. Yet the ripeness of the grapes in very good years is remarkable, helped by the reflection of the sun off the river, straight onto the vines.

THE RHEINGAU TASTE Riesling, of course, is the grape variety that counts, producing wines that blossom into fullness and smooth, plump, ripe, rounded maturity from the grapes' long, warm growing season. Yet the wines still have that characteristic and stubborn Riesling quality of refusing to go limp and flabby. Their minerally acidity is the engine-room, the power-house that drives them forward, kicking them into life; the spirit that animates the body.

These are wines flowing with fruit and honey, but the best, while intense and concentrated, are never too obvious or generous; they tease with the spicy promise of something more. No German wine is really big enough to qualify as a meal in itself, but Rheingau Rieslings are laid out like an elegant buffet that provides a complete and balanced diet. Only when we get to the *Beerenauslesen* and *Trockenbeerenauslesen* do the peaches and cream pile on such luxury and opulence that we wonder guiltily if we are having too much of a good thing.

CHOOSING RHEINGAU WINES Bereich Johannisberg covers the whole Rheingau, and by Bereich standards these wines can be reasonably good. But one cannot avoid the impression that they are mostly leftovers from the lordly table. It is better to take a proper seat and enjoy the best wines for their style and individuality.

The Charta group comprises 38 top-class Rheingau producers who share a common and easily recognizable symbol (a double Romanesque arch), yet whose wines are totally individual. Their message is that you can trust the symbol, so there is no need for anxiety about the quality, but you will not get pap or anonymity. Far from it. You will get some of Germany's top wines, and they will be dry. Indeed they are rather austere in youth – good Riesling needs time to develop its complexity and harmony – but be patient, this is the real thing.

Regional names to look for include Hochheim (whence the unspecific derivative English term Hock for more or less anything from the Rhine), Rauenthal, Eltville, Erbach (especially Marcobrunn vineyard), Hattenheim (with its excellent Steinberg vineyard), Oestrich (Lenchen vineyard), Winkel (Hasensprung and Schloss Vollrads vineyards), Johannisberg (Schloss Johannisberg vineyard) and Rüdesheim.

The best producers [★★ → ★★★ / ■■ → ■■■] include:

Aschrott	*Schloss Groenesteyn*
Becker	*Schloss Johannisberg*
Breuer	*Schloss Reinhartshausen*
Erben	*Schloss Schönborn*
Eser	*Schloss Vollrads*
von Mumm'sches	*Langwerth von Simmern*
Nägler	*Staatsweingut Eltville*
von Ötinger	*Wegeler-Deinhard*
Balthasar Ress	

The best Rheingau vintages include 1988, 85, 83, 79, 76 and 75.

RHEINGAU WINE AND FOOD Rheingau wines complement food well. Try some of the drier ones with a selection of cold meats, pork dishes or *Rheinischer Sauerbraten* – a pot roast of marinated beef.

WHERE NEXT? Cross to the **Rheinhessen** and beyond to the **Nahe** for earthier, more robust versions of the Rheingau taste. Better still, compare Rheingau Rieslings with Mosels (see **Mosel-Saar-Ruwer**) – lighter, less intense, more floral – and then with **Alsace** Riesling – heavier and stronger, but on the whole drier.

RHEINHESSEN

Some of Germany's most famous, and infamous, wine is produced in this rather amorphous region south of the Rheingau. Along with its soft, flowery Rieslings, the Rheinhessen produces some 55% of Germany's Liebfraumilch (see **Liebfraumilch**).

It is the home of Nierstein, a much borrowed moniker that shows just how cock-eyed the German Wine Law can be. Nierstein is a Rhineside village, in whose name wines as diverse as Niersteiner Hölle and Niersteiner Gutes Domtal are produced; the first a small vineyard of some 14 acres (5.5 ha), the latter applying to the produce of no less than 15 villages scattered to the west. So much for Teutonic precision.

How on earth we are supposed to know, or guess, whether a name refers to one particular vineyard or several very different ones is obviously something the German authorities couldn't care tuppence about. Furthermore, Bereich Nierstein covers about a third of the output of the whole of Rheinhessen. Too much Nierstein is called Nierstein for the producer's benefit, for marketing reasons, rather than on grounds of style or quality. The trouble is that the junk obscures our view of the good stuff. No wonder we scream for the simplicity of "RS" or "Riesling Dry" wines.

THE RHEINHESSEN TASTE When Rheinhessen wines are made from Riesling, and from a specific vineyard site or *Einzellage* (ideally beside the river in what is becoming known as the Rhein Terrase or Rheinfront), then they can have a flower-like fragrance and a beguiling, sunny softness that is denied to their nearest cousins in the Rheingau, yet be on a par with some of them for quality. Those from Bingen, opposite Rüdesheim, are closest to the Rheingau in style. Many can reach a refined and classy maturity. There is nothing brash or breezy about Rheinhessen Rieslings; mildness and softness are the keynotes.

When the wines are made from Müller-Thurgau or Silvaner, they will very likely appear (perhaps disappear is more appropriate) as bland Bereich Nierstein or Liebfraumilch, although the best producers can make them sing. New grape crossings tend to provide more interest than distinction.

CHOOSING RHEINHESSEN WINES Regional names to look for include the villages of Oppenheim, Nierstein and Bingen, with those of Nackenheim and Bodenheim in the second rank. The best producers [★★/■■ → ■■■] include:

Braun	*Gunderloch-Usinger*
Anton Balbach Erben	*Louis Guntrum*
Carl Koch Erben	*Freiherr Heyl zu Herrnsheim*
Dahlem Erben	*Rappenhof*
Gessert	*Villa Sachsen*

It is also well worth seeking out the dry RS (Rheinhessen Silvaner) wines, with their simple black and yellow labels. Over a hundred winemakers have joined forces in the region's stab at linking itself with a plain but sound everyday varietal.

RHEINHESSEN WINE AND FOOD These wines do not stake a claim to any particular form of food. However, a glass of Rheinhessen can be pleasant with ham.

WHERE NEXT? See **Rheingau** or **Rheinpfalz** for variations in the Rhine style, **Franken** for a drier German taste, **Alto Adige** for more spirit and brio with Riesling, or **Austria** for a similar rustic style with more depth and less sugar.

RHEINPFALZ

The gentle, ripe, plump-fruited, soothing style continues south from Rheinhessen into the rolling Rheinpfalz, where Riesling wines take on a more exotic and tropical character. They are worlds away from the crisp Mosel, as are the vineyards: instead of steep and unforgiving slate there are great tracts of rich agricultural land.

While Rheinpfalz Rieslings may lack the grandeur of Rheingau wines, they share something of their fullness. If anything, they build a bridge with the generous spiced mango flavours of some New World Rieslings. The best of them are still stamped with the hallmark of acidity, although instead of catapulting the wine forward with drive and power, it often just hitches a lift. The wines are benign, open-hearted, and the richer ones lazily honeyed.

Other grape varieties do well here too. Like Rheinhessen, Rheinpfalz is Liebfraumilch country, producing some 42% of German output, and the principal ingredient is usually Müller-Thurgau. Of the new crossings, Kerner, Morio-Muskat and particularly Scheurebe are in the forefront and often strikingly aromatic.

Village names to look for are exclusively in the northern half, in Bereich Mittelhaardt/Deutsche Weinstrasse: Wachenheim, Forst, Deidesheim, Bad Dürkheim. Among the best Rheinpfalz producers [★★→★★★/■■→■■■] are the following:

Bassermann-Jordan	Müller-Catoir
Biffar	Ökonomierat Rebholz
Bürklin-Wolf	Pfeffingen
Johannes Karst	Reichsrat von Buhl
Köhler-Ruprecht	Wegeler-Deinhard
Lingenfelder	Wolf-Erben
Mosbacher	

Rheinpfalz wines will happily accompany a wide range of different pork dishes and they combine well with the more difficult vegetables such as artichoke and asparagus.

WHERE NEXT? Try **Rheingau** for the classics – Rheinpfalz never quite manages the same class. **Alsace**, across the Franco-German border, offers a different philosophy. To take the style even further, try **Australian** and **California** Riesling.

New Zealand's interesting Rieslings owe something to Rhine tradition – but they are made with riper grapes.

RHONE

The Rhône Valley is predominantly red wine country. Although 80% of all France's AC wine is made between Vienne at the top end of the northern Rhône, and Avignon in the south, only 4% of it is white. The most interesting wines come, and in only the tiniest of quantities, from the steeply terraced vineyards of the north. Because of this some of them are very expensive.

THE RHONE TASTE The grape varieties are unusual. There is none of Burgundy's buttery Chardonnay; no incisive, aromatic Loire whoosh of Sauvignon Blanc; no rich, honeyed Sémillon such as we might find in Bordeaux. Instead there is shy, musky Viognier; delicately flavoured Roussanne; powerful, alcoholic Marsanne; and bland, barley-sugary Clairette.

As a group, the wines are rather short on bold definition. Many of them are dullish, matt flavours that we have to go in and yank out by the collar, or else be patient and sit outside the bottle for decades until they are ready. Only in a very few instances will our faces light up with wonder and delight.

BEGIN WITH CHATEAUNEUF-DU-PAPE OR LIRAC You could, I suppose, begin with Côtes-du-Rhône, or better still Côtes-du-Rhône-Villages, because they are not expensive. But frankly, many of them are not worth the candle. Why not begin instead with a wine that shows a bit more character?

White Châteauneuf-du-Pape is not exactly cheap, but since only 2% of the entire Châteauneuf production is white (amounting to an output of less than 250,000 bottles a year), the pressure of demand is on. The grape varieties include Clairette, Roussanne, Grenache Blanc and Bourboulenc among others, some of which are used to make red Châteauneuf-du-Pape too.

It is stainless steel and temperature-controlled fermentation that have brought these wines to life. Not only are they now made fresh and crisp, but they also draw out intense fruit flavours varying from apple and quince to pineapple and peach, including the peach kernel as well.

For freshness they are best drunk young, but age will round them out and increase the kernelly nutty flavours. The best Châteauneuf producers [★★/■■■] include:

Beaucastel	*Nalys*
Font-de-Michelle	*Vieux Télégraphe*
Mont-Redon	

Lirac, better known for red and rosé, makes a very similar style of white to Châteauneuf, which is also best drunk young to make the most of the fresh fruit. The best producers here [★★/■■] include:

J Assemat	*Segries*
Maby	*Testut*

OTHER RHONE WINES Côtes-du-Rhône whites too often lack any sort of fresh, crisp attack; they are best drunk young, simply because they are not going anywhere interesting. Côtes-du-Rhône-Villages, made from Clairette, Roussanne and Bourboulenc, has a lower yield, and is therefore fuller-bodied with a bit more concentration and flavour, plus an extra degree of alcohol, bringing it up to 12%. The great thing to be said in favour of the relative neutrality of these wines is that they don't get in the way of other flavours when they are drunk with food.

Very occasionally, somebody will pick early and ferment at a cool temperature to get some kick into it. Duboeuf [★★/■■] is a prime example; the wine is a delight, but nothing at all like traditional Côtes-du-Rhône. Chusclan, Laudun and Rasteau are the best village names to look for. Co-operatives abound (there are 65) and some of them, such as the Cave des Vignerons de Rasteau [★→★★/■■] produce a decent top wine. Look also for individual producers' names [★★/■■] like Jaboulet Aîné and Guigal.

The white wines of the northern Rhône are different. Quality is generally much higher and, in spite of the tiny output of Condrieu and Château-Grillet, quantity is up too: a quarter of all Hermitage is white (see **Hermitage** and **Condrieu & Château-Grillet**).

The Rhône's other white wines of note are either sweet or sparkling. The sweet wines include some of France's best *vins doux naturels* (see **Beaumes-de-Venise** and **Vin Doux Naturel**). Among the sparklers is St-Péray, a dry *méthode champenoise* blend of Marsanne and Roussanne from the northern Rhône; good producers [★★/■■→■■■] include Cave des Vignerons de St-Péray, Paul-Etienne Père et Fils and J F Chaboud.

Another good sparkler, Clairette de Die, comes in two styles: a dry *méthode champenoise* and a much more exciting *demi-sec cuve close* called Clairette de Die Tradition, made from Clairette and Muscat grapes with a taste half-way to Asti Spumante. Reliable producers [★→★★/■■] include Archard-Vincent, Cave Coopérative de Clairette de Die, Albert Andrieux and Buffardel Frères.

RHONE WINE AND FOOD Dry Rhône wines will be overpowered by rich sauces and strongly flavoured dishes; on the other hand, they won't steal the show from less pronounced foods. Good accompaniments are mild cheeses, delicate patés and veal.

WHERE NEXT? If you take to the Rhône taste, the whole New World is open for experiment: start, perhaps, with **California**. Closer, **Rioja** offers two styles: oaked and unoaked, with a similar hot-sun, stony-soil provenance. And search among the **Vins de Pays** of nearby regions for gems like the Chardonnay from the Ardèche.

RIESLING

It may seem surprising, but many people consider Riesling to be the world's most aristocratic white grape variety. Yes, they even put it above Chardonnay. Surprising – because it is Chardonnay, not Riesling, that makes such noble Burgundian wines as Puligny-Montrachet and Corton-Charlemagne; surprising – because it is Chardonnay, and not Riesling, that winemakers around the world love to make, that drinkers clamour for, that the press writes about.

There is nothing strange, though, about wanting to put Riesling at the top of tree. It makes magnificent wines in Germany along the Rhine and Mosel, culminating in rich, sweet, yet sometimes ethereally light wines with very, very long names. It has travelled to America, and to Australia and New Zealand. It is versatile, making wines that vary from very dry to very sweet. It can mature wonderfully well in bottle, developing intriguing scents and flavours over a decade or two. And it will match a great variety of foods; certainly more than Chardonnay.

THE RIESLING TASTE The styles of Riesling vary enormously, depending on how and where the wine is made. Even a fairly simple quaffer from Australia, however, will impress with its balance, depth, length and stylish flourish for the price. The grape produces complex wine that delights with its apparent contradictions.

Riesling is an aromatic variety, although its wines are rarely as pungent as Muscat or Gewürztraminer. Generally light- to medium-bodied, even rich and sweet wines can retain a feeling of lightness and freshness, thanks to a streak of acidity that is one of the grape's great characteristics. When grapes of most varieties approach maturity, their natural sugar level rises and acidity decreases. Riesling grapes, however, are capable of maturing further; unusually, as sweetness increases, acidity remains more or less stable. Even Riesling wines made from late-picked grapes, therefore, can taste very fresh.

When the grapes are affected by *Botrytis*, the fungus that shrivels the grape concentrates the sugar and the acidity. The balance between the two remains, so that even rich *beerenauslese* and *trockenbeerenauslese* wines are not cloying.

Riesling spans the sweetness scale from top to bottom. Dry Riesling is made by fermenting out all the sugar and bottling the result, while sweetness comes about in one of two ways. The most natural way is to leave some unfermented grape sugar in the wine; this is usually what happens in the case of *Beerenauslesen* and above (see **Germany**) and in the best New World late-harvest wines. It is the concentration of sugar brought about by *Botrytis* that makes this possible. This produces the most luscious and voluptuous styles of Riesling.

The second way of making the wine sweet is a short cut. Sweetness is added, normally in the form of unfermented grape juice or *süssreserve* of a similar quality or must-weight to the fully fermented wine. It has the advantage of rendering thin, acidic wines more palatable; the sweetness masks acidity and rounds out the wine, giving it more apparent body. This is how most medium-dry, medium-sweet and sweet Rieslings are made, including *kabinett*, *spätlese* and *auslese* wines (see **Germany**). Convention has it that sweetness increases in line with initial must-weight: so an *Auslese* will generally be sweeter than a *Kabinett*. But Germany's new wave of *trocken* and *halbtrocken* Rieslings now make it possible to choose between, for example, a dry *Auslese* and a medium-sweet *Kabinett*. Fortunately, labels give a clear indication when a wine is *trocken* or *halbtrocken*.

What is really remarkable about Riesling is the complexity of aromas and tastes that can develop. At its plainest it has a grassy, herby smell, but many wines are reminiscent of apricots, honey and nuts too. Richer and more mature wines take on a petrolly or kerosene smell; some become pleasantly cheesy.

Riesling has tremendous capacity for ageing; the better the wine, the longer it will last. The key to its ageing is its ever-present acidity, because high acid levels promote the development of complexity. Late-picked Rieslings deepen in colour with age and emerge with layers of flavour.

BEGIN WITH GERMANY Riesling is the great grape of Germany. It makes all styles from *trocken* (dry) wines to very sweet *Eisweine*. The quality scale, which runs from *Tafelwein* through QbA to QmP wines (see **Germany**), is based on the initial must-weight. But this can be manipulated during winemaking to produce a relatively drier or sweeter end result.

Trocken wines can seem rather austere until you acquire a taste for them; *halbtrocken* wines are probably a better place to begin if you are looking for a dry-ish Riesling. Dry QbA wines are particularly austere, so the extra weight of, for example, a *Spätlese* is more approachable. *Kabinetten* are dry or dryish natural (unsugared) wines of distinct personality and distinguishing lightness. *Spätlesen* are stronger, more full-bodied and often sweeter than *Kabinetten*; they are most often sweet, but dry *Spätlesen* are on the increase. *Auslesen* are sweeter and sometimes stronger than *Spätlesen*, often with honey-like flavours. *Beerenauslesen* are very sweet, intense and usually strong. *Trockenbeerenauslesen* are intensely sweet and aromatic. *Eisweine* are concentrated, sharpish and very sweet.

(See **Baden, Franken, Mosel-Saar-Ruwer, Nahe, Rheingau, Rheinhessen** and **Rheinpfalz**.)

OTHER RIESLINGS Alsace, across the border into France, makes excellent Rieslings, generally in a drier style than Germany, and with greater alcoholic strength (see **Alsace**).

Austria makes Rieslings in equivalent styles to Germany, from *trocken* through to *trockenbeerenauslese*, with an extra category called *ausbruch*. The best can compare with those of Germany (see **Austria**). Further to the east, Riesling is grown with varying degrees of success in Hungary, Romania, Bulgaria and Yugoslavia (see **Hungary, Romania, Bulgaria** and **Yugoslavia**).

In the New World, straight Riesling will generally be dry or medium-dry, though an increasing number of sweet to very sweet late harvest and *Botrytis* versions are now made (see **California, Australia** and **New Zealand**).

RIESLING AND FOOD Riesling wines are remarkably versatile and can match a greater range of food than, say, Chardonnay wines; try a rich *Spätlese* with duck or goose, or a *Trocken* with chicken. But they really come into their own with puddings, especially apple strudel. It would be difficult to better a *Beerenauselese* with *crème brûlée*.

WHERE NEXT? Having followed Riesling around the world, look at **Silvaner**, which can, in the right place, be equally fine; or try comparable styles of **Chenin Blanc** from the Loire.

RIOJA

Spain's white Rioja runs the whole spectrum from crisply refreshing new-style wines to traditional heavily oaked ones. Both styles can be delightful, and both can throw up duffers.

The major grape variety is Viura, known elsewhere in Spain as Macabeo. It is a gift to makers of the new style: high yielding with good lemony, grapefruit acidity, making the most of stainless steel fermentation to produce light if undistinguished wines. The problem at the moment is that Riojas lose their major asset, freshness, very quickly. If you don't catch them within a year, some of them are hardly worth drinking.

The other grape varieties are Garnacha Blanca, which turns into a heavy, plodding wine with more alcohol than flavour, and Malvasia, which has more subtlety and apricot-kernel character, but which does not yield very highly and oxidizes easily. Rioja producers have got the message that the world wants crisp fresh wine all right; but the world also wants it to taste of something interesting.

The future of white Rioja begins to look a bit iffy: only relatively few committed producers bother with Malvasia in a blend, and only a few wines perform at star level. But the ones that do are a clear indication that white Rioja could have an astonishingly bright future if only more producers followed suit.

Among the best of the zippily-fresh, unoaked wines are those from the trail-blazing Marqués de Cáceres [★★/■■], Viña Cumbrero [★★/■■] from Montecillo, and those from the hi-tech Martinez-Bujanda [★★/■■]. Do drink the youngest vintage available of Marqués de Cáceres, although the Martinez-Bujanda wines, which are a blend of Viura and Malvasia, will last rather better.

In the middle are wines that are still rather on the neutral side, but have enough oak-ageing to give them some body and a light creamy vanilla quality; the oaking is not overdone, so they are still balanced by the freshness. These [★→★★/■■] include:

CVNE, Monopole	Olarra, Añares
Bodegas Riojanas, Monte Real	Franco-Española, Diamante

At the other extreme are such classics as Marqués de Murrieta [★★★/■■→■■■] and López de Heredia Viña Tondonia [★★★/■■■]. Murrieta positively bounces with energy; the fresh lemon is as rich as lemon curd spread on thick butter, there is a hint of pine and plenty of body to stand up to the new oak flavours. This wine resembles nothing so much as good Burgundy or one of the better New World Chardonnays. Murrieta's Castillo Ygay Reserva [★★★/■■■] ages magnificently; Tondonia's Reserva [★★★/■■■] is more restrained and spicy, but equally long-lived.

Heavily oak-aged Rioja can take on most food and win handsomely, as shown by its local partnership with culinary delights such as cod cooked in olive oil, garlic and red pepper or *chorizo*, a spicy cured pepper sausage.

WHERE NEXT? For the light, fresh style try the **Loire** or northern Italy (see **Alto Adige** and **Friuli-Venezia Giulia**). To follow up on moderately oaked wines try any oaked Italian white (see **Italy**), two-to five-year-old **Sémillon**, or less expensive Burgundy (see **Côte Chalonnaise** and **Mâcon**). For the rich oaky wines try a top Burgundy (see **Côte d'Or** and **Chablis**), a New World Chardonnay (see **Napa Valley**, **Sonoma** and **Australia**) or **Retsina**.

ROMANIA

Romania's wines are rarely encountered outside the country, although political and economic changes will doubtless make exports more likely in future. A favourable climate and some investment in technology already suggest that potential for quality is extremely good. So far Cotnari [★/■] is perhaps the best-known, a sweet wine reminiscent of Hungarian Tokay or Sauternes. Muscat Ottonel [★/ ■■] is also good.

Apart from Romania's own Feteasca grape, there are widespread plantings of international varieties including Muscat, Gewürztraminer, Chardonnay, Riesling and Ruländer. Among the most promising regions so far are Murfatlar near the Black Sea; Banat, in the west towards Hungary and Yugoslavia; and Tirnave in Transylvania, for light, crisp, fresh wines.

WHERE NEXT? Bulgaria is streets ahead in terms of modern quality, while **Hungary** is a little closer to Romania in its collection of odd characters.

RUEDA

Although not well known, the white wines of Rueda in north-west Spain show considerable promise and are well worth seeking out. They owe their extra bit of class to the local Verdejo grape, and to modern winemaking by the few good producers.

The grape produces a lightly aromatic, softish, slightly nutty wine, and a combination of climate and careful winemaking ensures they are fresh and clean. Straight Rueda has less Verdejo than Rueda Superior (Viura and a little Sauvignon Blanc are the other permitted varieties), and some of the latter may be oak-aged. Among the best Rueda producers [★→★★/■■] are:

Alvarez y Diez	*Marqués de Griñon*
Bodegas Angel Rodriguez	*Marqués de Riscal, Reserva*
Castilla la Vieja	*Limousin*

These are modern wines, but the traditional Rueda style is still made. Palomino grapes produce light sherry-style *finos* and *amontillados* which undergo *flor* treatment but not the *solera* system (see **Sherry**).

WHERE NEXT? Head back to **Rioja** for the prototype, over to **Penedès** for perhaps classier and more interesting whites. The **Loire** provided much of the inspiration for this area, Sancerre especially (see **Sancerre & Pouilly-Fumé**).

SANCERRE & POUILLY-FUMÉ

On chalky slopes cut by the Loire, 200 miles (320km) up the river, Sauvignon Blanc thrives: it is best known when wearing its Sancerre hat. Like Muscadet and Chablis, the name caught on; the hat became one of France's most sought-after fashion accessories.

At its tangy best, with a whiff of nettles, gooseberries, grapefruit, blackcurrant leaves, asparagus, Sancerre should be clean as a whistle and deliciously, refreshingly drinkable. And it usually is, especially if you catch it within a couple of years of the harvest. But it should not be taken too seriously, and the *haute couture* prices are in danger of making it rather long-faced. They may also be in danger of diluting the quality of Sancerre itself, which would be even worse. Despite that, Sancerre does have a steely, flinty quality about it that nowhere else quite seems to manage, an almost British reserve about it that can make other Sauvignons seem as if they are vulgarly showing off.

Its neighbour Pouilly-Fumé has had a different sort of success. The grape is the same, the style similar, but with a slightly more pronounced smokiness (hence the *fumé*), and a little more body and roundness, slightly riper fruit perhaps. These too are exciting wines; the only question mark over them is the price. Wonderful as Baron de L [★★/■■■] from de Ladoucette may be, most of us have to stop and think carefully before paying the equivalent of first-growth claret prices for a bottle; all it takes is a little voice to whisper "It's only a drink," and we are done for.

Other good producers [★★/■■→■■■] include:

Didier Dagueneau	*Roger Pabot*
Jean-Claude Guyot	*Michel Redde & Fils*
Domaine Laporte	

Pouilly's nominal success owes a lot to the New World; some credit the Mondavis of California with the idea of borrowing the evocative word "Fumé" to help convey the impression of light toasty smokiness in their Sauvignon. Since then Fumé has been pressed into service by all and sundry, and is generally taken to mean that the Sauvignon has spent some time in oak (see **Sauvignon Blanc**).

There are other wines in this part of the region based on Sauvignon Blanc, notably Menetou-Salon [★★/■■], Reuilly [★★/■■] and the under-valued Quincy [★★/■→■■]. Coteaux du Giennois [★→★★/■■] is a VDQS with promise.

Sancerre is fairly adaptable as far as food goes: from crisp vegetables to tender shellfish to richer fish, or it's interesting to drink as an aperitif. Pouilly-Fumé seems to work well with river fish, mixed fish dishes, and smoked trout and eel.

WHERE NEXT? Sauvignon de Touraine can, in the right hands, provide the pleasure of Sancerre at half the price (see **Touraine**).

SARDINIA

Writers seem to agree that Sardinia, though *in* Italy, is not *of* it. The wines too show this "unItalian" quality. Even the mainland's ubiquitous Trebbiano no longer holds sway; it is now outgrown by the Malvasia, Vernaccia and Nuragus grapes.

Nuragus is probably the least exciting variety. Nuragus di Cagliari [★/■], made in large quantities around the port of that name, is a fairly neutral wine, a thirstquencher more than an exciter of tastebuds. Much of it is made by the giant Cantina Sociale Marmilla co-operative. Other white wines of Cagliari are on the sweet side and are definitely an acquired taste.

Vernaccia di Oristano (no relation of the Tuscan Vernaccia) is a sherry-like wine [★★/■■] which is aged in wood and develops *flor* (see **Sherry**), but which is not fortified. Its flavour is nutty and slightly bitter with a lingering finish. The best brand, made by the Cantina Sociale della Vernaccia, is Sardinian Gold.

At another point on the coastline is the winery of Sella & Mosca, a substantial and much-lauded operation which manages to combine quantity with quality. Its model white is the light, agreeable, bone-dry Torbato di Alghero [★/■■], made from a blend of local grapes, which goes well with fish. The other white bestseller from Sella & Mosca is the dry yet powerful Vermentino di Alghero [★→★★/■], made from a variant of Malvasia and other varieties. The traditional Vermentino has an assertive, earthy style, but a considerable quantity is now made as light, fresh *vino da tavola*, much of it widely distributed by the Dolianova co-operative.

Of the sweet wines, the most prized is Malvasia di Bosa [★/■■], made near Alghero; this sherry-like wine is made either dry, to serve as an aperitif, or more commonly rich and sweet with a bitter note like Spanish *oloroso*. Various Moscato wines are also made.

Other Sardinian producers [★/■→■■] include:

Attilio Contini	*Cantina Sociale Riforma*
Cantina Sociale Cooperativa	*Agraria*
Dolianova	*Vini Classici di Sardegna*
Cantina Sociale di Dorgali	

Sardinian whites are just the thing for fish soup. Torbato di Alghero goes well with grilled rock lobster.

WHERE NEXT? **Spain** inspired a good part of the Sardinian taste, so follow the sweet trail to **Sherry** and less well-known wines like **Málaga**.

SAUMUR

Like its neighbour Anjou to the west, Saumur's main white grape is the Chenin Blanc, whose acid nature gave rise to a whole new industry. In 1811 Jean Ackerman founded the sparkling wine house of Ackerman-Laurance, and now *méthode champenoise* Saumur [★★/■■→■■■] is one of the best French sparklers made outside Champagne.

With its fresh, clean bite and a sharp wake-me-up tingle, this wine is more in the nature of a jangling alarm clock than a gentle nudge in the back. Some houses, like Bouvet-Ladubay [★★/■■], owned by the Champagne firm of Taittinger, make 100% Chenin wines. But most prefer to blend with some Chardonnay and Sauvignon Blanc to take the acid edge off. Another good producer, Langlois-Château [★★/■■→■■■], is part-owned by the Champagne firm of Bollinger.

Chardonnay and Sauvignon add their lift of fruit to the still wine too; up to 20% of other varieties are allowed in Saumur Blanc, although it remains bone-dry and can be unpleasantly sharp. One of the best is made by the co-operative Cave des Vignerons de Saumur at St-Cyr-en-Bourg; daisy-fresh, edgy and racy, but with clean and sharply defined fruit.

Sparkling Saumur makes a fabulously appetizing aperitif, while the acidity of the still wines cuts sharply through pork.

WHERE NEXT? Crémant de Loire (see **Loire**) is usually recognized to be a bit better than straight Saumur, and **Vouvray** sparklers, from nearby, are worth a try. For the same sort of value, in a fuller and fatter style, try **Cava**.

SAUTERNES & BARSAC

Sauternes is one of the great, one of the classic, white wine styles, much copied around the world but rarely equalled. It is such a high-risk drink to produce that some proprietors claim it as a hobby rather than a business; certainly any accountant worth his salt would warn off anybody daft enough to even consider thinking about the possibility of maybe looking into the idea of producing Sauternes for a living.

Because these wines are difficult and expensive to produce, we have to pay a lot for them. We should not begrudge that – within reason. What we should avoid are any cheap Sauternes that cut corners, because they will not come within a thousand miles of the real thing.

Sauternes is an *appellation* within Graves, at the southern end near Langon. Next door across the little River Ciron is Barsac, making similar wines that can call themselves either Barsac or Sauternes. Between them they cover five communes – Barsac, Preignac, Bommes, Fargues and Sauternes – which constitute the First Division. The very demanding conditions of warmth and humidity that help to make these wines special are not quite matched by the neighbouring *appellations* of Cérons, (see **Graves**), Ste-Croix-du-Mont, Cadillac and Loupiac (see **Bordeaux**); they can make good wines, but they rarely have the intense lusciousness of Sauternes.

THE SAUTERNES TASTE The appeal of these wines is their honeyed, sweet, glycerine-smooth, concentrated richness. The fruits they evoke are peaches and apricots, sometimes raisins in a very mature wine. Sauternes is, if anything, bigger, richer and more luscious than Barsac. Alcohol is high in both (around 13-14%), but despite all this unctuous stand-a-spoon-in-it goodness the best do not feel cloying. Their just-balancing acidity keeps them animated.

With oak age, Sauternes develop spicy, toasty flavours, and a remarkable change in colour takes place, from golden-syrup yellow through russet and coppery-bronze to deep tawny. They are wines that definitely need maturing to allow the depth and spectrum of flavours to emerge. Ten to 20 years is normal; a few, especially from the lighter vintages, can be enjoyed at six or eight years; some top wines from better years soldier on for longer than the patience of most drinkers.

Sauternes and Barsac are special for a number of reasons. Autumn mists rise from the Rivers Garonne and Ciron, and are shooed away by the sun as the day wears on. Damp, warm, humid weeks are the breeding ground for a fungus that thrives on the grapes, turning them rotten. Not just any old rotten, though: special rotten – "nobly" rotten, as the French have it. The fungus *Botrytis cinerea* pierces the skin of the grape, allowing water to evaporate. But not sugar. And not acidity. Well, not all of it. As the grape dehydrates, they become relatively more concentrated.

The grapes are not a pretty sight: they are squishy, mouldy and shrivelled. They do not rot evenly: sometimes a whole bunch will go; more often just a few grapes. Since only rotten grapes are used, the pickers have to traipse through the vines several times over the course of a few weeks, harvesting stickily and virtually berry-by-berry.

Because of the concentration, each vine yields maybe a couple of glasses of wine rather than the bottle or two that some growers elsewhere might expect to harvest. Permitted yield is 25 hectolitres per hectare – Château d'Yquem normally produces nearer to 10 – and this compared to typical Bordeaux yields of 40 hectolitres per hectare. The prices asked begin to seem more reasonable.

Sémillon is the mainstay grape, valued for richness, body, and prime susceptibility to *Botrytis*, while Sauvignon Blanc supports with balancing acidity; the third grape, Muscadelle, is less distinctive than the other two, and is invariably kept to about 5% of a vineyard's plantings. Although declining in popularity it does add an attractive whiff of liquorous honeyed perfume.

All that sugar is too much for the yeasts to convert to alcohol. If they could do it, the wine would be stronger than port. Beyond 13 or 14% they are killed by the alcohol. The grape sugar that remains is what makes the wines sweet, and the effect of *Botrytis* is to give the wine a distinctively honeyed smell and flavour.

This is all very well when Nature is smiling, but producers still have to make a living when She is not. It is quite possible for prolonged autumn rain to ruin a crop that looked to be progressing well. By then it is too late for the producer to do anything about it, so, in anticipation of this, he would probably not gamble the whole crop. He would pick some grapes under normal conditions and make a dry bread-and-butter wine to keep his accountant happy, hoping that, if conditions turn out right and *Botrytis* occurs, he will have jam on it.

Alternatively, if the vineyard were only partially affected by *Botrytis*, and the producer had neither the money nor the skilled labour to collect grapes individually, he might harvest the whole lot, ripe and rotten together, and make a neither-this-nor-that sort of wine. These partially botrytized wines are rarely successful, and make the least exciting Sauternes. Sorry, second least exciting. Some producers just chaptalize (add sugar) before fermentation.

CHOOSING SAUTERNES Sauternes is expensive and often available in half-bottles. The region was classified, along with the Médoc, in 1855. Its only *premier grand cru classé* is Château d'Yquem [★★★/ ■■■], and there are 11 first growths, 14 second growths and quite a number of *crus bourgeois*.

The best Sauternes vintages include 1988, 86, 85, 83, 79, 76, 75, 71, 70, 67, 62 and 55. Among the best châteaux in Sauternes and Barsac [★★→★★★/■■■] are:

Broustet	Lafaurie-Peyraguey
Cantegril	Lamothe-Guignard
Climens	Liot
Coutet	de Malle
Doisy-Daëne	Nairac
de Fargues	Rabaud-Promis
Gilette	Rayne-Vigneau
Guiraud	Rieussec
Guiteronde	Suduiraut

Especially good-value producers [★★→★★★/■■■] include:

Bastor-Lamontagne	Mayne des Carmes
Doisy-Vedrines	St-Amand

Though the dry wines produced in neighbouring Cérons are entitled to the Graves AC, those made in Sauternes and Barsac as "insurance" wines are entitled only to straight Bordeaux. They might sound humble, but from a good producer they can be extremely good. The noblest château of all, d'Yquem, calls its dry wine "Y" (Ygrec in French) and it is well worth the search – and expense – to try a bottle [★★★/■■■] for a hint of the honey and grapefruit of the famous wine, but without the sweetness. The first growth Château Rieussec also uses an initial – R – for its dry wine, which is another fine example of this rare breed [★★★/■■→■■■], as are the dry wines of Coutet [★★/ ■■→■■■] and Doisy-Däene [★★/■■→■■■].

SAUTERNES AND FOOD Sauternes is the ultimate dessert wine, as well as a classic accompaniment for *foie gras*. It is lovely with summer fruit dishes, bread and butter pudding and fruit flans.

WHERE NEXT? A number of other regional *appellations* make sweet wines in a similar (though lighter) style to Sauternes, from the same trio of grapes, but at a fraction of the cost. For cheaper, less syrupy versions, try the nearby wines of **Monbazillac** or Cérons (see **Graves**); or the tiny *appellations* of Loupiac, Ste-Croix-du-Mont and Cadillac (see **Bordeaux**).

Outside the Bordeaux region, try lighter and fresher German *Auslesen, Beerenerauslesen* and *Trockenbeerenauslesen* (see **Germany**). Other comparable styles include some **Muscats**, Alsace *Sélection des grains nobles*, **Vouvray** *moelleux* from the Loire, Hungarian **Tokay** and **Orvieto** *abboccato*. Compare Y and R with Noble Dry Sauvignon from Kumeu River (see **New Zealand**).

SAUVIGNON BLANC

Sauvignon Blanc is one of the most aromatic of all grape varieties. It makes simple, direct, easy-to-understand wines that have a crunchy green freshness – rather like biting on a just-picked pea-pod. Most are dry. A little sweetness is sometimes left in to help take the edge off the sharp acidity, but this rarely amounts to a medium-dry wine.

Sauvignon is perfectly in tune with the exciting pin-sharp flavours currently in demand. Widely travelled and responsive to new surroundings, the grape takes on different characteristics depending on where it is grown and how it is made. Although it has been around for ages, its successful varietal career is a recent phenomenon.

THE SAUVIGNON BLANC TASTE Sauvignon doesn't just smell; it pongs – of nettles, gooseberries, crushed blackcurrant leaves, asparagus, tropical fruit … even cat's pee. Indeed, it appeals as much to the nose as to the palate, and does so immediately: brittle, sharply defined, pungent aromas jump out of the glass to meet you; if you have to go in and look for them, you've got the wrong Sauvignon. Like Gewürztraminer, Sauvignon also has a powerful and easily recognizable taste.

Pure Sauvignon Blanc wines are generally light to medium in weight, and at their best when young. If this grape has a fault, it is in resembling a film set. There is little to back up the impressive façade, so it needs shoring up with planks of some other grape. Depth is traditionally supplied by Sémillon, which is often blended in with Sauvignons. This not only gives more body, but prolongs the wine's lifespan and helps to moderate excessive pungency. Even with a dollop of helpful Sémillon, though, Sauvignon Blanc is not going to develop with time like, say, Chardonnay or Riesling into something that is unrecognizably superior.

In a bid for longevity and respectability, or perhaps to make up for a lack of elegance, some producers give it a few months in oak, calling it "Fumé" and asking a higher price. It is debatable whether it warrants the extra cost. The best Sauvignons *are* elegant; over-oaking merely gets in the way. Oak-aged Sauvignon can begin to take on flavours of tinned asparagus or peas as it matures, losing the focus of its great appeal – its freshness.

BEGIN WITH NEW ZEALAND The home of this grape variety is in France. During the 1980s, however, warning bells began sounding from across the globe. Chile's Maipo Valley [★/■■] makes Sauvignon Blanc, but it is disappointing: the sound wasn't coming from there. California has adopted it as a kid brother to Chardonnay and produces some excellent examples: yet the sound wasn't coming from the northern hemisphere either.

The source of this big clanging noise was New Zealand – which has redefined the flavour of this grape variety. Marlborough, at the northern tip of the South Island, is now the centre of the Sauvignon Blanc universe. Screamingly pungent, razor-edged, leafy-green, varietally pure flavours burst out of the glass with an intensity that is unmatched elsewhere. Ardent supporters of French Sauvignons might complain that these New Zealand wines are too obvious and lacking in subtlety. And they may have a point, but it is a pedantic one – a bit like winning a Bentley in a raffle and refusing it because you don't like the colour (see **Marlborough**).

In the North Island of New Zealand, Sauvignon changes into a lusher, richer, broader, more tropical fruit style of wine (see **Gisborne** and **Hawke's Bay**).

OTHER SAUVIGNON BLANCS Sauvignon thrives in cool regions, which is why the Loire is its natural habitat. Sauvignon de Touraine is a sound, lively, inexpensive, youthful stuff with more zip and flair than many a Muscadet at the same price (see **Touraine**). Further upriver it has put Sancerre and Pouilly on the map. Until the meteoric rise of New Zealand's Sauvignons these twin towns achieved the finest expression of this grape's character. The grape's affinity with the Loire is further emphasized by wines from Menetou-Salon, Reuilly and Quincy (see **Sancerre & Pouilly-Fumé**).

Sauvignon de St Bris, to the south-west of Chablis, is a worthy VDQS. Packed with Sauvignon style, it is now becoming more pricey. Names to look for [★★/■■] include Bersan, Albert Defrance, Domaine Grand Roche and Labouré Roi.

In Bordeaux it is often blended with Sémillon. Its most successful manifestation here has been in the sweet wines of Sauternes and Barsac, playing second fiddle to Sémillon (see **Sauternes & Barsac**). Elsewhere, the region has tended to produce dull, fruitless, character-less dry whites. Fortunately Bordeaux has woken up and now makes some dry Sauvignon worthy of the name (see **Bordeaux, Graves** and **Entre-Deux-Mers**).

Sauvignon's New World success is not limited to New Zealand. Australia makes an increasing number of interesting Sauvignons, and some successful wines have been produced in California, especially in the Napa Valley. Robert Mondavi borrowed the term "Fumé" from Pouilly and it has since been passed around the world like a copy of *Playboy* around the locker room. "Fumé Blanc" is now tacitly taken to refer to a Sauvignon that is either fermented or aged in oak (see **Australia** and **Napa Valley**).

SAUVIGNON BLANC AND FOOD The stronger a wine's personality, the more difficult it is to match successfully with food. New Zealand Sauvignon is a classic example: though excellent by itself or as an aperitif, is a hard act to follow. The less exuberant French Sauvignons, however, have a more tolerant relationship with food.

Sauvignon will accept a good measure of acidity in food, although you may need some practice to match the level accurately. Flavour-some cheese makes a good partner; goat's cheese is a perfect match. Other accompaniments are *salade Niçoise*, shellfish and grilled tuna.

WHERE NEXT? After the intensity of Marlborough Sauvignon it would seem there is nowhere left to go. And if it is the powerful, pungent, penetrating pong that attracts, then there is little to touch it. But Sauvignon's lack of real substance may leave you hankering after something chunkier. If so, the next logical step is **Sémillon**. It too can develop a grassy, herbaceous smell, but this grape variety fills out into a more rounded wine.

SAVOIE

There seems little reason in principle why Savoie should not do what Alto Adige did during the 1980s: make a name for itself with snappily crisp, ultra-light, dry and utterly refreshing alpine wines. As it is, most of them are too ordinary to grab the world's attention. There are encouraging signs of life, but one of the big handicaps seems to be the duff hand of grape varieties that the *appellations* have been dealt.

Grapes grow between the *pistes* from Val d'Isère to Lake Geneva, and similarities with the wines of neighbouring Switzerland are not hard to detect. Crépy seems to be made from melted snow; it is one of the few wines that can make Muscadet seem big, flavoursome and full-bodied, and the Chasselas grape (Fendant in Switzerland) is the reason why. Alcohol is around 11% and some wines are bottled, like Muscadet, *sur lie* to give them a prickle and a bit more life. Drunk with *raclette* (the Alpine dish of melted cheese and potatoes), after whooshing down a mountain-side, what could be better? The best Crépy producers [★★/■■] include Goy, Mercier and Métral.

Seyssel, which incorporates the Roussette grape (aka Altesse) is earthier, spicier, fuller and richer, with a quince-like flavour. The reputation, though, is for an attractively yeasty *méthode champenoise* sparkling wine, Seyssel Mousseux. The best Seyssel producers [★★/■■] include Mollex and Varichon et Clerc.

Such excitement as there is in Savoie is currently provided by Chignin, a village making dry, clean, light- to medium-bodied wine from the Bergeron grape (the Roussanne of the Rhône) which has some ageing potential, and by Apremont. Rather like the Côtes de Gascogne, Apremont has an unpromising start – the local Jacquère grape is a bit of a plodder, very high-yielding and thus rather dilute – but the simple ski-fresh pleasure is just right for the mountain setting. Other ACs include Abymes and Montmelian. Best producers from Chignin and Apremont [★★/■■] include:

Pierre Boniface	Savoyard
Caveau du Lac	St-André
Coopérative Le Vigneron	Michel Tardy et Fils

WHERE NEXT? For Crépy try **Muscadet**; for Seyssel try a white **Rhône** or Furmint from **Hungary**; for Chignin and Apremont try a wine from **Alto Adige**.

SEKT

Germany produces a lot of sparkling wine, but nearly all of it is consumed by Germans. This is no great loss to the rest of us, however, as much of it is ordinary in the extreme. Almost all *Sekt*, as it is called, is made by the *cuve close* method and has precious little character, since much of it is made from imported base wine trucked in from other parts of Europe. The situation has improved somewhat of late, though: partly as a result of the EEC regulation that all bottles labelled *Deutscher Sekt* should contain wine made entirely from German grapes; and partly due to the increasing use by producers in Germany of the *méthode champenoise*.

The grapes used in *Sekt* include Silvaner, Riesling, Chardonnay, Pinot Noir, Trebbiano, Chenin Blanc, Sauvignon Blanc and Colombard (the foreign varieties coming mainly from France and Italy). The better producers [★★/■■] include:

Bernard-Massard	Kessler
Deinhard	Kupferberg
Deutz & Geldermann	Rudolf Müller
Fürst von Metternich	Treis
Gräflich von Kageneck'sche	

WHERE NEXT? Many New World sparkling wines equal the quality of good all-Riesling *Sekt*: a little sweetness, lots of fresh fruit. Most other sparkling wines, such as **Saumur** and **Cava** are better value.

SEMILLON

Wines labelled simply Sémillon are generally dry, though heavy oaking and high alcohol can combine to give an impression that some are off-dry. Yet the grape is perhaps best known as the principal ingredient in the sweet wines of Sauternes and Barsac.

Sémillon appears, as often as not, in a double bill with its partner Sauvignon Blanc. It is the "fat one" of the Laurel and Hardy duo which lends weight to the partnership and, by dint of its ability to age gracefully, prevents many a thin Sauvignon from falling embarrassingly flat on its face before the end of the first reel. It also appears as a supporting player in many dry wines labelled Sauvignon Blanc, although it is rarely listed in the credits.

As a result of this, Sémillon has long been under-appreciated as a varietal in its own right. There are some successful dry Bordeaux wines made from the grape, but they are traditionally labelled with the property name rather than the grape variety. It has taken Australia, in particular the Hunter Valley in New South Wales, to show the heights that dry Sémillon can achieve.

THE SEMILLON TASTE It is difficult to believe that the light, lemony taste of a young Sémillon will ever progress to anything more substantial. Its role as a poor man's Chardonnay, which it more closely resembles, gives a clue to how much potential is packed into this grape variety.

After 15 or 20 years Hunter Valley Sémillon puts on a lot of weight and develops a roundness and butteriness very reminiscent of Chardonnay. The amazing thing is that it can do this without any ageing in oak. The citrussy tang of youth is not wasted either: that is what keeps it lively, holding the flabby middle-aged spread at bay.

But long-lived Sémillon is rare; few people can be bothered to mature it for the decade or more it needs. There is a short-cut, though – oak-ageing. This creates a rich, mellow, rounded style in a fraction of the time. It is by no means as classy as the real thing, but for most purposes, and most pockets, it will do nicely.

Sometimes young Sémillon can display an aromatic, herbaceous, grassy smell very reminiscent of Sauvignon Blanc. The difference is on the palate: Sémillon has noticeably more weight and body. While Sauvignon will peak relatively early and rarely improve after a couple of years, Sémillon goes from strength to strength. This is why the two varieties are often blended together. Sauvignon seduces with its aromatic power, masking its partner's initial shyness, while Sémillon makes up for Sauvignon's lack of body and fills out the wine when Sauvignon begins to flag.

BEGIN WITH BORDEAUX A native of France, Sémillon is the country's second-most-widely-planted white grape after Ugni Blanc (Trebbiano). Traditionally the principal grape used to make the sweet wines of Sauternes and Barsac, its susceptibility to "noble" rot, *Botrytis cinerea*, combined with its ageing potential, make it the most aristocratic French white grape variety after Chardonnay (see **Sauternes & Barsac**).

In combination with Sauvignon it also turns out dry Bordeaux from great to indifferent (see **Bordeaux, Graves, Entre-Deux-Mers**).

OTHER SEMILLONS One significant point in Sémillon's favour is its ability, when Chardonnay stumbles in the market place, to pick up the baton and run. As Chardonnay prices increase, with greater demand chasing a shortage of grapes, so the less expensive Sémillon – which shares something of the weight, the complexity and even the oakiness of its aristocratic competitor – is widely considered a reasonable and worthy alternative.

The Hunter Valley in New South Wales is the mecca for lovers of mature, unoaked dry Sémillon. The wines it produces here (losing its

Old World accent along the way) are unique, developing a distinctive rich, toasty style after long ageing in bottle (see **Hunter Valley**).

The grape's popularity is now spreading to other Australian wine-growing regions. South Australia, Victoria and Western Australia all produce Sémillon in styles varying from light, fresh and herbaceous to full, weighty and oaky (see **South Australia**, **Victoria** and **Western Australia**).

Chile's Sémillon wines, which often lack acidity, make an interesting contrast to those of Washington State (see **United States**), which have a savage green-grass character.

SEMILLON AND FOOD Although the lighter, fresher styles can be drunk as aperitifs, the weight of Sémillon reserves it a place at table. The lemony quality of young wines can partner a wide range of fish, including the oilier kind. Older Sémillons, while delightful on their own, can match more buttery sauces as well as the buttery, biscuitty richness of pastry.

Their weight makes Sémillons ideal for white meats like chicken or veal, although it is often the sauce rather than the meat which determines the effectiveness of a match.

WHERE NEXT? Sémillon provides a logical step on the way to **Chardonnay**. It does not always have the full, flavoursome, stylish completeness of Chardonnay, but it is the grape variety that comes closest to it. The different Sémillon styles – young and lemony, young and oaky, or mature and buttery – easily find an equivalent among the various styles of Chardonnay. But generally this will involve moving upwards in price.

SHERRY

Psst! Do you want to know a secret? Well never mind, I'll tell you anyway. What is one of the best-value wines on the market at the moment? Begins with S.

Absolutely right. Not the cheap stuff, not the sweet stuff, not the inexpensive brands of sherry from the off-licence that granny buys to make the trifle. Cheap sherry is cheap sherry and simply isn't worth drinking. But *real* sherry, from tangy dry *fino* through nutty dry *amontillado* to rich dry *oloroso*, is fabulous to drink, unbelievably underrated and is almost given away when you consider the time and effort that goes into making it.

What they all have in common, you notice, is dryness. There are a few rare exceptions, but as a rule of thumb all good sherry is dry. And it all comes from the south-west corner of Spain around the town of Jerez de la Frontera.

THE SHERRY TASTE The taste of sherry, a fortified wine, derives largely from the way it is made: differences in the process account for differences in style. White Palomino grapes, grown on the dazzlingly white *albariza* soils reminiscent of Champagne country, are the common raw material. It is after fermentation that the wine's future course and style is plotted.

A decision is taken to send each cask on a particular path through the *bodega* that will determine its eventual style. Traditionally the barrels were classified into two groups: the finer, more delicate ones destined to become *fino* sherry and the fuller, heavier ones for *oloroso* sherry. The practice is sometimes short-circuited nowadays – the wines are told how to develop rather than asked – but the basic principle remains the same.

Fino derives its unique yeasty character from a pale, wrinkly, yellowish mould called *flor* which grows on the surface of the wine. The mould ensures that the wine undergoes a partial and very slow oxidation, and increases esters and aldehydes, giving *fino* its fresh tang. *Fino* sherry should be light, with a delicately yeasty smell and a slightly austere bite.

Pale cream sherry is made to look like *fino* for snob reasons. The dilemma of those who are slaves to fashion is that they must be seen with pale drinks, although they don't really like anything too dry. There are obviously plenty of them because sherry companies have designed a wine that looks dry but tastes sweet. It is not in the same class as the dry sherries.

Flor is a naturally occurring phenomenon, and the various strains help to account for slight differences in style from one barrel to the next and from one *bodega* to another. The most marked difference in style occurs in Sanlúcar de Barrameda at the mouth of the Guadalquivir river. The sea makes Sanlúcar cooler, humidity is greater, the *flor* grows more profusely, and therefore oxidation is slower while aldehydes increase. The style produced here, *manzanilla fina*, is thus zestier, fresher and more pungent than *fino*, and has a salty, savoury edge to it.

The *flor* yeast thrives best when the wine has an alcohol level of around 15-16%, so the *fino*-to-be is fortified to this level. The wines will stay like this for about two years, during which time the *flor* will fluctuate in vigour and depth. It is more likely to continue growing if the barrel is continually refreshed with new wine. *Oloroso*-to-be is strengthened to around 18%, safely out of the reach of *flor*.

Oloroso is dark and rich, with a deeper, more sultry nutty fragrance and raisiny maturity, sometimes with the bitter-sweet flavour of burnt caramel. It is usually dry, though sometimes the bitter edge becomes so shockingly brutal that a little sweetening wine is added to the *oloroso* for balance: not enough to obscure the flavours of the sherry, just enough to harmonize them.

Some of the driest *olorosos* are matured in small quantities by doctors, lawyers and others with spare cash and time on their hands, more as a hobby than a business. Unlike the blends from big *bodegas*, with hundreds of butts in a *criadera*, these may have no more than half a dozen. They are called *almacenista* sherries. Originally they were sold to the large *bodegas* to give depth and character to some of their blends, but in the last few years firms like Emilio Lustau have done a great service by bottling some of them unblended, straight from a single cask [★★★/■■■]. Most of these are uncompromisingly dry; each is in a different and unrepeatable style.

Sherry is produced by fractional blending in a *solera* system, whereby a quarter to a third of the wine is drawn off and replenished with younger wine from another barrel; this in turn is replenished with younger wine still, and so on. The last butt or barrel in the line-up, from which sherry is drawn off for bottling, is the *solera*, which is fed from a variable number of *criaderas*.

Sherry is thus a blended wine, and this system makes vintage sherry an impossibility. What it does, however, is to ensure a consistency of style and quality, evening out any idiosyncracies in the flavour between barrels and years.

In some instances, particularly when the butt is not refreshed with wine from other *criaderas*, or if the wine is fortified up to 18%, the *flor* will die off and sink to the bottom of the cask, thus allowing increased contact between wine and air. These oxidized *finos* become *amontillados*, darkening in colour to amber-brown and developing a powerful nuttiness and great length of flavour. *Fino amontillado* (and its equivalent *manzanilla pasada* from Sanlúcar) is a kind of half-way stage between the two styles.

Another half-way style is *palo cortado*, which develops into something between an *amontillado* and an *oloroso*.

In this, their natural state, *amontillados* are completely dry, and that is how the best are sold. Even if the real thing costs five times as much as sweet *amontillado*, it is worth the difference. It is not always possible to distinguish between them from the label, but *seco* usually indicates the real thing.

CHOOSING SHERRY Among the best *fino* sherries [★★→★★★/ ■■→■■■] are these from the following producers:

Tomás Abad	Emilio Lustau
Domecq, La Ina	La Riva, Tres Palma
Garvey, San Patricio	Valdespino, Inocente
Gonzalez Byass, Tío Pepe	Don Zoilo
Harvey, Tío Mateo	

The best Sanlúcar *manzanillas* come from Barbadillo [★★★/■■] in particular, and from Delgado Zuleta [★★/■■] and Hidalgo [★★/■■]. Since freshness is paramount with *fino*, it should be drunk as soon as possible after bottling, which means it is best bought from an outlet with a rapid turnover.

The best *amontillados* [★★→★★★/■■→■■■] include:

Tomás Abad, Don Tomás	Harvey, 1796 range
Domecq, Botaina Amontillado Viejo	Emilio Lustau, Almacenista Amontillado
Garvey, Tío Guillermo	Sandeman, Bone Dry Old Amontillado
Gonzalez Byass, Amontillado del Duque	

Good *amontillados* from Sanlúcar [★★→★★★/■■] include Barbadillo, Delgado Zuleta and Hidalgo.

Top *olorosos* [★★→★★★/■■→■■■] include:

Luis Caballero, Heavenly Cream Rich Old Oloroso	Sandeman, Dry Old Oloroso
Gonzalez Byass, Apostoles Oloroso Viejo	Sandeman, Imperial Corregidor
Gonzalez Byass, Mathúsalem Oloroso Muy Viejo	Valdespino, Don Gonzalo
Diez Merito, Victoria Regina	Williams & Humbert, Dos Cortados

Good *olorosos* from Sanlúcar [★★→★★★/■■→■■■] include Barbadillo's Oloroso Seco and the sweeter Sanlúcar Cream.

SHERRY AND FOOD The Spanish serve sherry before, during and after the meal. Dry sherry can hold its own with anything from lobster to baby shark. Try a glass or two of dry *amontillado* or *oloroso* with a wedge of mature cheddar on a Sunday afternoon.

WHERE NEXT? Apart from **Montilla** (and a few lesser Spanish versions), there is nothing else quite like sherry. There are sherry imitators of course, from **Cyprus** and **South Africa**, and some can be reasonable. But it is a pity they are allowed to be called sherry. Try other fortified wines, including **Málaga**, **Madeira**, **Marsala** and Australian stickies (see **Liqueur Muscat & Tokay**), or Hungarian **Tokay** or *vin jaune* (see **Jura**).

SICILY

The wine industry of this island has undergone something of a sea-change of late. Where once the sweet, fortified dessert wine Marsala (see Marsala) was the sole wine exported in any quantity, today Sicily is the centre of a giant table wine industry. That said, few of the wines are of any great distinction.

As with all hot-climate areas, the various dessert wines made are sometimes more successful than the dry wines. Three major Moscato names to watch for [★→★★/■■→■■■] are Moscato di Noto, Moscato di Villa Fontane and Moscato di Siracusa, which have a characteristic spicy Muscat aroma and a caramel finish.

Moscato di Pantelleria is made on the island of Pantelleria to the south-west of Sicily from the Alexandrian Muscat grape, known locally as Zibibbo. The best style is *passito*, made from sun-dried grapes, which give a raisiny quality to this golden, sweet and naturally strong (14%) but still fresh dessert wine. Bukkuram [★★/■■■], the best version, is made by de Bartoli; the co-operative makes a version called Tanit [★/■■■].

Of Sicily's dry wines, Corvo [★/■■] is a soft, popular wine made in two styles: light and delicate style (with a yellow label) or more pungent and rounded (with a green label); there is also a *spumante* version [★→★★/■■■]. Other drinkable dry wines are made by the giant Settesoli and Regaleali companies [★/■■] which produce light, fairly acidic styles. Regaleali's best dry white, Nozze d'Oro [★★/■■■], includes Sauvignon Blanc in the blend. Look also for Villagrande's fruity Etna Bianco Superiore [★→★★/■■].

Malvasia delle Lipari is a rich, honey-and-apricots wine from a group of tiny islands to the north of Sicily. The best example [★★/■■■] is made by an ex-pat Swiss, Carlo Hauner.

Other Sicilian producers [★→★★/■■] include:

Camilleri	*Rapitala*
Coria	*Cantina Sociale Enocarboj*

Try Regaleali's Nozze d'Oro with swordfish, Corvo with sardine and fennel pasta, Moscato di Pantelleria with *cassata*.

WHERE NEXT? **Sardinian** dry wines provide contrasts, and some similarly interesting sweet wines. Compare the sweeter Sicilian wines with Tuscan **Vin Santo**.

SILVANER

This is the man-in-the-street of white grape varieties, a kind of Teutonic Trebbiano that generally makes very ordinary wines indeed. Like all non-aromatic wines, though, it compensates with other qualities, and has an important place in the drinking hierarchy.

Silvaner is sprinkled around central Europe, where it probably originated, but has made its home in Germany – particularly in Rheinhessen and Franken – and in Alsace; it also makes very creditable wines in Alto Adige. Its career as a "stud" is rather more impressive than its track record as a wine. It has been crossed numerous times with Riesling, notably to sire Müller-Thurgau, Rieslaner and Scheurebe.

THE SILVANER TASTE Silvaner wines generally have so little smell that they are described as "neutral". Occasionally there are hints of earthiness or flintiness, especially in Germany. Some are faintly smoky, others very lightly spicy, but all share a quality of being grapey rather than fruity or flowery.

Most wines have good body and crisp acidity, but little personality of their own. We tend to notice these characteristics all the more because there is not much else to deflect our attention. Nevertheless the backbone and structure they can bring to a blend with lightly aromatic but limp Müller-Thurgau is mutually beneficial; they support it like an iron truss, in return for a flowery button-hole.

Silvaner wines have legendary ageing capacity, especially those from the Rheinhessen; some bottles have been known to survive, and thrive, for up to 30 years.

Strangely, there is very little sparkling Silvaner, although it seems to have precisely those qualities – neutral nose, good acidity, medium weight – that take well to being fizzed up.

BEGIN WITH GERMANY Germany has more Silvaner vines than any other country, just under half of these planted in Rheinhessen. Franken, while producing less, often squeezes a bit more finesse from the grape. In both cases the heavy clay soils account for Silvaner's characteristic earthiness.

Producers in Rheinhessen are approaching Silvaner sensibly. A hundred of them, ranging from small estates to big co-operatives, have now adopted a common logo and label. Rheinhessen Silvaner, or RS, gets to the heart of Germany's organizational problems at a single stroke (see **Rheinhessen**).

Silvaner reaches its apogee in Franken, where it fills many a Franken *Stein*. It is still earthy, steely, flinty, but often clear-cut and with some finesse. Along with Baden, where some Silvaner is also made, this is one of the most ungermanic wine-producing regions of Germany (see **Franken** and **Baden**).

Rheinpfalz is less important than it was for Silvaner, but still makes some excellent examples, including bone-dry wines of high must-weight; a little is made in Nahe too (see **Rheinpfalz, Nahe**).

OTHER SILVANERS Beyond Germany, Silvaner becomes Sylvaner in Alsace, where it produces a basic varietal wine (see **Alsace**). Unremarkable versions are also made in Austria and Switzerland (see **Austria** and **Switzerland**).

SILVANER AND FOOD Silvaner is a good savoury accompaniment to savoury food. Try it with pork.

WHERE NEXT? Compare Silvaner with a good German **Riesling** for a major boost in style and personality.

SOAVE

Soave is Italy's biggest-selling dry white DOC wine, the country's cheap, mass-produced answer to Germany's Liebfraumilch. But instead of being light, sweet and flowery, it is light, neutral and dry.

Made in the Veneto region, it is a sister to the red wines of Valpolicella and Bardolino. Originally the hills around the walled and castle-crested town of Soave, east of Verona, produced good everyday drinking wine for the city of Romeo and Juliet. These hills now constitute the central Soave Classico zone, but it is the flat surrounding plains, where year after year characterless wine is produced on an industrial scale, that have diluted both the wine and its reputation.

Much of this wine, served from litre bottles in countless Italian restaurants around the world, has been as memorable as the wallpaper. But Soave need not be so.

THE SOAVE TASTE The principal grape of Soave is Garganega. If it is bursting with anything, it is juice and not flavour. Up to 30% Trebbiano di Soave, another of the world's underwhelming grapes, may be incorporated in the blend. As a result, straight Soave is as often as not bland and anonymous.

Soave Classico from the best producers derives its medium weight from the greater concentration produced by lower yields. It is very lightly perfumed, almondy and dry, with a feel variously described as creamy or oily. Owing to the lower yields, these wines cost more, but it is worth paying extra for the real thing: good Soave grows on you.

A traditional but neglected style of Soave is coming back into favour. It is called Recioto and, as with Recioto di Valpolicella, is so concentrated that you can barely believe it has any connection with the standard stuff. Bunches of grapes are laid out to dry on racks in a shed. Early picking ensures good acidity; drying and shrivelling concentrates the sugar. The result is a rich, golden, honeyed wine. Though rarely as luscious as Sauternes, it bears some resemblance to German *auslese*, and, like it, can vary in sweetness.

CHOOSING SOAVES Be careful when shopping for Soave; there are precious few good bottles. Look for single-vineyard names and for the Classico designation. The best producers [★★/■→■■] include:

Anselmi	Tadiello
Boscaini	Tedeschi
Pieropan	Zenato

OTHER REGIONAL WINES A number of other light wines made in neighbouring areas from local grape varieties bear a family resemblance to Soave.

Gambellara, just to the east, is a lightweight wine produced from the Trebbiano di Soave grape; it has some comparable characteristics at only two-thirds of the price. Look for wines of the local co-operative, the Cantina Sociale di Gambellara [★/■→■■].

At the southern end of Lake Garda, Garganega is blended with Tocai, all-purpose Trebbiano and other grapes to give the lively Bianco di Custoza a lift. The wine has a slightly "oily" quality. Reliable producers [★→★★/■■] include Cavalchina, Portalupi, Santa Sofia and Villa Medici.

Next door is Lugana, an elegant though somewhat bland wine made from Trebbiano di Lugana. The best have a certain nutty power which can withstand salami or *polenta*, two tasty local specialities. Producers to look for [★→★★/■■] include Fraccoroli, F Visconti and Podere Co'de Fer.

Over to the east, the Garganega grape crops up in the wines of Colli Berici [★/■■] and Colli Euganei [★/■■].

SOAVE AND FOOD Soave is very accommodating; it really doesn't mind what you eat with it, although it prefers mild flavours. It is good with pasta, providing the sauce is not too powerful, and with mild cheeses. If anything, it is most at home with seafood, from grilled fish to *risotto*. Recioto makes an interesting partner for lobster, and for stronger cheeses.

WHERE NEXT? Any of the wines from Collio, Colli Orientali and Grave del Friuli (see **Friuli-Venezia Giulia**) are worth exploring. Outside Italy, **Pinot Blanc** and **Pinot Gris** will extend the Soave drinker's horizons, as will **Silvaner**; these grapes share its lack of distinctive varietal flavour.

SONOMA

Sonoma, like Napa Valley, lies north of San Francisco Bay. The region was one of the first to be colonized by the vine back in the immediate post-Gold Rush days of the 1850s. The climate here is similar to that of Napa, with hot summer days and colder evenings which help to prevent over-ripening. Many of the best wineries are to the north, in Alexander Valley, Dry Creek and Russian River Valley. As in Napa, every conceivable grape is grown here, but it is Chardonnay and Riesling that stand out.

Start with the old-established wine firms such as Sebastiani and Pedroncelli [★→★★/■■→■■■], many of them founded by Italians. These wineries make generic "jug" wines to high standards, as well as varietals. Lovers of Sauvignon Blanc should seek out the Dry Creek label, and Kenwood [★★/■■■] makes some attractive wines from Gewürztraminer and Chardonnay.

Higher up in quality [★★/■■→■■■] are wines from:

Chateau St Jean	*Iron Horse*
Clos du Bois	*Jordan*
Hanzell	*Sonoma-Cutrer*

Chateau St Jean, a mock-colonial mansion with palms and all, makes gloriously rich Chardonnay, sparkling wines and a rare, sweet *Botrytis*-affected Riesling.

Iron Horse makes some of the zippiest wines in the state from Chardonnay and Sauvignon Blanc. Its *méthode champenoise* fizz [★★★/■■■] is as zingily, bitingly fresh as any outside Saumur: the wonderfully clean, racy, incisive, electrifying energy hits you like a bolt of lightning.

Jordan makes a ripe and attractive, but very expensive Chardonnay. Sonoma-Cutrer is a Chardonnay specialist, producing three distinct styles from three different vineyards; Les Pierres is the classiest and longest-lived of these.

Clos du Bois also plays the vineyard game, particularly with Chardonnay, some of which is also barrel-fermented; Calcaire Vineyard is big and creamy, Flintwood lean and stylish. Hanzell is a collector's item, producing Chardonnay to superlative standards.

Sonoma boasts California's oldest winery, Buena Vista [★★/■■→■■■], which once belonged to "Count" Agoston Haraszthy, the founding father of California wine; it makes some good Chardonnay and Riesling.

To the north of Sonoma, in Mendocino, Fetzer [★★/■■→■■■] also makes particularly good-value wines.

Fine Sonoma Chardonnays, when full and ripe, do no harm to an asparagus starter and positively flourish next to buttered lobster tails and loin of pork.

WHERE NEXT? Next-door **Napa Valley** uses much the same grapes to make wines typically weightier and often less refined. South of the Bay, areas like **Monterey** and Santa Barbara (see **California**) offer further variations on Sauvignon and Chardonnay.

SOUTH AFRICA

South Africa's vineyards have suffered from the political climate but certainly not the weather at home. For the Cape has marvellous grape-growing conditions and enthusiastic, well-funded winemakers.

Steen, or Chenin Blanc, is South Africa's everyday white grape, making rather ordinary wines. The best that could be said about them is that they are clean, fresh and modern. They vary from dry to sweet, and the acidity keeps most of them lively enough, but South Africa has failed to address the problem of how to draw real varietal character from this grape. Only when it is made rich and intensely sweet, as in Nederburg's *Botrytis*-affected Edelkeur [★★/■■■], does it approach the Loire for quality.

South African Constantia [★★/■■], a Muscat dessert wine, was once legendary. Dry table wines have always been drinkable, notably those from the state organization KWV [★→★★/■■]. Other producers [★★/■■] include:

Groot Constantia	*Spier*
Hamilton-Russell	*Twee Jongegezellen*
Klein Constantia	*Union Wine*
Nederburg	*Zevenwacht*

Nederburg is also notable for its Paarl Riesling [★★/■■].

WHERE NEXT? **Australia** does a better job with similar conditions, and **California** is streets ahead, though neither matches South Africa's prices. The really adventurous might go so far as to seek out the wines of Zimbabwe.

SOUTH AUSTRALIA

South Australia is far and away the largest wine-producing state in Australia, churning out some two-thirds of the country's wines. The Riverland region alone, sprawling along the banks of the Murray River towards the state border with Victoria, is responsible for over a third of all Australian wine, much of it in the form of cheap "cask" wines. But, if this sounds to you like an emphasis on quantity rather than quality, think again, for the beauty of Australia as a wine-producing country is its ability to pin down every section of the market, to produce gems alongside the dross – and South Australia is the prime example of this.

Some of Australia's finest wines are produced here: in the great clearing-house of the Barossa Valley; in the rarified *terra rossa* of Coonawarra and its neighbour Padthaway; in the maritime-influenced Southern Vales and hot Clare Valley; and in the Adelaide Hills, one of the country's up-and-coming cool-climate regions (see **Barossa Valley, Coonawarra, Southern Vales, Clare, Adelaide Hills**).

And then there is the Riverland. Production here is vast. The region is basically a desert through which the wide, sluggish Murray River ambles like a wandering strand of rogue spaghetti. If it rains, it makes national headlines. Irrigation is everything, quantities are astonishing and quality never gets a proper look in. In the Riverland's defence, inexpensive everyday drinking is not to be sneered at and Australian technology ensures that there are few duffers. Even at this humble level it is possible to enjoy a bit of fruit. But it is only a bit, because the climate and environment are impressive obstacles.

Berri-Renmano [★→★★/■■→■■■], a coupling of two co-operatives that were already giants in their own right, spews out over a million bottles a week. It would probably crush the equivalent of England's annual grape harvest in a matter of 20 minutes. But among all this the Renmano Chairman's Selection range [★★/■■→■■■] stands out as a lesson for all mega-producers: delightful Chardonnay, Rhine Riesling and Traminer at affordable prices, with decent Sauvignon, Colombard and Chenin to back them up. It also owns the Barossa Valley Estates label [★/■], which produces some of Australia's best-value low-priced wines.

The other Riverland property of note is Angove's [★→★★/■■].

WHERE NEXT? Follow the same producers up the quality scale to the **Barossa Valley** and other quality areas within the state. California's Central Valley is another area making good-value, good-quality wines on a comparable scale.

SOUTHERN VALES

Boundaries and regional names in Australia are not always as precise as they are in Europe's carefully mapped, regulated and controlled appellations. Southern Vales, to the south of Adelaide, encompasses McLaren Vale, and the names are sometimes used more or less interchangeably to describe this wine region.

The climate here is warm, but modified by the waters of the Gulf of St Vincent, and although it has traditionally made some hefty beefy styles, it is re-emerging as a producer of more modern cool-climate wines. The standard is generally good, but there are signs that the best wines are still to come. Chardonnay, Sauvignon, Semillon and Rhine Riesling are the principal varieties.

Thomas Hardy & Sons, Australia's second-largest wine company, is based at Reynella just south of Adelaide. It has a long string of labels: Chateau Reynella Chardonnay [★★/■■■], from McLaren Vale fruit, is made in a soft, full style with plenty of new oak; Siegersdorf Rhine Riesling [★★/■■] from Padthaway starts off light and attractive, and matures well; the Bird Series and Stamp Collection brands [★/■■] are good, sound, reliable wines; superior Hardy Collection [★★/■■→■■■] includes grassy, aromatic Semillon/Sauvignon Blanc and melony toasty Chardonnay, both from Padthaway, and a honey-and-raisins-style Rhine Riesling Beerenausleise; the Eileen Hardy label [★★/■■→■■■] is top of the range.

Geoff Merrill [★★/■■→■■■] is one of the star producers, making very good Chardonnay and Sauvignon Blanc. His Mount Hurtle label contains entirely McLaren Vale fruit, while the Geoff Merrill wines may incorporate grapes from Barossa and Coonawarra.

Other good producers [★→★★/■■→■■■] include:

Blewitt Springs	*Pirramimma*
Coriole	*Ryecroft*
Andrew Garrett	*Shottesbrooke*
Richard Hamilton	*Wirra Wirra*
Middlebrook	*Woodstock*

Nearby Langhorne Creek has a long history of winemaking, which probably explains its reliance on fortified and dessert wines. Bleasdale and Temple Bruer [★→★★/■■] are the producers.

WHERE NEXT? Nearby **Barossa Valley, Clare, the Adelaide Hills** and **Coonawarra** compete to offer South Australia's best wines. There are some parallels with the wines of California's **Napa Valley**.

SPAIN

Peter Ustinov once explained that he reached the top of his profession very quickly because he didn't have any qualifications to detain him at the bottom. Lesser mortals, those with humble certificates of cycling proficiency or doctorates in theoretical astrophysics, will therefore be able to sympathize with Spain.

Spain is a hot country, which makes it inherently difficult to grow white grapes with enough acidity to keep the wines tasting fresh. High temperatures at fermentation time have generally only added to the problem, making wines that are flat, lifeless, dull and oxidized, without any fruit flavour. But hang on a minute – what about California's

Central Valley or Australia's Murray River and Hunter Valley? They can be at least as hot as Spain. How can they make brilliant wines full of fruit and character? They can do this because they don't have any qualifications to detain them at the bottom.

Spain, on the other hand, is wonderfully qualified in terms of tradition. Many wineries still ferment in giant Ali Baba jars or *tinajas*, which have changed little since Roman times. If your family has been making and drinking coarse alcoholic wines for generations, then it seems natural to carry on in the same old way. Communities have been self-supporting, neither selling wine to others nor buying any in. They have thus been deprived of a second opinion on their wine.

Now that their isolation has been breached, producers are becoming aware of how far behind in the race they are. Fortunately the solution is very often simple. Just by picking the grapes earlier in the year, before the acidity plummets, and fermenting at cool temperatures in stainless steel tanks, enormous strides can be made. Many co-operatives are well-placed to do this, provided they also persuade their members that quality of grapes matters more than sugar level. It has been traditional to pick as late as possible, when sugar is highest: this makes foul wine, but it pays the bills. The re-structuring, the oenological *perestroika* that is necessary to overcome this, is hard for many to take.

There are increasing numbers of co-operatives and other producers taking these kinds of steps. The results are dramatic, and some of the wines, even from La Mancha, are now extremely drinkable: fresh and lively, inexpensive – just the ticket for everyday mealtime quaffing (see **La Mancha**). Because progress is piecemeal, good wines occur sporadically; it is the occasional go-ahead producer, rather than an entire *Denominacion de Origen* (DO) that determines the best choice of wine.

One excellent example of this comes from an unlikely spot down in Andalucia. The traditional wines of the Condado de Huelva have been either sherry look-alikes or dull, fat, oxidized and fairly alcoholic table wines. But a group of private producers mucked in together to set up a modern winery; and the enormous local co-operative at Bollullos, under new management, modernized itself drastically. The wines – Viña Odiel [★/■■] from the former, Privilegio del Condado [★/■■] from the latter – are clean, fresh and very pleasantly drinkable, provided you catch them young.

That is the easy bit. Spain's other great problem is grape varieties, and unfortunately it was dealt a duff hand. Native varieties are not packed with powerful fruit, or aromatic pungency, or bright individuality, or any of the things we look for in a really classy wine. Foreign varieties (Chardonnay especially) are beginning to make inroads, particularly in Penedès. The remarkable firm of Torres (see **Penedès**) is experimenting with others, and attempting to give them a distinctive Catalunian twist by blending with local grapes.

But it is not all doom and gloom, not all unrealized potential. Spain has a few excellent white wines – among them Rioja, Cava and Spain's greatest and most individual white wine, sherry. If you doubt that, just look at the imitators around the world. Nobody tries to copy the wines of La Mancha or Navarra. Just sherry. And so far the best sherry has successfully fought off the competition. It is one of the most underrated wines in the world.

WHERE NEXT? See the specific entries on Spanish wine styles: **Málaga**, **La Mancha**, **Montilla-Moriles**, **Navarra**, **Penedès**, **Rioja**, **Rueda** and **Sherry**.

SPARKLING WINE

Sparkling wine of one sort or another is produced in Argentina, Australia, Austria, Brazil, Bulgaria, Canada, Chile, Colombia, Germany, Hungary, India, Israel, Italy, Luxembourg, Mexico, New Zealand, Portugal, Romania, South Africa, Spain, Switzerland, the USSR, Venezuela and Yugoslavia; it is made in California and more than 20 other American states (including Hawaii), in France of course, and even in England.

Its sheer ubiquity is testament to the almost magical alliance of wine and carbon dioxide – and that is what the bubbles are made of, whether the wine is a cheap brand into which the gas is injected or Champagne in which the fizz develops in bottle. The gas ensures that alcohol reaches our brains quickly, thereby getting the proceedings off to a swift and uninhibited start.

There is only one way to become a serious contender in the fizz game, and that is to use the *méthode champenoise*. The advantages are a fine mousse of pinhead-sized bubbles, the development of biscuitty flavours and a reasonably long life (see **Champagne**).

It is possible to make cheaper sparklers by less time-consuming methods such as *cuve close* (also known as the Tank or Charmat Method). Wines made in this way are not destined to achieve the same age or complexity of flavour; the mousse, too, is less fine, and the bubbles don't last as long. Cheaper still is the injection method, which produces big, fat, lazy bubbles. Carbon dioxide is pumped into the base wine, and lasts for about a minute after you open the bottle.

CHOOSING SPARKLING WINES There are three French regions outside Champagne that make *crémant* sparklers by the *méthode champenoise*: the Loire, Alsace and Burgundy.

Some of France's best *méthode champenoise* wines come from the Loire, around Saumur and Vouvray. They range from searingly bonedry to sweet, from light to full-bodied, and are invariably less expensive than Champagne. Saumur makes the nerviest, edgiest, liveliest wines; Vouvray is slightly fuller and softer; Crémant de Loire is creamier and gentler (see **Saumur**, **Vouvray** and **Loire**).

The Crémant d'Alsace *appellation* was introduced a year after France's other two Crémants, in 1976, and some good sparklers are produced, though quality is variable (see **Alsace**). Crémant de Bourgogne is a full and quite soft wine (see **Burgundy**).

Some pockets of sparkling wine production elsewhere around France are hallowed by long tradition. Blanquette de Limoux, made just south of Carcassonne, claims to have invented the sparkling process a century before the Champenois (see **Blanquette de Limoux**). Gaillac in south-western France makes three different kinds of youthful sparklers, of which its *perlé* version is the best-known (see **Gaillac**). In the Rhône Valley a rather unsubtle St-Péray *méthode champenoise* is made near Valence, but from further east comes a real gem, Clairette de Die Tradition (see **Rhône**). Other French regional sparklers include Seyssel from Savoie, Chardonnay *méthode champenoise* from the Jura, and Blanc de Blancs from Provence (see **Savoie**, **Jura** and **Provence**).

Italy is one of the fizziest countries in the world. There are some exceptionally fine dry *méthode champenoise* wines that give as much pleasure (and cost as much) as Champagne. Ferrari [★★★/■■■] in Trento, and Ca' del Bosco [★★→★★★/■■■] from Franciacorta in Lombardy, two of the very best, produce lean, steely, austere and very dry wines from Pinot Bianco (Pinot Blanc), Pinot Grigio (Pinot Gris), Pinot Nero (Pinot Noir) and Chardonnay.

Germany, on the other hand, produces very little *méthode champenoise* wine. The vast majority of German *Sekt*, as it is called, is made by the *cuve close* method (see **Sekt**).

Spanish Cava is a broad, full style of *méthode champenoise* wine, which can be a little unexciting. But these are wines of great value, and they are getting livelier by the minute (see **Cava**).

Portugal's sparklers are on a level with Spanish Cava. Almost all are *méthode champenoise*, although J M da Fonseca makes unusual sparklers by the "Russian continuous" method (see **Portugal**).

Some of the best *méthode champenoise* sparklers are made in California, especially by Schramsberg (see **Napa Valley**) and Iron Horse (see **Sonoma**). Other good indigenous producers of sparkling wine [■■→■■■] include:

Chateau St Jean	*Paul Masson*
Mark West Vineyards	*Sebastiani*
Mirassou	*Wente*
Monterey Vineyard	

There has also been an influx of prestigious Champagne firms, including Domaine Chandon (see **Napa Valley**) and others. In spite of this, there is still some way to go before California matches the right grapes to the right soils and climates.

Elswhere in the USA, the Finger Lakes region in upper New York State makes some *méthode champenoise* wine (see **New York State**). But the most promising region outside California is the northwest, because of its climatic suitability for Chardonnay and Pinot Noir. Washington's Chateau Ste-Michelle [★→★★/■■■] and Oregon's Knudsen-Erath [★→★★/■■■] are among the leaders.

Australia's *méthode champenoise* industry is even more fledgling than the USA's, but catching up fast. As in California, Champagne firms are now carving themselves a slice of the action – hence the choice of cool growing regions such as Tasmania, where Roederer has joined Heemskerk (see **Tasmania**) and of the Adelaide Hills where Bollinger has a share in Petaluma (see **Adelaide Hills**). Other notable Australian *méthode champenoise* producers [★★/■■] include:

Chateau Remy	*Seppelt, Great Western*
Penfolds	*Yalumba*
Rosemount	*Yellowglen*
Seaview	

New Zealand, which has lately become so adept at growing quality white grapes with high acidity, may well prove an even more impressive producer of sparkling wines than Australia. The Champagne house Deutz has linked up with Montana [★/■■], New Zealand's largest wine company, and the potential is enormous.

There is no limit, it seems, to the number of French fingers in other people's *méthode champenoise* pies. The most unusual is India's attractively soft and fragrant Omar Khayyam [★/■■→■■■], produced with Piper-Heidsieck know-how.

SPARKLING WINE AND FOOD   Some people could live on sparkling wine and hors d'oeuvres, and no doubt some people have. Champagne is the ultimate aperitif and almost any *méthode champenoise* worth its bubbles makes an excellent pre-prandial drink – and a pretty excellent post-prandial drink if it comes to that.

Sparkling wines are mood-lifters: a glass or two of fizz not only tantalizes the tastebuds but makes the world (or at least your living room) a friendlier place.

WHERE NEXT? See the specific entries on sparkling wine styles: **Asti Spumante, Blanquette de Limoux, Cava, Champagne, Gaillac, Saumur, Sekt** and **Vouvray**.

See also the introductions to the main wine-producing countries and the following entries: **Adelaide Hills, Albana di Romagna, Alsace, Barossa Valley, Burgundy, England, Jura, Loire, Marlborough, New York State, Oltrepò Pavese, Piave, Rhône, Savoie, Sicily, Sonoma, Tasmania, Verdicchio** and **Yarra Valley**.

SWITZERLAND

Like Austria, Switzerland has loads of potential, but not a lot to show for it. This is partly because the Swiss drink the wine all themselves, paying prices that leave visitors gasping (and turning to beer). But there is also a feeling of missed potential. If you were designing a vine-growing country on the back of an envelope, you might place it somewhere between France, Italy and Germany, making sure to give it a cool climate. You would hope for wines with Burgundy's class, Piedmont's character and perhaps the Mosel's delicacy. Instead, you get Swiss wines.

They can be light and wonderfully fresh, no doubt about it, but the Swiss give themselves a handicap from the start. Their equivalent of Grüner Veltliner is Chasselas, a table grape variety the French barely even bother to make into wine. Given a little *pétillance* from bottling *sur lie* like Muscadet, its youth and freshness constitute most of the appeal. It does best in the French-speaking part of Switzerland, particularly under the name of Fendant in the Valais, and also as Dorin in the Vaud, and as Perlan in Geneva and Neuchâtel. Good winemakers, with good sites, can persuade Chasselas to make some age-worthy wines.

Johannisberg, the local name for Silvaner, can have more character, as can Traminer, which goes under the name Savagnin.

Eastern Switzerland, the German-speaking part, makes interesting but even rarer wines, most of which never leave their home canton.

Reliable producers [★→★★/■■■] include:

Château de Trévelin	*Orsat*
Hammel	*Testuz*
Domaine du Mont d'Or	

Frankly, though, Switzerland is better at making money than wine, as you will appreciate when you come to buy a bottle.

WHERE NEXT? **Austria** has a wider range of tastes, lower prices and at its best alpine freshness and bite. **Savoie** does a French version of Swiss wine at, again, more sensible prices.

TASMANIA

This could become Australia's own doorstep equivalent of New Zealand. Its cool climate is conducive to making fresh, lively, elegant and distinguished wines which have a family resemblance to those of northern Europe.

Louis Roederer of Champagne has joined forces with Tasmania's Heemskerk [★★/■■■] to make *méthode champenoise* fizz from Pinot Noir and Chardonnay. Piper's Brook [★★/■■→■■■] Chardonnay and Riesling are showing the island's potential to be exciting, but these are early days yet.

WHERE NEXT? Head east to **New Zealand**; back to **France** to compare prototypes; or across the Pacific to **Oregon** for similar conditions and aspirations.

TOKAY

Hungary's greatest white wine is Tokay, made in a range of styles from dry to very sweet. It has nothing to do with the Tokay of Alsace (which is Pinot Gris), but is made from Furmint and Hárslevelü grapes, up in the north-east corner of the country near the Czech border.

THE TOKAY TASTE The grapes for Tokay are picked when very ripe, and the conditions – long sunny autumns and dampness rising from the Bodrog river – resemble those around the River Ciron near Sauternes. This combination of humidity and dryness encourages the development of *Botrytis cinerea*, which shrivels the grapes and concentrates the sugar. Some grapes are picked earlier in the season before *Botrytis* gets a grip, and are made into Tokay Szamorodni, which can be either sweet or dry.

The *Botrytis*-affected grapes are used to make the sweet style called Tokay Aszú. They are thrown into a wooden tub and forgotten for a week. The drops of free-run, top-quality juice that collect in the bottom are used to make the legendary Tokay Essencia, which had the reputation of reviving Tsars (the only people who could afford it) from their deathbeds. It ferments painfully slowly, taking years to reach a mere 2-3% alcohol. Due to an acute shortage of Tsars, Essencia is rarely sold but used to sweeten other styles.

The mouldy grapes remaining in the 7.7-gallon (35-litre) wooden tub (or *putton*) are mashed into a paste and added to a *gönc* of dry base wine. A *gönc* is a 31-gallon (140-litre) cask, and the number of *puttonyos* of sweet mash that are added will determine the sweetness of the eventual wine; the scale for Aszú goes up to six.

During fermentation a wrinkly, yellowish yeast called *flor* develops on the surface of the wine, just as with *fino* sherry; so the wine is rather like a cross between sherry and Sauternes. The sweeter it is, the longer it is left to mature in wood: take the number of *puttonyos*, add two, and that gives the number of years it will be aged.

CHOOSING TOKAY Tokay retains enough acidity not to taste cloying. The freshest and grapiest styles are the less sweet ones, and a wine of two or three *puttonyos* is probably the best place to begin, since it can be drunk fairly young and is also relatively inexpensive. Wines of six *puttonyos* and Essencia (which today is made with the equivalent of eight *puttonyos*) have a more intense, raisiny character which can develop in time into a thicker, more caramel-like and treacly style. These wines really do need to mature, and two or three decades would by no means be inappropriate.

At present all exports of Tokay are bottled by the State winery [★★→★★★/■■→■■■]. Quite a bit is made, but not bottled, by private winegrowers. They sell wine locally, and may begin to trade more widely as and when the politics of the country allows it.

TOKAY AND FOOD Tokay is one of the very few wines to marry well with chocolate. A lovely summer companion is peaches and cream; an exotic winter one is Australian macadamia nuts.

WHERE NEXT? There is nothing else like Tokay, though there are similarities with **Sherry**; those with a sweet tooth can try **Sauternes** and the intensly sweet wines of **Austria**, or **Vin Santo**.

TOURAINE

Up the Loire past Anjou and Saumur, Sauvignon Blanc begins to muscle in on Chenin Blanc territory around Tours. The climate is among the mildest in France – fruit and vegetables grow so well that the region is known as the garden of France, a name adopted by a vast *vin de pays*. The wines themselves could be said to have a vegetable garden smell: fresh, green, grassy and crisp.

Among the very dry Chenins are those from Coteaux du Loir [★/ ■■] and its slightly better neighbour Jasnières [★/■■], to the north of Vouvray; and those of Touraine-Amboise [★★/■■], Touraine-Azay-le-Rideau [★★/■■] and Touraine-Mesland [★★/■■]. Touraine's most famous Chenin is, without a doubt, Vouvray (see **Vouvray**).

This leaves the general Touraine *appellation*, most of which is spoken for by Sauvignon. Simple Sauvignon de Touraine, especially when made by a consistently good producer such as the co-operative at Oisly-et-Thesée [★→★★/■■], delivers most of the flavour at half the price of Sancerre. Inexpensive, youthful, it has more zip and flair than many a Muscadet or dry Chenin Blanc. Other good Sauvignon de Touraine producers [★→★★/■→■■] include:

Albert Bescombes	Domaine du Pré Baron
Delannay	Domaine de la Presle

WHERE NEXT? Pay the premium for **Sancerre** to see if it is deserved; then jump to **New Zealand** for Sauvignons of similar value. It is also well worth searching out the VDQS Sauvignon de St-Bris (see **Sauvignon Blanc**) for a tasty rarity.

TREBBIANO

One cannot help feeling a little sympathy for this high-yielding grape variety, in spite of the fact that it produces some of the world's most boring wine. In countries where, for centuries, the water has been suspect, Trebbiano has provided a perfectly satisfactory and safe alternative: the wine is colourless, odourless, tasteless, but with a refreshing tang of acidity, and is available in copious quantities.

Its freshness, inconsequential lightness and anonymity have been great attractions in societies where wine was regularly drunk at least twice a day. But these qualities in a wine are no longer highly valued outside southern Europe, and it is rather frowned on these days. In a world where wine is drunk for pleasure rather than necessity and is expected to exhibit a distinctive presence, poor old Trebbiano has few friends among drinkers.

However much we knock it – and most people do – we cannot hide the fact that it is Italy's most widely planted white variety. In fact, under the name Ugni Blanc, it is France's too, but the French have the sense to turn this thin, acid little wine into much more palatable Cognac and Armagnac.

THE TREBBIANO TASTE This is rather a contradiction in terms. The grape is one of the world's biggest croppers (and tastes like it) for which reason it is very popular with growers. It has good acidity, which endears it to the spirit producers, but little else of note beyond a sort of vaguely winey feel; it varies from light- to medium-bodied.

BEGIN WITH ITALY Begin and end with Italy, in fact. Wherever it travels, the grape adopts the name of the region; wisely, very few wines adopt the name of the grape. Thus Soave contains some Trebbiano di Soave, and Lugana is made from Trebbiano di Lugana. There are very few wines in which Trebbiano does not feature. It turns up in one form or another in Bianco di Custoza and Gambellara (see **Soave**); in Frascati, Verdicchio and Orvieto (see **Frascati, Verdicchio, Orvieto**); in Est! Est!! Est!!! [★/■■], Bianco Vergine della Valdichiana [★/■■], Bianco dei Colli Maceratesi [★/■→■■] and many more, often sharing the bottle with other varieties. Any white Italian wine that is not called by a varietal name stands a good chance of containing some Trebbiano.

The grape's home is in Tuscany, where, as you might expect, it is called Trebbiano Toscana. Along with the more respectable Malvasia it has been a small but traditional component in the region's most famous red wine, Chianti. As this particular role has declined, however, other uses have been found for it. Modern vinification techniques came to the rescue in the late 1970s to produce a light, fresh, clean, everyday drinking wine called Galestro, re-packaging and re-launching central Italy's white Trebbiano/Malvasia blend (see **Tuscany**). In Italy these wines fulfill perfectly the need for a glass of white something-or-other at meals.

Trebbiano d'Abruzzo is a bit different. It can be made using either the Trebbiano Toscana or Bombino Bianco grape, the latter of which produces a richer, fuller taste. Valentini's wines [★★/■■■] are streets ahead of anything else labelled Trebbiano.

OTHER TREBBIANOS As Ugni Blanc, Trebbiano is also grown in Provence and the Midi, but it almost invariably disappears into anonymous table wines. Some is grown in Australia too, but even there it has never amounted to more than a blending component or a base for spirits and fortified wines. That, perhaps, is the clincher. If the Australians can't make anything interesting from it, then there really is no hope that some hitherto undiscovered quality will burst out and surprise the world.

TREBBIANO AND FOOD Most Trebbiano is for those occasions when you can't be bothered with flavour. The grape's total lack of character makes it an ideal, if unexciting, house food wine. It is the vinous equivalent of a tomato ketchup bottle; whatever you are eating, just up-end it and splodge a little into a glass. It can take on strong, spicy flavours because there is absolutely nothing in the wine to obscure.

WHERE NEXT? From the humble Trebbiano-based *vini da tavola* virtually any grape is a step up. Try Italian wines in which Trebbiano plays a part but where the dominant variety – Malvasia, Grechetto, Garganega etc – calls the tune (see **Italy**). Further afield, lightness, freshness and the imposition of a maximum alcoholic degree are all characteristics of **Muscadet**.

TUNISIA
Tunisia's wines bear a certain resemblance to those of Sicily, which is a relatively short hop across the Mediterranean. Muscat is widely used for both sweet and dry wines. Vin Muscat de Tunisie [★/■] is a rich, sticky dessert wine in the mode of Sicilian Muscats, which goes well with rich Arab pastries.

The major producer is the Union des Coopératives Viticoles de Tunisie [★/■], known for its spicy dry Muscat de Kelibia. Other producers [★/■] include the state-owned Office des Terres Domaniales, the Societé Lomblot and the Societé des Vins Tardi.

WHERE NEXT? Try a Muscat from **Sicily**. **Algeria** produces wines with a stronger French accent.

TURKEY

Turkey grows a lot of grapes, but over 95% of them are intended for eating, either fresh or dried. The few white ones that are pressed and fermented do not make wonderful wines. Some Sémillon is produced in Thrace; Villa Doluca, the country's best winery [★/■], makes both Sémillon and Johannisberg Riesling. There is, as throughout the Mediterranean area, some Muscat, while dry Urgup and sweet Narbag are made in Anatolia. Tekel [★/■] is the brand name used by the Turkish state drinks monopoly.

WHERE NEXT? **Greece** makes wine with more conviction.

TUSCANY

Tuscany is, of course, famous world-wide for its red wines – and in particular Chianti. Sweet Vin Santo is the white wine most revered by the Tuscans themselves (see **Vin Santo**). Strictly speaking, there is no "Chianti Bianco", but this is a region of many excellent winemakers, so Tuscany's white wines certainly bear tasting and several have classic features in their own right.

Vernaccia is a local grape apparently unrelated to others of the same name in Sardinia and other regions. Within the confines of San Gimignano, a glorious medieval turreted town, the grape becomes a fine and unusual white wine made without the addition of any Trebbiano. The traditional style was praised by Michelangelo; in his day the wine took on a bronze colour with age and had a distinctive woodiness like fine sherry. There is still a "note" of nutty sherry about the wine today, especially on the slightly bitter finish, but the first impression it gives is of a stylish and elegant, fresh-tasting, slightly creamy wine. It makes a good aperitif, and is excellent served with light fish dishes.

Good producers of Vernaccia di San Gimignano [★→★★/■■] include the following:

Cusona	*Fattoria di Pietrafitta*
Castello di Pescile	*Fattoria della Quercia*
Falchini	*Teruzzi & Puthod*

Galestro, by contrast, is a thoroughly modern white wine created by a consortium of notable Tuscan producers in 1980 to demonstrate what can be done with dull old Trebbiano when money is spent and expertise used. This low-alcohol white (maximum 10.5°) blends Sauvignon Blanc, Chardonnay, Pinot Bianco (see **Pinot Blanc**) and Trebbiano with very pleasant results – and without a hint of the flabbiness that can mar some Italian whites. Among the best producers of Galestro [★★/■■] are:

Antinori	*Ricasoli*
Frescobaldi	*Ruffino*

Torricella is an unusual dry white wine made by Ricasoli [★★/■■] from Malvasia grapes, then aged in wood and bottle for up to ten years. Light, flinty Bianco Pisano di S Torpe, which became DOC in 1980, is made near Pisa with Trebbiano and Malvasia grapes. Producers to watch for [★→★★/■■] include:

Gello	*di Piedivilla*
Gaslini	*Salvadori*

Bianco Toscano is, as its name suggests, the "workhorse white" of the region; a table wine made from Trebbiano and Malvasia. It sometimes has a hint of fizz to give it a lift. Reliable producers [★/■■] include:

Amorosa	*Capezzana*
Brolio	*La Massa*

This is soup rather than pasta territory: a chilled glass of Bianco Pisano di S Torpe with a bowl of home-made *minestrone* can be close to perfection.

WHERE NEXT? Tuscany faces stiff competition within Italy from **Friuli-Venezia Giulia**, **Alto Adige** and even nearby **Orvieto**.

UNITED STATES

The great glory of the US wines is their consistency. As the sixth-largest wine producer in the world, the USA makes excellent generic or "jug" wines to a standard not always maintained elsewhere. Above this basic level, though, the picture is less clear. California has a way of charming the palate in international wine tastings, but for the price of a fine wine from Napa and Sonoma you might just as well be comtemplating Burgundy or the best Rheingau wines. The climate does not always work in the winemaker's favour either. In California, the sun certainly shines but the fog also rolls in to the North Coast and Central wineries bringing mould in its wake, and in the vast Central Valley the scorching heat is an enemy to quality that technology struggles to combat.

What all American winemakers have in common, it seems – from the largest "refinery" to the smallest home concern – is enthusiasm for the vine. They really care about the wine and the consumer and will spend time explaining both, hence the proliferation of neck labels, back labels and wine-tasting classes. They also have a certain humility (apart from the "demi-gods" of the "boutiques" in California) and are always ready to experiment with a wide range of grape varieties and winemaking methods. It is an industry which changes each year and expands all the time.

Like all things American, taste is built on a large scale. The flavour of an American wine, be it from New York State or Washington is obvious from the outset. There is no struggle to detect nuance. If the wine has a fault, it is a tendency to overkill – so Chardonnay is more buttery than European versions, Semillon is heavy on the vanilla, and Sauvignon Blanc smells of green peppers. Once your nose is accustomed to this, the wines grow on you.

The vast bulk of US wine, of course, is produced in California, but a number of other states such as Oregon and New York have made their mark with quality wines (see **California**, **Oregon**, **New York**) and others again show promise. A full range of white varieties is grown in Washington State, including Chardonnay, Semillon and Riesling. Although many grapes are still sold to California and Oregon, there are some good Washington producers [★★/■■→■■■]:

Arbor Crest	*Latah Creek*
Chateau Ste Michelle	*Mount Barker*
Columbia	*Preston*
Hogue Cellars	*Salishan*

For the future, there are areas of the eastern seaboard and Texas which are bidding for stardom, together with Idaho in the west and even New Mexico to the south-west. Among the best fledgeling Texan producers [★→★★/■■→■■■] are:

| Fall Creek | Llano Estacado |
| Ste Genevieve | Pheasant Ridge |

All of these new regions have potential but it is still California which holds sway and which has the charm and marketing skills to export its wines in quantity.

WHERE NEXT? See the specific entries on United States wine styles: **California, Monterey, Napa Valley, New York State, Oregon** and **Sonoma**.

USSR

In this era of *glasnost* Soviet wine may well move forward on the world stage, but as yet it remains essentially a mystery to the Western drinker. Although the USSR is the world's fourth-largest producer, its wines are consumed at home and they tend to be sweet. Good Soviet dessert wines are made in the Crimea but the most renowned region overall is Georgia, known for its sweetish but drinkable Champanski [★/■] and for still white wines made with recognizable grape varieties such as (Italian) Riesling and Pinot Gris.

WHERE NEXT? Try **Bulgaria** for proof that a modern industry can be established, and produce good wine, in similar conditions.

VERDICCHIO

This wine produced in the unfashionable Marche region on the eastern flank of Italy is made from the local Verdicchio vine, said to date back some 1,500 years. It yields an attractive wine, which is light and delicate in style but which is known world-wide not so much for its taste as for its bottle – a curvaceous amphora cleverly promoted by local exporters.

Verdicchio is a fragile vine to grow amid the region's other crops and the resulting wine is fresh and delicious but does not keep for more than an average of three years. It is made in still, *frizzante* and *méthode champenoise* versions. A *classico* version is named Verdicchio dei Castelli di Jesi after the picturesque local fortress towns, and this is the quality name to look for. Good producers [★→★★/■→■■] include:

Cantina Sociale di	Fazi-Battaglia
Cupramontana	Garafoli
Cantina Sociale Val di Nevola	F Torelli

Drink Verdicchio young, as it does not keep beyond about three years.

WHERE NEXT? Cross the Appennines for **Tuscany**'s whites, or go north to **Friuli-Venezia Giulia**.

VICTORIA

Australia's Garden State is perhaps best-known for the classic, unique flavours of its Liqueur Muscats and Tokays, produced in north-east Victoria (see **Liqueur Muscat & Tokay**). But not everything made here is sticky.

Victoria's most fashionable cool-climate region, the Yarra Valley, is producing wines of increasing stature (see **Yarra Valley**). Elsewhere, in the north-east, Brown Brothers [★★→★★★/■■→■■■] makes an impressive and extensive range of varietals of extremely high quality. Muscat is one of its specialities, and it produces an appealing quartet: aperitif-style Dry Muscat Blanc, Late-Picked Muscat, aromatic Late Harvest Orange Muscat & Flora (perfect with puds) and Liqueur Muscat. A late-harvested, *Botrytis*-affected Noble Rhine Riesling is good too. Its King Valley vineyard has been in production for some time, but a new higher site, Whitlands, has a long, cool growing season which enhances flavour and acidity. Brown Brothers wines from here, which include Rhine Riesling, Gewürztraminer, Chardonnay and Sauvignon Blanc, have a vibrancy and intensity which puts them in a different league from the rest of the whites.

By an odd quirk of viticultural history, Victoria grows around 70% of the world's Marsanne, most of it in the Goulburn Valley, and most of it shared between two neighbouring properties: Chateau Tahbilk and Mitchelton. The wines [★★/■■■] are partially barrel-fermented, and begin with a light honeysuckle and peach flavour; but over five to ten years they can develop more honeyed and resinous, gum-like flavours, with a rich sweet scent like jasmine.

Tahbilk and Mitchelton also produce Chardonnay, Sauvignon Blanc and Rhine Riesling. Mitchelton's range extends upwards from the everyday Thomas Mitchell label [★/■■] through Mitchelton and Print Label [★★/■■→■■■] to Classic Release [★★/■■■]. Further north in Echuca the Tisdall winery [★★/■■■] does a good line in Chardonnay and other varieties grown in the Strathbogie Ranges, called Mount Helen. The Chardonnay is oaky, spicy and appley, but full and rounded.

Big, bold, beefy Chardonnay flavours are produced by Balgownie Estate [★★/■■■]. Yellowglen [★/■■■] specializes in sparklers, while Delatite's [★★★/■■] Rhine Riesling and Gewürztraminer are racy, beautifully defined, varietally pure and deliciously exciting.

Victoria's Murray River region, also known as Mildura, is the equivalent of South Australia's Riverland. Irrigated vines here produce table grapes, dried grapes, and lots of fairly undistinguished wine, most of which is destined for the "cask" market. Big companies such as Lindemans, McWilliams and Mildara have wineries here.

Although Mildara has a foot in Coonawarra, the juice comes to the larger operation here at Merbein for fermentation and further processing. The Flower Series wines [★/■■] are made from Murray fruit and include everyday light, fresh Colombard/Chardonnay, and straightforward Fumé Blanc. Jamieson's Run [★★/■■] is a Coonawarra blend of Sauvignon Blanc, Chardonnay and Semillon; and Coonawarra Rhine Riesling [★★/■■] is good too.

Other Victorian producers to note [★→★★/■■] include:

Bannockburn Vineyards	*Idyll Vineyards*
Best's, Great Western	*St Leonards*
Chateau Remy	*Taltarni*

WHERE NEXT? Range around **Australia** for equal value and interest, across to **Western Australia** in particular; compare the Brown Brothers range of Muscats with those of João Pires and J M da Fonseca in **Portugal**.

VIN DOUX NATUREL

Vin Doux Naturel (VDN) is France's answer to the fortified wines of Spain and Portugal. The French ones are not as famous but they are made in a similar way. Fermentation is stopped by the addition of alcohol, so the wine has a high strength and its sweetness comes entirely from the unfermented grape juice remaining in the wine.

The Mediterranean coast and the Rhône Valley are the centres of production. Some are red (usually made from Grenache) but the best-known are white and principally made from the Muscat grape.

The best wines are made from Muscat à Petits Grains (see **Muscat**), the aristocrat of the Muscat family and the same variety that makes frothy Asti Spumante. In fact, if you can imagine a cross between the taste of Asti Spumante (without the froth) and white port, then fortified Muscats are something like that. Frankly, I can't. It is much easier to open a bottle.

Muscat de Beaumes de Venise, from the Rhône Valley, is the lightest, floweriest and freshest-tasting of all (see **Beaumes-de-Venise**). Those from the Mediterranean coast are less flowery, more raisiny, more serious, weightier. Here the light citrus flavours have become slightly cooked, like marmalade or candied orange peel, and they often seem flatter because acidity is less pronounced. Nevertheless, some can have an attractive honeyed flavour.

Muscat de Frontignan, from the town of that name along the coast from Montpellier, is the pick of the Mediterranean bunch, with those of Lunel, Mireval and Rivesaltes close behind. Muscat de Rivesaltes can also be made from Muscat of Alexandria, which produces a heavier, coarser wine; there is also a plain Rivesaltes which is a blend of grape varieties.

A curiosity, for those who have been through all these VDNs and come out smiling, is the "Rancio" style, which has been oxidized by leaving the casks open to the air.

The two principal producers of Muscat de Lunel [★/■■] are the Cave Coopérative and Domaine de Belle Côte. For Mireval, the main producer is the Cave Coopérative [★/■■]. The best Rivesaltes comes from Château de Rey [★★/■■→■■■]. Other producers [★/■■■] include Domaine St-Luc and Cazes.

Banyuls comes from isolated, rocky country in the Pyrénées-Orientales. Obligatory ageing produces a style half-way between Madeira and port. The best is Banyuls *grand cru*. The Cellier des Templiers [★→★★/■■→■■■] is the biggest producer. Other producers [★→★★/■■] include Domaine de la Rectorie and Domaine du Mas Blanc.

A variation on the VDN theme is Vin de Liqueur (VDL), which is "muted" with alcohol before the fermentation has a chance to get going. These are usually sweeter and simpler wines, but the fresher fruit taste can be welcome. Pineau des Charentes from over near the Atlantic coast is made in this style, but muted with Cognac rather than just plain grape spirit (see **Pineau des Charentes**).

WHERE NEXT? The strong, sweet Portuguese Moscatel de Setúbal of J M da Fonseca is produced in a similar way to VDNs (see **Portugal**). Muscat of Samos (see **Greece**) is perhaps the Mediterranean's most venerable Muscat.

VIN DE PAYS

French wine laws always have to steer a middle course. On the one hand they could give the producer so much freedom that there might as well not be any controls at all; before 1973 Algeria was a recognized source of "Burgundy", for instance. On the other they could hedge him about so much that he has no room for manoeuvre, no chance to improve his Colombard with a little Chardonnay, should he deem it necessary or desirable. The *appellations contrôlées* take the stricter route; *vin de pays* allows more leeway for experiment (see **France**). Growers can plant Chardonnay and use it for a *vin de pays*, even if the local AC forbids its use. The gamble has paid off, the freedom has not been abused, and some quite spectacular wines have been produced at very reasonable prices.

It is the volume of *vin de pays* produced, allied to the quality that some (but not all) can achieve – plus the fact that most of us can afford to buy a bottle – that make them such an exciting group of wines. They have exploited temperature-controlled fermentation and an armoury of shiny gadgets to put the fruit flavours where they belong, out front. Many of them are simple, clean, fresh, unpretentious wines that must make the previous generation of drinkers weep when they recall what they had to put up with.

Vins de pays come in three levels of geographical precision. The largest can cover whole regions and take in several departments. Jardin de la France (see **Touraine**) covers most of the Loire Valley, Comté Tolosan occupies a great chunk of the south-west, and d'Oc takes in the Rhône, Provence and Languedoc-Roussillon (see **Coteaux du Languedoc**, **Côtes de Roussillon**). The second tier is departmental, and the third is more specifically zonal. Few wines are worth keeping: if you don't catch them while they are dew-fresh, you will have missed the boat.

Many of the most exciting white *vins de pays* [★/■→■■] come from the south-west. SICAREX, which acts as a research station and supervisor of co-operatives in the area, has done much to help with new plantings, and offers advice on varieties and blending. Its own wines from the Domaine de l'Espiguette are sometimes bottled under the Espigou label.

The giant Listel company is one of the most go-ahead in the entire south of France, producing high-tec, dry Vin de Pays des Sables du Golfe du Lion from all sorts of grape varieties grown in reclaimed sand dunes at the mouth of the River Rhône. Its sweet, fragrant fizz, Pétillant de Raisin, is one of the best low-alcohol wines on the market at only 3.5% alcohol.

Other good *vins de pays* [★/■→■■] from the south-west include Coteaux de l'Ardèche, Coteaux des Baronnies, Comte de Grignan, Vin de Pays du Gard, Côtes de Thongue (which makes interesting *maceration carbonique* wines), Coteaux de la Cité de Carcassonne, Catalan and Côtes Catalanes. In the south-east and centre of France, other good *vins de pays* are also made in Gascogne (see **Côtes de Gascogne**) and Yonne.

WHERE NEXT? For similar value and up-front flavour, try the New World's cheaper regions: **Chile**, California's Central Valley (see **California**) and the Riverland in **South Australia**. Try also the wines of **Bulgaria** and the less-fashionable wines of **Italy**.

VIN SANTO

Italy's "holy wine" is a rich, sweet, earthy concoction traditionally made by hanging bunches of grapes to dry from the beams of smoky country kitchens before fermenting. Today the grapes are still dried before vinifying and the "real thing" still has real status in Italy, especially in Tuscany. Unfortunately, there are quite a few wines that claim to be the real thing and are not.

The wine is made from Trebbiano and Malvasia grapes and has a spicy richness which marries with the flavours of cakes and pastries. Its colour starts as gold and ages to deep bronze. The best wines are aged in small barrels called *caratelli*, which are sometimes kept under the rooftiles for four years or so.

Good producers of Tuscan Vin Santo [★★/■■■] include:

Antinori	*Frecobaldi*
Avignonesi	*Isole e Olena*
Cappelli	*Villa di Vetrice*
Castello di Volpaia	

Other good Vin Santo is made outside Tuscany in the Marche region, the Gambellara area of the Veneto and in Umbria; in fact, the wine is made all over Italy on an *ad hoc* basis for family use.

WHERE NEXT? Tokay has a certain resemblance, although it is always sweet. Other Mediterranean wines such as **Málaga** and the odd Greek Mavro (see **Greece**) offer similar tastes.

VINHO VERDE

Vinho Verde, the "green wine" of northern Portugal, does not look green; in fact more than half of it is red. It is not named after the lush countryside where the grapes are grown, although the vigorous foliage does contribute to the overall effect. Nor is it grown organically, although vines here are traditionally manured by cows rather than by bags of chemicals. It is called green wine because it is made to be drunk young.

This is Portugal's largest demarcated wine region, stretching nearly 100 miles (160 km) from just south of Oporto and the River Douro up to the Minho River. But the land is not intensively cultivated with vines. Vinho Verde was, and for some producers still is, a cottage industry. Vines are planted around the edges of fields, climbing up trees or slung between posts, leaving room for maize, tomatoes, cabbages and kiwi fruit underneath. Farmers in this region have traditionally used the grapes to make a simple, fresh rustic wine, largely for home consumption.

THE VINHO VERDE TASTE Vinho Verde is not a single varietal wine, nor even a standard blend. Given the small scale and diffuse nature of winemaking here, a large number of different grape varieties are used in varying combinations, few of which are encountered elsewhere: Alvarinho, Loureiro, Trajadura and Avesso are among the best. Most are characterized by high acidity.

In Portugal white Vinho Verde is dry and, because of its very high acidity, almost tear-jerkingly refreshing. It is pale in colour, light and lemony, and varies in perfume according to the grapes used. The freshness of flavour recalls grass, apples and mint. It is relatively low in alcohol, generally around 9%. Traditionally, the wine was bottled so soon after fermentation that it underwent a secondary, or malolactic, fermentation in bottle.

A by-product of this activity is carbon dioxide, which, as it cannot escape into the air, dissolves in the wine. When the bottle is opened, it produces a very light sparkle or *pétillance* – a slight prickle on the tongue which enhances the wine's refreshment value.

That is how it used to be made. Faced with the need for larger-scale production triggered by wider demand, growers and winemakers modified their methods, planting proper vineyards and standardizing carbon dioxide levels. This has made for greater consistency, but something of the creamy quality of traditional Vinho Verde has been lost in the process.

Commercial Vinho Verde was also sweetened to reduce the searing tartness for the "international palate". This has produced wines that are less distinctive, but still light and pleasant. More recently, some producers have recognized that modernization may have gone too far, particularly with regard to sweetness. There are now drier Vinho Verdes available internationally, some from single estates, which are closer to the original style.

CHOOSING VINHO VERDES Vinho Verde with character is difficult to find. Look out for single-quinta designations. The most reliable producers [★→★★/■] include:

Amarante
Aveleda
Casal Garcia
Champalimand

Gatão
Palacio da Brejoeira
Solar das Boucas

VINHO VERDE AND FOOD Wines perceptibly high in acidity like Vinho Verde have two roles as far as food is concerned: on the one hand they can match the acidity in, for example, a light vinaigrette or a sharp lemony sauce, and on the other hand cut through the richness of fatty or oily foods such as sardines, mackerel and herring, or roast pork with crackling.

Dishes such as these are typical of Portugal, and demonstrate the merits of partnering a region's wine with its food: in particular Portugal's powerful, salty dried cod dish, *bacalhão*, makes a good case for drinking Vinho Verde by the pint.

WHERE NEXT? If high acidity is the attraction, then try a young Chenin Blanc from the **Loire**. If the acidity is too much, consider **Muscadet**. Generally refreshing wines are made in Italy's **Alto Adige**. If the prickle appeals, then the Italian options increase (see **Italy**); if the modest alcohol level appeals then so may the Tuscan blend Galestro (see **Tuscany**). Also try **Gaillac**.

VOUVRAY

All Vouvray is white, and all of it is made from the Chenin Blanc grape. In the absence of any distraction from red or rosé, with not even a Sauvignon to break the monotony, and with two millennia to practice, you would expect this small French town to be good at making Chenin wines by now – and it is.

Vouvray, situated on the Loire a few miles upstream from Tours, deserves some sympathy for being lumbered with such a difficult grape variety. The high acidity, the reluctant fruit, the lack of an easy, approachable style, the patience needed to wait for quality wines to mature – all these factors make life difficult for grower, producer and drinker.

THE VOUVRAY TASTE Vouvray can be dry, medium or sweet, still or sparkling. The dry is often a bland fruitless disappointment, especially when drunk young, and especially if it is cheap. Even dry Vouvray needs ageing (like Hunter Valley Semillon) for a decade before you can see what it is driving at. Then the acidity begins to loosen its grip, and a gently nutty flavour emerges in the wine, swelling to fill the glass.

Vouvray *demi-sec* is that rarity in the wine world, neither dry nor sweet, but a true medium wine, plum in the middle of the spectrum. Forget the cheap stuff, which at worst is completely uninteresting, and at best has a distant, indistinct, muffled feel, as if you were trying to play the piano with boxing gloves on. But from a good producer *demi-sec* Vouvray will develop the delicate and juicy fruit tastes of pears and quince. And it still has a streak of clean, refreshing acidity, even after the 15 or 20 years you have waited.

Although Vouvray *moelleux* does not usually have the *botrytis* richness of Coteaux du Layon wines, it can be sensational after its decade or two in bottle: beautifully balanced between soft richness and firm freshness, with flavours of honey and hazelnuts piling on to the pears and quince.

CHOOSING VOUVRAYS The drinker has to address four questions when choosing Vouvray. The first, the sweetness level, will largely depend on weather conditions. Given a warm, dry summer and a long sunny autumn, the grapes will ripen fully; in a particularly good year they may even be affected by *Botrytis*. The rich, sweet, full-bodied, honeyed *moelleux* wines that result are the best that Vouvray produces, with a characteristic refreshing streak of Chenin Blanc acidity. The best vintages for these sweet wines include 1988, 86, 85, 83, 82, 79, 78, 76, 71, 64, 61 and 59. In years when conditions are not good enough to make sweet wines, the grapes are picked earlier and made into dry wine.

The second question, that of age, is crucial. It would be a waste to drink *moelleux* wines young: they take decades to mature. But then so do most of the dry wines. The grape's acidity stamps a long "sell-by" date on Chenin Blanc wines and, being picked earlier, the dry wines have even more acidity than the sweet wines. The same applies to medium-dry wines: any good Vouvray needs time to come into its own – a decade or more. Since top-quality medium-dry wines are in short supply around the world – most producers tend to aim for one of the definitive extremes – a good, mature *demi-sec* Vouvray should occupy a place in any serious wine cellar. As for buying cheap Vouvray to drink young, I wouldn't bother. There are always more interesting alternatives available for the price.

The Vouvray drinker is also faced with a choice between still and sparkling wines. When grapes here have to be picked green and barely ripened, and the sharp acidity is just too much, then sparkling wine comes to the rescue. This may sound as though fizz is a last resort for the grapes, but fully sparkling *méthode champenoise* Vouvray *mousseux* can be as frisky as a racehorse. Like its half-pressure sibling Vouvray *pétillant*, which can also be very good, it is medium- to full-bodied and can be either dry or sweet.

Finally, there is the matter of choosing a producer. The best [★★/■■→■■■] include:

Bidaudières	Huet
Brédif	Jarry
Foreau	Poniatowski
Freslier	

Montlouis, across the river, has its own *appellation* and a similar range of styles which play second fiddle to Vouvray.

VOUVRAY AND FOOD Dry Vouvray goes well with most kinds of fish and with piquant cheeses such as goat's cheese.

Demi-sec Vouvray is the answer to Chinese sweet and sour dishes, and other savoury foods that are cooked with sugar (braised red cabbage) or caramelized (onions, carrots).

Sweet Vouvray is just the job with cheesecakes, sweet soufflés, and strawberries and cream.

WHERE NEXT? Explore the other **Loire** *appellations* nearby such as **Touraine** and **Anjou**, and try also the *méthode champenoise* sparklers of **Saumur**.

WESTERN AUSTRALIA

Western Australia is *the* up-and-coming wine-producing state of Australia. First planted with vines in 1829, its viticultural history is older than that of South Australia and Victoria, but its reputation as a quality wine area has only emerged over the last decade or so.

WA's most lauded wine region, and justifiably so, is the Margaret River in the south-west corner of the state, and some remarkable white wines are produced here (see **Margaret River**).

Elsewhere in Western Australia, the Lower Great Southern region, which incorporates Mount Barker and Frankland River, has a long, cool growing season well suited to varieties such as Riesling and Gewürztraminer. These produce fresh, crisp, sometimes racy and often fragrant styles, with some peachy, honeyed Late Harvest wines for extra interest. Chardonnay and Sauvignon Blanc are made in small quantities. The best producers [★→★★/■■→■■■] include:

Alkoomi	*Jingalla*
Chateau Barker	*Karrelea*
Forest Hill	*Plantagenet*
Howard Park	*Redmond*

Swan Valley is in complete contrast. One of Australia's, indeed the world's, hottest wine-making regions, it was the birthplace of WA winemaking. In the old days when strong, macho, highly alcoholic hooch was the height of good taste it thrived. Today, although a few good producers manage to overcome the climatic obstacles, principally by irrigating and turning down the dial on their temperature-controlled fermentation tanks, grape growers prefer to go in search of more amenable sites.

Chenin Blanc and Verdelho supplement the more usual Chardonnay and Semillon varieties. Houghton is the top producer. Its Supreme Dry White blend [★→★★/■■] is a bestseller, but it also makes good varietals including Chardonnay and Verdelho [★★/■■→■■■]; a diagonal gold stripe on the label indicates the superior wines, and Moondah Brook Estate [★★/■■→■■■] and Show Reserves [★★/■■→■■■] are particularly good.

Other good Swan Valley producers [★→★★/■■→■■■] include Evans & Tate, Olive Farm and Sandalford.

In the South-West Coastal Plain, Capel Vale [★★/■■→■■■] makes very good Chardonnay, backed up by other varietals including Riesling, Gewürztraminer, and a Semillon/Sauvignon blend.

WHERE NEXT? Victoria makes similar wines. Many WA winemakers have California in their sights, in particular the north coast counties of **Sonoma** and **Napa Valley**.

YARRA VALLEY

Victoria's buzz region is currently the Yarra Valley, which starts just 20 miles (32 km) out of Melbourne. It has come back into fashion, after decades of decline, because the climate is relatively cool. With just the sort of conditions that make for a fairly long and slow growing season, the more delicate flavouring components in the grape are given a chance, and varieties such as Chardonnay can show something of the elegance they do in northern France. As the era of bold, sock-it-to-'em flavours has given way to a desire for more "complexity" in wines, so regions like the Yarra Valley have been able to offer winemakers better raw material than some of the more traditional and hotter regions of the country.

One of the modern fledgling trailblazers is Coldstream Hills, just beginning to turn out Chardonnays with classically restrained but firm and well-defined flavours, backed up with good acidity. The Lilydale label [★★/■■→■■■] is fleshy and pineappley but the Four Vineyards label [★★→★★★/■■→■■■] is where the future of this style lies. And talking of northern France, Domaine Chandon [★★/■■■], an offshoot of the Moët & Chandon Champagne company, is just beginning to come on stream with a *méthode champenoise* Pinot Noir/Chardonnay blend, and a Cuvée Chardonnay.

Other good Chardonnays [★★/■■■] come from:

Mount Mary	Tarrawarra Vineyards
St Huberts	Yarra Yering

Yeringberg [★★/■■■] also makes a Rhône-like Marsanne.

WHERE NEXT? Other fashionable white wine areas in Australia are **Margaret River** in Western Australia and **Clare** in South Australia, or try the cool-climate wines of **Tasmania**. A similar degree of care and skill is exercised in California's **Sonoma** region.

YUGOSLAVIA

For Yugoslavia read Lutomer Riesling [★/■], a light Liebfraumilch-like creation from Slovenia which regularly outsells all other white offerings on Britain's supermarket shelves. Beyond this, there is life, in the form of some powerful dry white wines produced in the south and some far superior Riesling in the north.

The wines vary from rather subtle and fragrant in the Traminer and Riesling of the north, near the Julian Alps, to earthy, rich and Rhône-like in the high-alcohol wines of Dalmatia. Pinot Gris can be perfumed and agreeable as can Pinot Blanc.

Yugoslav wines seem far better on home territory than abroad; perhaps the Yugoslavs keep the best for themselves. Grk [★/■→■■], in the south, is not an expletive deleted but a heavy, tired sherry-like offering with an oxidized taste. But the best wines are made on the Dalmatian islands. Names to look for include Posip, Bogdanusa and Vugava [★/■→■■]. All distribution here is state-controlled.

WHERE NEXT? Try **Bulgaria** for a more modern approach to central European winemaking.

ZINFANDEL (WHITE)

The Zinfandel grape isn't white – but there is white Zinfandel. It is the invention of a colour-blind marketing man.

It is a common experience that pink wine tastes wonderful on holiday: sun, sand and sea ensure a thirst that red wine cannot satisfy, and for which white wine, since we are on holiday, is somehow inadequate. Rosé, therefore, is drunk by the bucketful. Back home, however, rosé goes the way of 17 rolls of film and the seaside romance: remembered once in the depths of winter, and then forgotten about for ever. Except by marketing men.

Extensive research indicated that people buy more white wine than rosé, obviously because of the name. It was a simple matter to re-name the "product" and, since we have all learnt long ago that any connection between a product and the claims made for it are at best tenuous, we found nothing remotely odd about asking for a white wine and being sold a pink one.

It is a variation on the old dry-sweet conundrum. Many people who like sweet wine don't like other people to know that they do; pale cream sherries, to take one example, have succeeded largely for this reason. They look dry, just like a *fino*, which smart drinkers are supposed to prefer; yet they taste sweet, which gives some people who like to be thought of as smart drinkers infinitely more pleasure.

In the case of White Zin, the simple but brilliant deception has been more than vindicated by buoyant sales. Everybody is happy, except for the inventive marketing genius who thought up the idea; he has been unjustly denied a Nobel prize for too long.

THE ZINFANDEL TASTE California's red Zinfandel grape is a high cropper, which means that producers can make lots of it quite cheaply; it has good sugar levels, which means they can make a medium-dry to medium-sweet wine with a moderate alcohol level, simply by stopping the fermentation before it is complete and leaving some residual sugar in the wine; and it has reasonably good acidity, which makes for a fresh wine.

The formula is not new: inexpensive, medium-sweet, fresh wine is the traditional "way in" for many drinkers. White Zinfandel can be thought of as pink Liebfraumilch, or as a high-strength Cooler. But the packaging is supercalifragilistically successful, and positively prestidigitational in its effect on sales.

CHOOSING ZINFANDELS Drinkable White Zinfandels are made in California by the following producers [★/■■]:

Beringer	*Mirassou*
Fetzer	*Mondavi*

ZINFANDEL AND FOOD This is not a particularly good idea.

WHERE NEXT? If it is the medium sweetness of White Zin that appeals, rather than the colour, then there are white – really white – alternatives such as **Liebfraumilch**.

INDEX

Page numbers in **bold type** refer to main entries.